Public Secrets, Public Spaces

Public Secrets, Public Spaces

Cinema and Civility in China

Stephanie Hemelryk Donald

ROWMAN & LITTLEFIELD PUBLISHERS, INC.
Lanham • Boulder • New York • Oxford

ROWMAN & LITTLEFIELD PUBLISHERS, INC.

Published in the United States of America
by Rowman & Littlefield Publishers, Inc.
4720 Boston Way, Lanham, Maryland 20706
http://www.rowmanlittlefield.com
12 Hid's Copse Road
Cumnor Hill, Oxford OX2 9JJ, England

British Library Cataloguing in Publication Information Available

Library of Congress Cataloging-in-Publication Data

Donald, Stephanie Hemelryk, 1961–
  Public secrets, public spaces : cinema and civility in China / Stephanie Hemelryk
Donald.
    p. cm.
  Includes bibliographical references and index.
  ISBN 0-8476-9876-9 (alk. paper) — ISBN 0-8476-9877-7 (pbk. : alk. paper)
    1. Motion pictures—China—History. 2. Motion pictures—Social aspects—China.
I. Title.

PN1993.5.C4 D66   2000
791.43'0951 21—dc21   99-044346

Printed in the United States of America

♾™ The paper used in this publication meets the minimum requirements of
American National Standard for Information Sciences—Permanence of
Paper for Printed Library Materials, ANSI/NISO Z39.48-1992.

Contents

Preface

> The words civil society name the space of uncoerced human association and also the set of relational networks–formed for the sake of family, faith, interest, and ideology–that fill this space.[1]

The idea for this book was in no small part prompted by Michael Walzer's definition of civil society. I was uncomfortable with the circularity of arguments around the question of civil society in 'new' China. I had also become acquainted both with Chinese cinema and the small, but insistent, field of international scholars who debated its nature and significance with such flair. I acknowledge here, and throughout the following pages, those scholars and film critics who, first, have made viewing Chinese cinema possible at all, and second, have developed the pleasure into an intellectual challenge: Chris Berry, Nick Browne, Chen Xiaomei, Rey Chow, Paul Clark, Mary-Ann Farquhar, Dai Jinhua, Gina Marchetti, Sheldon Lu, Tony Rayns, Esther Ching-mei Yau, and Zhang Yingjin are a few names that spring to mind.[2] Their work has encompassed histories, gender analyses, and most recently, discussions of transnationalism and diaspora in relation to Chinese film production and practice.[3] Where I hope to contribute a different perspective is in my focus on the notion of the public, and particularly on cinematic public space. I will be arguing in this book that, before we settle on terms such as 'national' or even 'transnational' cinema, we need to acknowledge the publicness of cinema. Cinema's contribution to, say, the concepts of the national and transnational, lies in the wide-ranging possibilities of cinematic cultural space. Cinema is both discursive and creative. Films not only explore individual and social fantasies, they also produce the space in which those fantasies become available in public. Cultural spaces are as important a factor in the consideration of citizenship-formation as they are in the study of identity-politics and cross-cultural fluidity. To discuss them adequately involves an awareness of institutional practice, governmental and social context, and industrial conditions of production, but it also requires an attention to the texts themselves. My task in this book is to ask the question: What can we see in film, and when can we see it? When is film political, and how do we know, or surmise, that it might be?

The complementary analysis of film and civil society that I propose takes as its grounding then the idea of space rather than a political ideology. Walzer is describing an ideal and in the following analyses I will search for the ideal in moments of cultural production. I will suggest that, whether or not there is an operating, institutionalized civil society evident in China in the 1980s and 1990s, it is possible to discern moments of *public space* in cultural productions (films) of the period. Within such a moment lies an articulation of a contemporary public imaginary, which may not be foregrounded in the narrative of the film but which is discernible in the structure *and texture* of the narration.[4] The usage of the term imaginary is developed from Lacan's Imaginary. This is a psychoanalytic term that describes pre-Symbolic experience, generally infantile and associated with the primacy of the image. Here, the application of the term moves it into the social and political realms, so that the incomplete grasp of experience through cultural practice may be understood as a *collective* enterprise. The term can therefore be used to describe that which is not fully expressed in the Symbolic (language and communication), but which is nevertheless essential to the ways in which people understand themselves individually and as a group.

As part of the intention of this study, I am necessarily questioning the concept of civil society as *the* indicator of publicness. The release of the concept of publicness from the straitjacket of a liberal-democratic definition of autonomy, informality, and nonstate-institutions (wonderful as all those things may be) yields a wider, wilder, and more optimistic field of vision. In order to do this, I will utilize some key terms throughout the book (*the political imaginary, symbolic public spaces, textual disruptions, contemporaneity*). Rather than attempt decontextualized definitions here, I would like simply to signal these concepts, and request that they are understood alongside empirical notions of political organization, places of public assembly, generic mistakes in filmmaking, and the 'new', but that they are not mistaken for these ideas themselves.

My argument has grown from the ideas, concepts, and interests of various academic disciplines. While the research of sociologists, historians, and political scientists provides a context for my analyses of Chinese film, the analyses that they provoke offer an alternative way of thinking about contemporary Chinese culture. This alternative is not without precedent. It is inspired and informed by the possibility of cultural studies, and in particular the work of pioneers of subaltern studies, those who have invented and problematized the concept of the postcolonial. In my engagement with these strains of thought, I intend to give a political analysis of film that is valid as an interpretation of the symbolic sphere of cultural production, but which does not reduce filmic texts to transparent accounts of politics and society.

The earliest of inspirations comes from Walter Benjamin, and from his insistence that film lies at the heart of all our modernities. Benjamin recognized in the early 1930s that film was where people went to find the 'new', but to escape the 'present'.

> Our taverns and our metropolitan streets, our offices and furnished rooms, our railroad stations, and our factories appeared to have locked us in hopelessly. Then came the film and burst this prison world asunder by the dynamite of a tenth of a second, so that now, in the midst of its far-flung ruins and debris, we calmly and adventurously go travelling. With the close-up, space expands; with slow motion, movement is extended. The enlargement of a snapshot does not simply render more precise what in any case was visible, though unclear: it reveals entirely new structural transformations of the subject.[5]

This quotation from *The Work of Art in the Epoch of Its Technical Reproducibility* is well glossed by Howard Caygill, who understands, as did Benjamin, that the secret of film is that it does more than it knows, and that it makes possible more than it does: "It reveals the absolute which is immanent to experience but which manifests itself in inconspicuous and indirect ways." [6] What needs adding here is that the subject might be both collective and individual, and that the "entirely new structural transformations" are as much the work of the audience as the film text itself. The one needs the other to mark a moment of spectatorship as significant, and its significance is in its contribution to a publicness shared by some, but not necessarily all, of those who see the film.

The concept of public space is not new, and it is developing fast. It is now central to disciplines that were once far removed from one another. Philosophy and geography have been brought together to produce an adequate *intellectual* space in which to discuss space as a criterion and phenomenon of the public.[7] In a recent anthology we find the philosophical politicization of space, as developed in the work of Henri Lefèbvre, accompanying a critique of British government practice with regard to public access to common land.[8] It is both the philosophical and ideological contention of such arguments that public space is a prerequisite for human association. By analogy, I take it as a premise in this book that psychic space is necessary for a shared imaginary. Taking these two ideas together, it is arguable that the perception of public space in the symbolic sphere of cultural production offers an important insight into the meaning of contemporary experience. Arguments in this vein are not new to thinking about cultural production. They have, for instance, been made regarding the photograph. Victor Burgin's book of essays on the image in space, *In Different Spaces*, is the product of his work as a thinker, filmmaker, and photographic artist. He makes the point that space is noticeable when our bodies move through it, but also that our psyches use space in all processes of thought, memory, and visualization. "The child learns that . . . spatial coordinates are relative to the body, rather than objective properties of the physical environment." [9] What we describe as physical space is part and product of the pattern of our human actions in mind and body. Burgin also makes the connection between the creation of space and the film. He looks for the "shape-shifting hybrid objects that coalesce in psychical space," from visual culture, including films.[10] Although his interest is partly in the political import of these objects, he does not conceive of them as created in public, but more as targets of identification in the processes of spectatorship.

So why do I reiterate the public space debate in the context of cinema? Cinema offers the most visible and highly charged cultural products of the twentieth century. Films are the stuff of life, or, at least, they are designed to convince an audience that this is the case. The phenomenon of film relies on a cluster of responses and inputs from its spectators for its effect. Watching film involves processes of intellectual investment, cognitive activity, and some kind of identification, with human characters, with ideas, or with a visual rendition of the sublime: beauty or agony. In many cases, these responses entail a corporeal abandonment to the filmic world, as we draw fear, eroticism, human empathy, or righteous social anger from the film's surface. There is also a sense in which watching a film with others is an act of making oneself visible with others. The screening of the film invites the convention of an audience, and the presence of the audience gives the film its meaning. Without them, it is a story waiting to happen, a collection of images waiting to be seen. Together with the audience, however, the film makes publicness possible. Depending on the film, the context of its exhibition, and the ideological position of the critic, some audiences might have been dismissed as masses, or some films described as propaganda. But people in public always retain the possibility of making themselves visible, of making space.

THE COLOR OF EXPERIENCE

A public and political account of spectatorship must recognize both the psychic imaginary and corporeal knowledge, coming together to form what Howard Caygill, has termed, "the color of experience." [11] That expression is philosophically loaded but can also be taken literally to some degree. For Benjamin, colors of experience are visible in the paintings of children, but are continually deepened and refreshed as we pass through time. The same is so for art objects, including film. When we watch films, we watch the colors and patterns on their own account, as much as we concentrate on the cues to its social, psychological, and political signification. The color of experience is the color of mutual recognition, public acknowledgment, and a sense of *something*, perhaps expectations, being altered through the process of spectatorship. Caygill argues that Benjamin held to a philosophy of art as both textual and contingent, thus reminding current film theory of its origins in the philosophies of everyday life. This also brings us back to film as the symbolic center of modern experience, around which a certain kind of public may group and regroup as spectators.

Complicating my own spectatorship is my subjective position outside both China and the Chinese diaspora. I pick up on cultural cues according to the limits of my experience. As a British woman working in Australia, whose earliest memories are of a childhood in Singapore, I am unable to claim Chineseness or any kind of corporeal, experiential authenticity. Rather than sighing at this I have addressed the possibilities, and problems, of cross-cultural work in two of the chapters here. In chapter two, *Seeing White*, I stray between British and Chinese filmmaking in a debate on ways in which different film traditions use whiteness as a symbolic indicator. In chapter five, *Authenticity and Silence*, I question the value of a total hegemony of the authentic in work on film. This is a defense of the hybrid; the person and position which is both this and that, or neither one thing nor the other. More and more intellectuals need to consider their nothingness as we move across the globe in search of work and intellectual sustenance. The problem for me and arguably for all of us is to find and teach our wares in a pocket between the absolute and the absent.

It is anyway important for non-Chinese scholars and students to make efforts to look at Chineseness, partly as an intervention against diasporic experiences of ignorance and racism in white societies, partly to help us realize the historical limitations of our methods of analysis. Film scholarship must take hold of political theory as part of its remit, but in doing so it must also take note of the politics of these theories. Underlying my analyses here is the argument that we must transcend the Habermasian model (although not necessarily Habermas himself, who is often poorly represented) when looking at political space. This is because political space is not complete without cultural space, and neither makes sense without some analysis of the meaning of publicness in a particular place and time.

The color of my own experience has been greatly enhanced by many people who have helped me think about film, art, politics, and the phenomenon of visual politics. I take this opportunity to say thank you to Anne and Robert Benewick, Erica Carter, Rangan Chakravarty, Yingchi Chu, Tracey Crawcour, Craig Clunas, Harriet Evans, Stefan Feuchtwang, Kate Lacey, Jo Law, Laura Marcus, Jill Morris, William Outhwaite, Wendy Parkins, Ana Reynaud, Krishna Sen, Roger Silverstone, Margot Thüfner, Lubica Ucnik, Jeffery Wasserstrom, Zhang Wei, Gordon White, the University of Sussex, the University of Westminster, Murdoch University, many Murdoch undergraduates, and especially,

James Donald. Thanks too to Susan McEachern, Matt Hammon, and Collette Stockton for making it a book, not just an idea; and to Yingchi Chu, Garry Gillard, and Lubica (again) for seeing the mistakes. This book is dedicated to the people who watch more films than anyone I know, and like *Little Sisters of the Grasslands* best of all, Morag and Ellen.

1

Form and Content

"Ta gaosu wo dianying 'Hongse niangzi jun' de neirong hen hao."[1]

Red Detachment of Women (1961), a Liberation classic, is indeed a very nice piece of revolutionary romanticism.[2] It tells the story of a young servant girl, Qionghua, who runs away from her master's house on Hainan island, only to be recaptured and beaten on several occasions. Finally, Hong Changqing, a Communist Party activist in disguise, frees her, and takes her to join a detachment of woman fighters. Under his guidance, Qionghua learns to put the interests of the collective before her own desire for revenge. At the end of the film Hong dies, but Qionghua has matured into a hardened fighter for the Revolution, and can continue without him. The plotline is very familiar to Chinese audiences. The theme of transformation from victim to fighter, and from personal to collective motivation is a common one. It is a dialectical progression from servitude to personal freedom to the desired servitude of collective action, and is quite often focussed on a female protagonist. Moreover, the female star, Zhu Xijuan, was an affective inspiration to young women who appreciated her beauty as well as her strength in the role.[3]

In *Corruption* (1950) a pleasure-loving woman learns to value principles over personal satisfaction. In *The White-haired Girl* (1950) a village girl is sold into slavery, escapes into hiding, and is finally reunited with her family under the banner of Liberation and the People's Army. In *Daughter of the Party* (1958), three young women overcome personal animosities to establish a Party cell (figure 1.1). The inspiration is Li Yumei (played by Tian Hua, the same actress who plays the eponymous 'white-haired girl' in the 1950 classic), who, having led the women in their collective endeavor, dies a martyr.

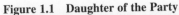

Figure 1.1   Daughter of the Party

A focus on content is not, however, the only way of articulating political meaning in cinema. The form of the narrative and the modes of its telling are as important to the project of education, or legitimation through film. The synopses I
offer sadly lack the heart of the films I describe. The reader cannot see and feel
the beauty of the actors, nor the effect that such beauty has on an audience's reception of the violence in the films. A mere synopsis cannot give the thrill of
recognition within a star system; without her screen presence Tian Hua becomes
merely a name rather than a phenomenon. And although a careful elucidation of
narrative patterns and themes gives an idea of what is going on in a film culture,
it cannot quite grasp the emotional force of repetition at the scale of full-length
features. Yet it is *content* to which international audiences are often invited to
reduce films outside their immediate cultural experience. It is an unfortunate
emphasis that takes away from the formation of filmic texts as visual objects of
pleasure, and study. Or, more worryingly, it encourages filmmakers to concentrate so hard on the surface visuality of the text, that any sense of a *visual subtext*
or a symbolic level of visual conceptualization (as opposed to a 'hidden meaning' that must be explained in terms of allegory), is lost before we start to watch
and look. In the same process of beautifying and dumbing the 'foreign film',
'content' has also been taken up by international distributors as a means of explaining the ideological (read 'non-Western') workings of a particular text. This
is in no small part a marketing strategy. International, and perhaps especially
Western, international film audiences tend to know very little about China. It is

frightening, for example, to face a roomful of Media Studies undergraduates who do not recognize the names of Mao Zedong or Deng Xiaoping. One of the off-shoots of these blank faces is a film market that has to mobilize, and then conflate, the entire range of popular knowledge about China in order to attract attention to its cultural production. Thus, Zhang Yimou's period pieces (*Ju Dou*, 1989; *Raise the Red Lantern*, 1991; *Red Sorghum*, 1987) are taken as allegories, and much of the later work of the so-called Fifth Generation (at least the men in that cohort), which is targeted at the international market—and often partly funded by offshore producers—is overtly politico-historical. The prime examples are Zhang's *To Live* (1993, Era International HK with Shanghai Film Studio), Chen Kaige's *Farewell My Concubine* (1993, Tomson HK Film Corp. with Beijing Film Studio), and Tian Zhuangzhuang's *The Blue Kite* (1993, Longwick HK Film with Beijing Film Studio). The content of these films is, in part, designed to entertain and educate the international spectator, as well as to give voice to memories from within Chinese imaginations, but the one is not quite the same as the other—and sheer content does not fulfill both objectives. It seems to me that an excessive concentration on content denies the importance of film as art (to borrow David Bordwell and Kristin Thompson's key phrase from their much reprinted classic *Film Art*).[4] It also ignores the possible subtleties of symbolic form and meaning in a film text, and the phenomenological possibilities of spectatorship. This has not been the fate of Hong Kong cinema, where Abbas's theories of disappear-ance have focussed specifically on the notion of symbolic space in the produc-tion of local memory, nor Taiwanese cinema, where the poetics of Hou Hsiao-hsien (*The Time to Live, The Time to Die*, 1985; *Dust in the Wind*, 1986), and the minimalism of Tsai Ming-liang (*Vive L'Amour*, 1995), demand integrated theo-retical and political attention.[5] In this book I will endeavor to accord Mainland cinema the same courtesies.

In setting up my analytic perspective, I argue that the current scholarly con-cern, with the existence or not of civil society in contemporary China, is frus-trated by a fundamental conceptual problem. This is that the concept of civil so-ciety originates in Western political thought and is dependent on ideas of liberal democracy.[6] Therefore, research into the existence of civil society must be linked to an investigation into the possibility of liberal democracy in China. This is not in itself a problem, except insofar as it precludes the researcher from wondering about other modes of human association, or autonomous, or spontaneous, politi-cal actions that do not fulfill the criteria of liberal democratic models of organi-zation or behavior. There is also a lack of attention to the symbolic sphere, and to the public imaginary, in research into civil society.

The form of film is one of the ways in which the public imaginary is articu-lated. Cinematic form produces a look, a feel, and a method of attraction, all of which combine in making space. It is this cinematic space, which invites and requires public participation, or spectatorship. Of course, spectatorship must be understood in context, both immediate and historical. I will briefly describe the ways in which Chinese cinema can be historicized, and indicate how I understand the divisions. I aim to combine sparse synopses with a wider frame of reference, but there is no substitute for seeking these films out and seeing them anew and afresh.

GENERATIONS

International spectators have become used to thinking about Chinese film as a history divided into generations. 'Generation' nametags are descriptive and convenient, but they should not be taken as absolute delineations of the form, or content, of the directors' films. The third and fourth generations have worked simultaneously, the fourth and fifth, and the fourth, fifth, and sixth. Their coincidences will produce as much similarity as their histories produce difference. The first and second generations are taken to mean the pioneers of the 1890s, and those who developed the medium in the first two decades of this century.[7] Very early films (1905–08) were operatic shorts; they were followed by short comic skits, and eventually by features. The first feature-length Chinese film was *Yan Ruishen,* (1921, China Film Research Society). In 1920, the Wan Brothers started the tradition of Chinese-animated film. In the same year Communist film units were set up in Shanghai, Guangzhou, and Beijing. In the1920s, dance artistes (Li Lili, Wang Renmei) were moved from variety onto the screen, although not to unanimous acclaim. A critic wrote in 1931 that "Unfortunately, the film world as a whole (and especially Hollywood) is pursuing a dangerous trend of turning anything that moves on stage into a film."[8] This critic turned away from the vulgarity of the musical to the exquisite performances of Ruan Lingyu. Her artistry exemplified the passionate social conscience that had developed, through May Fourth sensibilities, into film practice. In *The Peach Girl* (1932, Lianhua Studios) the potential of the melodrama for political storytelling was well appreciated.

> However you look at it, and by general reckoning, *Taohua qi xue ji* (*The Peach Girl*) is Lianhua's best picture to date. Especially from the point of view of Ruan Lingyu's performance. . . . There's passion in her every expression. . . . China still has many feudal influences and *Taohua qi xue ji* (The Peach Girl) ruthlessly targets and draws lessons from the downside of old Confucian ethics and feudal ways of thinking. . . . The present writer genuinely believes Ruan Lingyu's artistry will one day serve all mankind, and not simply be a means of lining the pockets of a chosen few.[9]

Sadly Ruan Lingyu committed suicide in March 1935. The dialectic of collective virtue, which she would doubtless have played out on screen alongside (or in competition with) Tian Hua, had she lived, came too late. According to her suicide note, she was in despair at gossip about her private life. It is very much a story of a Shanghai Hollywood, and not the saving of China from feudal oppression envisaged by the reviewer quoted previously.[10] Yet Ruan's story, seen from the perspective of the end of the twentieth century, is but a whisper of the theme of divorce and scandal that is in full flower in contemporary films and soaps on the Chinese mainland. The passion of Ruan Lingyu has survived at least as well as the political aspirations of Lianhua Studios.[11]

Sang Hu and Shui Hua are representative figures of the third generation of Chinese filmmakers.[12] Sang's films include *Joys and Sorrows of Middle Age* (1949), *A Peaceful Spring* (1950), the scripting of *A Make-Believe Couple* (1947), and *New Year Sacrifice* (1956). All show evidence of Hollywood-style camera set-ups and editing techniques. In particular, the films of the 1940s use the tricks of fast action detective movie narration: two- to three-head dialogue sequences to introduce and develop story lines, jump cuts, and cuts on action to keep several narrative strands in place without losing momentum or suspense, and dream sequences or flashbacks. *Joys and Sorrows of Middle Age* deals with fatherhood and the demands of national politics. Its content is contemporary and local to China, although the emphasis on private priorities would surely have shifted had the film been made a year or two later. Indeed, this film is more easily understood in the context of filmmaking in Taiwan under Guomindang rule than in post-Liberation China. *A Make-Believe Couple*, released two years previously, also deals with the social concerns of the May Fourth tradition and the radical movement, but through a comic story line. Class inequalities are displayed. The hero is a woman's hairdresser looking for a rich wife, and the heroine is a young single mother looking for a rich husband. They both engage in deception and end up with each other. It is a familiar romantic comedy of the Hollywood mode, and self-consciously so: the female characters dress in American 1940s film fashion, and the heroine's make-believe persona is based on the lie that she has just returned from the United States.

The last film, *New Year's Sacrifice*, is a definite departure from this unabashed adoption of recognizably Hollywood stylization, although the pessimistic humanism of the narrative would not have been approved ten years later in the era of revolutionary romanticism. Based on a famous short story by the May Fourth intellectual writer, Lu Xun, it deals with the suffering of a woman whose husband's family has discarded her after her baby son has been carried off by wild animals, and who is now working as a servant and due to her misfortunes, is considered too unlucky to take part in ritual sacrifices and religious ceremonies. Although the treatment is familiarly melodramatic, the solemnity of the adaptation suggests that the director has appreciated the developing requirements of socialist realism in Communist China.[13] Sang Hu's name also appears in much later productions. In 1975 he made *The Second Spring* (an anti-Soviet naval drama), and in 1979 *Twins Come in Pairs* reprises the farcical misunderstandings of *A Make-Believe Couple* in a twins' romance comedy.

Shui Hua is mainly known for *The White-haired Girl*, which he made in 1950. It uses melodrama and socialist realism in a fine mix of drama and ideology. His later films push this mixture of melodrama and politics to the breaking point. *Land*

(1954) tells the story of land reform in the 1930s. The efforts of a local activist are thwarted by the 'Devil' and his brother, a couple of evil landlords, who burn the hero to death. He is avenged twenty years later, by his son. It is an unremarkable tale of revolutionary heroism and the inevitable defeat of feudalism. In terms of Shui Hua's oeuvre, it can also be seen as a clever reworking of traditional narrative structures to new ends. The avenger of the father is pitted against evil brothers. The retention of the family at the center of the narrative eases the transition from individualism to collective revenge. In *Lin Family Shop* (1959) a middle-class family shopkeeper in Chejiang is under pressure from all sides. It is 1931 and the Japanese have taken Shanghai. Student leaders are calling for a boycott of Japanese goods. Lin and his competitors relabel the goods they have in stock, but at home his own daughter complains that she has only Japanese clothes and will be mocked if she wears them to school. Meanwhile, agents of the ruling KMT (GMD—*Guomindang*—Nationalist Party) are using the boycott as another excuse for extortion, and the bank is threatening to foreclose on Lin's debts in the face of the crisis. Despite a few good marketing ideas when refugees come to town (dollar packages of basins, soap, brushes, and towels), Lin's future begins to implode. As the unnamed narrator has warned us: "the big fish eat the little fish and the little fish eat the shrimps." Lin runs away, taking his daughter, and leaving his wife and son-in-law to lie their way out of trouble. So far, this synopsis might suggest a regular family melodrama. Perhaps at this point we are sympathetic towards Lin, or his wife, or even his rather petulant daughter. Shui Hua is more interesting than that, however. *Lin Family Shop* exploits the genre to its full potential, but retains an extra political edge by multiplying the melodramatic focus across competing family units. The Lins are hounded by the Nationalists and the bank. They in turn victimize at least three other groups of people. One is a stall-holder, who is forced to return basins to them for their 'cheap dollar packages'. He has a young family, and will have to sell his children to survive this petty disaster. Lin also has two investors. One is an old lady, whose own greed is not attractive, but understandable as her investment is her only source of income. The other is a single mother with a baby boy to raise. At the end of the film, as the bank and Shanghai traders close up Lin's shop to strip the assets, she and the other minor creditors are left outside beating on the door (figure 1.2). A voice-over cuts in again, reminding us of the didactic direction of what we might have mistaken for a middle-class family melodrama: "it is the poor who really suffer." The climax of the film is not Lin's pathetic retreat on a boat into the sunset; it is the death of the baby boy as he is trampled under the feet of the poor retreating from the brutality of the police. Shui's facility with melodrama is fully explored here. He takes an international cinematic formula, and recasts it in such a way that the genre sustains the story, but at the end is trumped by its own denouement. The generic flexibility of Sang Hu's and Shui Hua's work warns us against categorizing film directors too stringently. They work within political

Figure 1.2 Lin Family Shop

constraints, but their professionalism plays a major role in the enduring interest of their films.

The fourth generation refers to filmmakers, who trained before the Cultural Revolution, but who have continued to work in the 1970s, 1980s, and 1990s. Several of these directors had served apprenticeships in the early 1960s but have only made their first features in the last twenty years. They were active in the late 1970s in promoting new Chinese film and have been rather unfairly overlooked by the international film market in the wake of the fifth generation, whose emergence was arguably made possible by the efforts of this group of older directors. Xie Jin is especially popular with domestic film audiences, and his success spans twenty-one films and three decades of filmmaking. He has won several awards in the Chinese 'Golden Rooster' ceremonies.[14] His films are melodramatic epics of personal suffering, and particularly successful examples of the wound (*shang hen*) genre, stories of individual tragedy and eventual triumph that deal with the experiences of the Cultural Revolution in cathartic and personalized narratives. Titles include *Woman Basketball Player No. 5* (1957), *Young Masters of the Great Leap Forward (Service)* (1958), *Red Detachment of Women* (1961), *Two Stage Sisters* (1964), *On the Docks* (1972) (with Xie Tieli), *The Legend of Tianyun Mountain* (1980), *Herdsman* (1982), *Hibiscus Town* (1986), *Twilight Star* (1992), and *Women's Valley* (1995). The leading Chinese film critic, Ni Zhen, makes it clear that, as an onlooker who has been familiar with Chinese film before the Chinese New Wave broke on the shores of international film criticism, he judges the fourth generation to be the innovators, and the fifth their inheritors (although he also fails to mention Xie Jin):

Yellow Earth was made in the summer of 1984, a time when the group experiments, dominated by middle-aged directors from 1979 to 1983, had reached a comparatively stable stage. The first wave of Chinese new film, which lasted four years, had subsided, and filmmakers such as Wu Yigong, Hu Bingliu, Huang Jianzhong, Zhang Nuanxin, and Teng Wenji were experiencing an interval of meditation, reorganization, and renewal before launching a second breakthrough.[15]

The fifth generation, or the 'new-wave' cinema, refers to the filmmakers who graduated from the Beijing Film Academy in 1983. They were the first group to train since the Academy reopened in 1979 after the Cultural Revolution. The most famous of the group are undoubtedly Chen Kaige, whose films include *Yellow Earth* (1984), *The Big Parade* (1985), *King of the Children* (1987), *Life on a String* (1990), and *Farewell My Concubine* (1993); Zhang Yimou: *Yellow Earth* (cinematographer) (1983), *Red Sorghum* (1987), *Ju Dou* (1989), *Raise the Red Lantern* (1991), *The Story of Qiu Ju* (1992), *Shanghai Triad* (1995); and Tian Zhuangzhuang: *On the Hunting Ground* (1985), *The Horsethief* (1986), *The Blue Kite* (1993). These filmmakers were fortunate in having the opportunity to work on 'experimental' (*tansuo*) projects in the Beijing Youth Film Unit or under the guidance of Wu Tianming at the Xi'an studio.[16]

There are also lesser-known, but extremely skillful, women in the group. Notable of these are Peng Xiaolian, who in 1993 had decided to work as an independent filmmaker and lecturer in New York, and whose work includes *Me and My Classmates* (1985) (figure 1.3), and *A Story of Women* (1988); Hu Mei (co-director) of *Army Nurse* (1985), and director of *Far Away from War* (1987) that

Figure 1.3   Me and My Classmates

won prizes at festivals in Moscow and Salso, *A Marksman without a Gun* (1988), *An Emperor on the Run* (1991), and *Urban Gunman* (1992). As someone who has worked at the People's Liberation Army's August First film studio (her first three films were produced there), Hu Mei has managed to tell action stories, while dwelling on the erotic and painful aspects of military life. Li Shaohong, *Bloody Morning* (1990) (figure 1.4), *A Family Portrait* (1992) (figure 1.5), and *Blush* (1995), moves easily between the rural and the urban, the contemporary and the nostalgic.

Peng Xiaolian's work might be described as feminist-humanist. *Me and My Classmates* was made at the Shanghai (Youth) Film Studio, and concerns high school students. A class of students is looking for someone to take responsibility for the basketball team. Surprisingly, a girl is chosen. Her election is a joke, played by the class on their rather dour monitor. Yet, once elected, the girl takes her duties seriously; the monitor learns to listen to her classmates, and the boys learn to take women on as friends and classmates (*tongxue*). The visual rhetoric is clearly ideological. At the moment of reconciliation, students all sit on a rooftop praising the red sunset, discussing the positive qualities of the color red. The scene complements the theme of harmony between genders, while contextualizing these students' lives in late socialism. In her second film, *A Story of Women*, Peng deals with country women on a marketing trip to the city. There are no red setting suns, and there is no ideological rhetoric. But, then, these women are not at school, although at least one is young enough to be so, had she not been poor and recently married off to a deaf mute. This shift is not simply a result of the

Figure 1.4   Bloody Morning

Figure 1.5   Family Portrait

director serving the interests of her producers in each case. She tells appropriate stories for the subject matter, but she establishes a feminist symbolic system in both texts.[17] As Mary Ann Farquhar has demonstrated in her account of *Chinese Children's Literature,* education and ideology are aligned in the practice of storytelling.[18] Had Peng avoided this structure of thought she would have, perhaps, denied the poignancy of adolescence in the arms of a grand discourse. For, as her scene conveys, redness is only visible *after* the young people have learned to listen to each other's voices. In *Bloody Morning,* Li Shaohong uses a Gabriel García Márquez story, adapting it as a vehicle to discuss the tensions between the peasantry and educated professionals. In her statement for the London Film Festival screening in 1992, Li wrote,

> For me, the film has an allegorical level to its simple storyline. On the surface, it can be read as a story about the conflict between civilization and human ignorance, the former's defeat by the latter. For me, the murder in the end may or may not be incidental. Through this incident, I want to lay bare the cross-section of a whole society and its culture, thus exposing the psychology of a people to whom existence means mere survival.[19]

Family Portrait looks at the relationship between a family man and his son by a previous relationship, highlighting the burgeoning incompatibility between the family values of Maoist China and those of the urban entrepreneurial society of the 1990s. *Blush* tells the story of two prostitutes from their reeducation after

Liberation to their sorry attempts at marriage and motherhood. Li's work is diverse and mature and prompts the question, Why is it that transnational spectatorship seems only really interested in the works of her male contemporaries, Chen and Zhang?

CENSORSHIP AND INVESTMENT

In China there have been major state studios since the1950s. The number jumped from four in 1952 to sixteen by 1962. There is a national animation/children's studio in Shanghai, and the People's Liberation Amy (PLA) studio, August First.[20] Until spring 1994, these were all heavily subsidized by the China Film, Broadcasting and Television Bureau (CFTB), to whose officials they would submit every treatment and screenplay before commencing with a project. If, having received approval, the film was made, it would then be resubmitted for release. Any problems at that stage would result either in the film being shelved completely, or in so few prints being authorized that it could be distributed only very selectively. Since 1994, there has been some de-coupling of the studios from central budgetary controls, and this has pushed them towards strong commercial prioritization with, ironically perhaps, far less economic scope for experiments than was possible in the early to mid-1980s. It seems that market forces can work as an effective source of censorship in the right conditions.[21]

Preventive censorship was most effective, or most damaging, at times of political uncertainty. During the Cultural Revolution, roughly defined as 1966–76, the pressure on workers in the film industry was intense. In 1969, many artists were expelled from the studios and sent to May Seventh Cadre Schools, which were basically labor camps for ex-officials. The Shanghai Film Bureau investigated 104 of 108 high-level cadres, and 31 of its contracted 44 directors were subjected to criticism. Shanghai was particularly badly hit as it represented an era of film history that predated Liberation and was tainted with the ideas of liberal humanism that characterized the literature and films that emerged from the thinking of the May Fourth Movement (1919).[22] The excesses of the Shanghai-based radical faction known as the Small Group (*xiaobang*) in 1966–68 effectively silenced the film industry for almost a decade.[23]

As a result few films were made, and those that were tended to conform to the factionalized aesthetics of Jiang Qing, Mao's wife, and a prime mover in cultural politics at the time. She carried forward the Maoist aesthetic ideal of combining revolutionary realism and revolutionary romanticism. Productions that were considered safe were screen adaptations of revolutionary model performances (*geming yangban xi*). The shortest plot synopsis I have read is slipped into William Kessen's work on childhood in China. In an interview with an 'ordinary' workers' family in 1973, the interviewer asks about a film they have just seen. S/he is told: "[It was] about bandits who wanted to dynamite a train. They were outwitted by the People's Liberation Army."[24] The implied undertone in Kessel's book is that the film sounded a touch boring. Yet, we cannot necessarily accept that judgment. It is very important not to write off films of the late 1960s and early 1970s as insubstantial. They had large audiences, who still remember them, and who even today are buying up the 'eight [opera] classics' on VCD, for replay in their homes. These extravagant romances of revolution were made in a time of confusion and mixed political emotions. Much about that time appears to have been destructive, both of individual personalities and of the collective psyche of revolutionary China. Many readers will have encountered the recent spate of memoirs, widely available from American and European booksellers, which recount tales of horror, victimization, and final 'escape' to the diaspora. They may therefore assume that those stories are the only ways of approaching the period. They should look further to the more finely ambiguous recollections of Chen Xiaomei and Rui Yang, but also to the films themselves. Chen remembers that her favorite color was red.[25] Looking at these films, with the fixed association of political strength and revolutionary honor with redness, that is not at all surprising. Nor would it be extraordinary if red became the favorite color of a whole generation of filmgoers. The making of redness on film is a question of publicness. To what extent was redness owned by totalizing political agents of the State, and to what degree was it at large in the imaginations of the people who lived with it? After all, redness has not disappeared from Chinese film culture since the death of Mao Zedong, or the suicide of his wife Jiang Qing. It is used to catch the breath of China-hungry filmgoers in many popular new films. Most people will be familiar with the color saturation techniques of Zhang Yimou—think of that last scene in *Red Sorghum* when the screen fills with red, denoting blood, the dying sun, the color of the earth, and connoting the rising sun of the revolution through the bloodline of bereaved male bodies. But its success as a sequence is dependent also upon an affective response to the color red. The cinematography expects that the audience will both recognize the textbook connotations, but will also have already taken the color as their own, giving it over time the personality of public ownership. This is also the personality of long-term usage; red meant celebration long before revolution became something to celebrate. But in any case, had it been purely within the limits of central semiotic direction, no one would wear it or think it.[26] Redness is beyond semiotics in Chinese film. It is one of the colors that dominates the landscape of the political, cultural, and social imaginaries of Chinese life on the mainland. Its publicness lies in the recognition of redness that relies on but is not confined to the transferable meaning of redness across time.

    Not everything is the right shade of red, and some films are described by the Bureau of Propaganda as 'yellow' (*huangse*—obscene). Since the opening up of the film industry in the late 1970s and 1980s, there has been a shift towards retrospective censorship (although of course it is difficult to guess at how many treatments, scripts, and early rushes have been culled for political reasons in this period). Retrospective censorship describes the suppression of films that are already completed. They are either not distributed at all, or are subjected to major cuts. In 1993, Tian Zhuangzhuang's *The Blue Kite* was made as an approved co-production with Japan, but the final version was not approved by the CFTB, and only exists because a copy of the negative was stored in Japan.[27] People close to the culture industry do not know, or profess not to know, of its existence. Yet Tian still has a studio within the central Beijing Film Studios' complex. In the same year, the fourth generation director, Zhang Nuanxin's drama of life on the buses in Beijing, *Good Morning Beijing (1991)* was suddenly pulled out of the London National Film Theatre's retrospective season on Chinese film, at the demand of the Chinese Embassy.[28] Other directors, chiefly the sixth generation, have avoided the studio system and worked independently. Zhang Yuan's films, *Beijing Bastards* (1993), and *East Palace, West Palace* (1996) (released in film festivals 1998–99), are unlikely to be distributed to domestic cinemas, but they have made an impact on the international art-film scene.[29]

This brief account indicates the complexity of analyzing cinema as an institution of civil society in China in the 1980s and 1990s. The level of central controls, administered in the interests of the state, is clearly not compatible with the ideals of parallel autonomy in a liberal democracy. Conversely, the industry and its workers were not, as yet, in the thrall of the same economic constraints that filmmakers contend with in the bear pit of capitalist freedoms. It would be similarly problematic to attempt some kind of audience analysis to determine the effects of certain films on certain audiences, especially taking into account the factors of uneven cinematic distribution in the Chinese film market. Both these conditions are further complicated by the emergence of Chinese cinema as another example of a national industry serving domestic and international audiences, drawing on finance and talent from inside and outside the territory of the People's Republic, and increasingly having to acknowledge and compete with Hollywood. The results are mixed. The remarkable *Farewell My Concubine* (1993) is a film that I do not particularly like, but of which I must always acknowledge its skill (and its profound effects on transnational Chinese and non-Chinese audiences). In August 1998 one of the 'big' films (after *Titanic* had closed) was *Red Hot Lover* (1998). The film, directed by Ye Daying, a son of Marshall Ye, is set in the 1930s and 1940s. It tells the story of a revolutionary martyr and his love for his young wife who shares his struggle. She is also loved in vain by an American doctor, who narrates. This is a film that hedges its bets. There are two male stars, one white and one Chinese. The Chinese is played by Leslie Cheung, a serious Hong Kong heartthrob, and star of many films of Wong Kar-wai. The Chinese hero dies, but so does the woman, so there is no transnational adultery, but no sentimental disappointment for the American audience either. She dies in childbirth, and the doctor undertakes to raise her daughter. This causes a slight blip when we are shown the Liberation of China and the child, Pearl, seeing the faces of her father and mother in those of the dancing celebrants from the People's Liberation

Army. How can a Chinese mainland audience put up with the American whisking this daughter of the Revolution back to the United States in 1949? He doesn't of course, and American spectators have to live with the sop (printed in English at the end of the film) that Pearl revisited her 'step-father' in the late 1980s and helped him write his memoirs of 'A Time to Remember'. This film is particularly outrageous in its attempt to please all of the people all of the time. On the one hand, it woos an international (American) audience, while on the other hand it tries to reinvent the magic of Liberation and martyrdom for a jaded domestic palate. I was told by friends, however, that most Beijingers liked the film because it was so funny to watch a Hong Kong star play a Communist so convincingly. The point of this story, for the present book, is that it exemplifies the possibilities in looking at Chinese film. *Red Hot Lover* could be analyzed for its return to the historical and military emphases of the August First studios. It could be thought of as politically sound marketing: an attempt to revitalize the ideological imaginations of domestic audiences, while telling a satisfying love story to everyone else. Or, given the purchase of the face of Leslie Cheung in revolutionary guise, the film could be seen as a glimpse into the symbolic structure of contemporary cinematic imaginations in China. It is not a very good film, but it affords a moment of public space in a coincidence of casting and timing. Leslie Cheung became an on-screen martyr within twelve months of the return of Hong Kong to Chinese sovereignty, and people noticed that, and enjoyed it.

PUNCTURES IN THE FILMIC TEXT

These readings are premised on the idea that narrative and narration are susceptible to tension and puncture, which inject meaning into the text as a whole, and which may not be immediately obvious in terms of story or plot. Such tensions or disruptions to the text are significant, in that they can render a film political by radicalizing the relationship between spectator and text. This suggests that it is possible to discover public space in a filmic text.

First, I have been influenced by Miriam Hansen's work on the silent film era, and in particular her writing on the question of spectatorship. For Hansen, a spectator is not simply a member of a specific audience, whose responses to a particular film may be studied through discourse analysis, ethnography, or other sociological methodologies. The spectator occupies a subjective position that is determined to a greater or lesser extent—and it is that relationship which is most open to debate—by the form and content of the film itself. Hansen makes a useful distinction between spectatorship after the establishment of the classical Hollywood mode of narration, and in the early period—up to about 1910. She shows that, although the suturing between spectator and text is characteristic of classic Hollywood narration, early films also achieved a complicity with the spectator through an open prioritization of the spectators' point of view: "With their em-

phasis on display, early films are self-consciously exhibitionist, whereas classical cinema disavows its exhibitionist quality in order to maintain the spell of the
invisible gaze."[30] She further suggests that the direct address of the early films,
where reality was filmed rather than being constructed *on film*, gave it a publicness that resembled the theatre, or any public 'live' event. This induced in the
audience "a sense of collective presence" and created a space-time continuum
between them and the events on screen.[31]

Hansen expands her hypothesis in a discussion of cinema as an alternative
public sphere in which identifiable audience groups exploit the subjectivity of
spectatorship to their own advantage. She gives the example of the vast numbers
of women (forty percent of the audience in 1910), who used the cinema itself as
an alternative public space, and who used film as a source of imaginary identification for relief from daily life and as a psychic space in which a collective sense
of dissatisfaction could be played with and developed into an alternative political imaginary . If one combines Hansen's identification of the "sense of collective presence" in early cinema, and her intuition of the political psyche developing in the symbolic sphere of film in the classical period, it is possible to conceive
of film which can be read as either *intentionally* addressing an alternative public, or as in doing so as a result of its inherent coherence with an 'alternative'
contemporary mood. The collectivity is reproduced by a return to direct, contemporary address, placed in the text in the form of a disruption to the classical mode,
or in the case of Chinese cinema, the classical mode as modified by socialist realism and revolutionary romanticism.

My second cue comes from Thomas Elsaesser in his essay on German silent
cinema. He gives an important warning against treating films as transparent social or historical documents. There may be films and genres that seem to mirror
historical or social circumstances, or the form of which seem to offer a paradigmatic or causal explanation of social phenomena. However, an analysis of such
films, and of others in which—and Elsaesser looks closely at Siegfried Kracauer's
study of the fantastic films of German Expressionism—the link is less obvious,
should refuse a neat reduction of filmic text to reality.

> If one therefore wants to avoid making analysis a self-fulfilling prophecy, any rea-
> soning about the social or political meaning of films . . . has to respect both the
> autonomy of the historical dimension and the autonomy of the textual level, and seek
> structures—not where they overlap or mirror each other—but at the points of con-
> tact, where there is evidence that the text has seized, worked over, displaced, or
> objectified elements of the historical or social sphere, in order to bring them to rep-
> resentation within the text's own formal or generic constraints.[32]

So how does one begin to recognize these points of contact? How do we start
elaborating on public spaces, which by virtue of their specificity must be a secret to anyone who is not a participant in their maintenance and formation?

Elsaesser writes of "objectified elements" and that is the lifeline that helps a great deal. Indeed, one of the problems with Kracauer's reading of German film with the hindsight afforded by the rise of Nazism, is that he relied too heavily on his own experience, and not enough on the bodies of the films themselves.[33] By the end of that treatise, the one becomes the other and it is impossible to either argue or concur with its conclusions. "Objectified elements" on the other hand, are presumably carved out of the text by the film analyst in consideration of both its phenomenal and historical construction. This work means that we need to identify possible markers of such elements, in order to discover their political, social, and above all contemporary dynamism. 'Redness' is central to a whole slew of films made in the 1950s and must surely be one such mediator.[34] The color that had long been used to celebrate marriage reemerges in the 1950s and 1960s to symbolize the energy and the glory of the liberated China, carry the continuity of traditional social structures as they are shifted into Party hierarchies, and made simultaneously worthy and sexy in the pursuit of nationhood. But, the films are more than the sum of these four elements, and 'redness' is more than the signifier of their presence in the body of the film. It is the autonomy of the signifier, red, as well as its efficacy in symbolizing and embodying exterior meanings, that Elsaesser reminds us to be careful of in our analysis. "Elements" are also "made visible" through means other than the literal color of experience. They are "worked over" in the generic structure; casting; tropes of performance; intertextual referencing; motifs; cueing; in short in any aspect of the narration which lends itself to commentary. The following chapters illustrate my interest is not so much in films in which political or historical or social elements are neatly limited to the textual level—after this 'working over' in the formation of the text. I am more concerned with the times when the work-over produces a dissonance, or political/cultural 'hiccup', between the film and the matter it tries to contain, when the audience may step in and actively recognize a change between what might once, ideally, have been a perfect fit, but is now a moment framing the dynamics of imperfection. These are the moments of space that the text offers to the spectator, and which the contemporary condition of the spectator makes possible within the text.

2

Seeing White: Methods and Arguments

In the previous chapter I began to address the problem of locating cultural space in a film text. I identified my starting points within screen theory and film history. Here I return to the problematic of the idea of civil society, and its roots in the models of the public sphere, in order to describe the concept of public space and how it might be understood in film.[1] In the following analyses I argue that the Habermasian ideal of communicative action can be understood as operative both within and across cultural boundaries, and that its manifestations may be described as *cultural public space*. This approach to textual analysis reveals mutual pathologies within modern experience, which resonate across very different cultural discourses. I look at the production of gender, as part of two separate discourses of whiteness, Chinese and British, in one of the foundation texts of revolutionary Chinese cinema, *The White-haired Girl* (1950), and in the British classic *Black Narcissus* (1947). In these films the transection relation of gender across local emphases, on class and race respectively, indicates structural likenesses between two semiotic systems of meaning. Cultural public spaces are sometimes, therefore, places of cross-cultural association and collision.

I choose a cross-cultural analysis for two reasons. First, I need to situate myself as a non-Chinese spectator, and this is one positive way of doing that. Second, and rather more importantly, I am concerned to emphasize that public imaginaries are not always how we might hope. I am not seeking to romanticize either the popular or the public. Rather, I want to investigate its symptoms, warts and all. As someone very concerned with the ways in which females and femininity are experienced in the symbolic sphere, I pay particular heed to ways in which publicness articulates the exclusion of women in cultural space. The following analysis suggests that strategies of containment of female agency are as much part of cultural practice as they are endemic in political and social organization.

I begin, however, with a short discussion of the very concept of the civil in political discourse. I will argue that Habermas is both inappropriate *and* extremely helpful in formulating a framework in which to look closely at Chinese film. This contradiction rests simply on a choice of sources. Instead of relying solely on Habermas's work on the public sphere, which may be familiar to many readers, I also want to open up his thoughts on communication. Between these two trajectories of his philosophy, there is a path that leads us to the excitement and danger of publicness in the cultural arena.[2]

CULTURE AND CIVILITY

Culture is . . . organization, discipline of one's inner self, a coming to terms with one's own personality, it is the attainment of a higher awareness, with the aid of which one succeeds in understanding one's own historical value, one's own function in life, one's own rights and obligations . . . man is mind, he is a product of history, not nature.[3]

The extensive literature in the debate on civil society in China covers many interesting political and social studies.[4] Yet, its most persuasive if often unstated conclusion is that the concept at issue *as formulated at present* is irrelevant to the Chinese case. Richard Madsen, an American sociologist who has written widely on the notion of culture in China, has identified the problem of a research agenda for China that relies on a non-Asian, let alone non-Chinese, premise. He notes the difficulties that arise from identifying groups and organizations that have their own agenda and are self-financing as 'civil'. He points out that the effect of these groups in a political arena where the state has previously held the monopoly of power may be to weaken that power, but it also may be to destabilize society. In which case do these groups really conform to the Western notion of civil society as the safeguard of democratic political structures? Madsen writes that the Habermasian public sphere, if properly "abstracted" and concentrated on "moral and cultural dimensions," is a good basis for understanding China's democratic future. He does not however make the most immediate abstractions, between public sphere and civil society, and so between public sphere and democracy. Moral and cultural dimensions are therefore still inflected by the European case model. As he says: "Some scholars are calling this whole range of associations—everything from democracy salons to organizations of private households (*geti hu*) to clan associations to *qigong* clubs—'civil society'. But some are certainly more civil than others."[5]

Madsen is on the right track, but does not go far enough in his inquiry into the disputed terms before reusing them in the Asian context. "Those with the quality of 'civility' might eventually contribute to the creation of a democratic public sphere (which would not necessarily require the establishment of a

Western-style liberal democracy). Those without it may simply push China closer to anarchy."[6] Madsen wants to keep hold of civility as a sovereign component of civil society, but without defining it. Despite his claim that a "Western-style liberal democracy" is not part of his equation for Chinese civil society, his expectations of civility are processed through those values that do indeed underpin liberal democracy. He does argue that it is the quality of human relationships that signals a civility on which democracy may be predicated, and that these relationships may be found in surprising cultural forms. He cites in particular work that has been done around the media of memory in public spaces. For Madsen there must, however, be evidence of a "voluntarily organized citizenry." In premising the emergence of a public sphere, on the existence of an already developed civil society Richard Madsen's argument effectively conflates communicated action, democracy, and the public sphere.[7]

The present argument moves in the other direction. Components of the concept of 'civil society' are used as referential clues in the analyses of the films. These components, interest (individual or group), virtue (standards normalized as 'civil'), and action (the cultural enactment of ideas in public), are markers of publicness, which emerge as symptoms of a symbolic sphere of film. The American sociologist Edward Shils has defined civil society as a threefold concept containing a "complex of autonomous institutions," a "part of society possessing a particular complex of relationships between itself and the state and a distinctive set of institutions that safeguard the separation of state and civil society and maintain effective ties between them, and a widespread pattern of refined or civil manners."[8] Paradoxically, Shils's definition is useful because its apparent clarity masks common assumptions that need to be questioned in a cross-cultural context. First, he writes of civility as though it were a universal fact of life, rather than a constantly changing product of culturally and materially effected value systems. Secondly, he takes the process of communication for granted, and does not separate it out as an intentional and meaningful act. He writes of institutions, relationships, and manners, but without identifying communication as the means by which all three are constructed and reproduced. Shils defines civil society, but he does not acknowledge the social and cultural specificities of the ways in which it is constituted, and in which that constitution functions. Shils writes of civil society as though it emerges as an institutional form of a natural 'pattern' of refinement. He writes of interest and virtue, but does not recognize that, while they give clues to the normative space of publicness in a symbolic world, they are not, of themselves, 'normal'. The third component of the concept of civil society is human action, and this is the key to unlocking the potential of public space. The idea is taken from Hannah Arendt's concept of action as the highest form of *vita activa*, but is also influenced by the pragmatic arts policies of Mao Zedong. Action as a component of civility has the dimension of the unpredictable. It is the process of enacting intention, but its outcomes are not as intended. More than that, to take action is to accept that the consequences are unknown. The contradiction at the center of socialist action, visualized in socialist-realist culture, is the explicit denial of this unpredictability.

In Mao Zedong's formulations of popular intervention, it was always the institutions led by Party policy who would interpret the people's views and return them packaged as the mass line.[9] Recent developments in Chinese public life suggest that Gramsci's version of 'hegemony and consent' can allow a more radical connection between twentieth-century Western ideas of publicity and participation, and Chinese political philosophy.[10] Gramsci's version of the superstructure is a sphere of catharsis. The determining factors of the base are recognized, interpreted, and acted upon through consciousness, and are maintained in this sphere. Communicated action not only gives subjective form to the human experience, but can actually effect the conditions of that existence by freeing human action to initiate its own meaning.[11] This insight gives determining power over to individual and collective will, at *the moment of recognition* of the material agents that bind the will. Therefore, civil consciousness is only politically active at those moments when the public can identify the conditions of its submission to the state. This interpretation allows for acts of radicalism within a seemingly closed society, such as China, while not demanding that signs of autonomy indicate a move towards Western-style liberal democratic freedoms.

Madsen's ideas on shared memories and illicit communication helps elucidate cultural texts, but only if the democratic agenda is put aside. A film will not, at least in my argument, produce democracy. It may, however, contain moments of publicity that give symbolic weight to the history, memories, and psychic organization of particular groups of people. Film can narrate the present, and the collective political mood of that present, in ways that are not available to more tangible forms of human organization. Such a 'mood' is contemporary and hard to express in full; it is *more* than its common expression but *less* than its psychic potential. This is before the point at which it becomes tangible in the political sphere through popular or institutional change.

What then are the questions to be reasked and reanswered before this cross-cultural and interdisciplinary analysis move may be made with any conviction? Not just, what is civil society, but what sort of concept is civil society. Is it a term that may be easily understood in one cultural and political tradition and then transposed for analysis to another? If not, what are the elements of civil society that can be translated as a kind of basic grammar of the concept? And, for my purposes, which model might be adaptable across cultures and to the particular task of identifying a specific political imaginary at work in films?

The Virtues of Civil Society

Gramsci comprehends that human personality, value, and function are matters of both individual obligation and collective endeavor.[12] If (wo)man is a product of history then s/he is a product of the collective mind, who yet must take responsibility for her/his own contemporary personal and political maturation. This demands forms of social and political intervention that are made effective by a constant interrogation of institutional interests, and the interests of the populace as defined by those institutions. In this way, political action should not be a struggle for crude domination, but a searching out of consent and appropriate hegemony. The Chinese political analyst, He Baogang, has translated Gramsci's work into a modern Chinese context, by calling again for a democracy which entails a healthy antagonism between state and society: "An opposition movement, a democratic strategy, and an antagonism between the state and society . . . to talk about civil society is to inquire into a new political theory of the state and to articulate a normative project for liberalization and democratization."[13]

His assumption that "to talk about civil society" is oppositional and antagonistic is true in the context of modern authoritarianism of which he writes.[14] In much contemporary political analysis by Chinese scholars and Western commentators, the twin focus on the events in Tiananmen Square, in April to June 1989, and on the Habermasian discourse around state-society relations makes the radical edge of 'talking about civil society' quite plain.[15] However, his further assumption—that talking about civil society will produce liberal, democratic political organization in producing a break between state and society—is problematic. The exact nature of this 'normative' project is unclear. If the articulation of normativity is to take place through agonistic public debate—wherever and however that is possible—why can He Baogang already propose that the project will necessarily emerge as liberal and democratic? Will 'talking about civil society' as a borrowing from Western political discourse produce a Western-style liberalization and democratization? If so, will this produce his sine qua non of a reformulation of state power as it exists in contemporary China? Will, in fact, 'talking about civil society' be radical enough to have any effect on current patterns of political domination? Both critical reflection and empirical observation suggest that, on the contrary, the institutions of civil society as organized in liberal democracy entail a series of close compromises between state and society.

His quest for normativity suggests that he has already dismissed the Gramscian notion of perpetual interrogation in favor of a different, but fixed, virtue system, and set of related legitimate interests. In his formulation the emphasis on consciousness and the development of individual and social personality is undermined.

Of course, the relative transparency of democracy, conceived as a marketplace of competing interests, held in agonistic abeyance by fixed procedures of representation and participation, does make the very different transparency of governmental surveillance impossible. Democratic transparency is maintained throughout state, government, and social organization and motivation, with de facto limits fixed for domestic privacy, national security, and capitalist protection.

Total(itarian) transparency entails a panopticism, in which the entire spectrum of political, economic, social, and private behavior is available to the sight of the leader, and the Party, which legitimates their absolute power. It is a condition of modernity that this legitimation is false insofar as the visibility does not have to be achieved to be believed. The subjects of panopticism behave as though they were under surveillance, whether or not that is actually the case. This is a different image from the purely authoritarian—as envisaged by China's Legalist philosophers for example—where the panopticon functions according to law, as described by the historian-philosopher Michel Foucault.[16] The populace is never able to observe the observer while always remaining—or imagining themselves to remain—under close scrutiny. Thus, the authoritarian leader attains absolute presence by disappearing, a disappearance effected once again by the self-propulsion of self-surveillance.

The totalitarian leader is *visible*, either through a personality cult or through the permeation of all public space by the Party and its organizations. In these ways, visibility is magnified, to such an extent that the leader's presence uses up the entire political and national imaginary. In his observations of the populace he expects to see himself. These lines of vision are strictly vertical, however, which allows the leader her/himself to mask the motivations and manipulations of the center from the populace, while requiring their total participation in narrating the present, and remembering the past, according to Party lines. Post-Maoist China may be described as on a systemic seesaw between authoritarianism and totalitarianism, and He Baogang's argument that 'talking about civil society' is radical is fair enough in that context. I wonder, however, whether it is radical enough to tip the seesaw over and build a whole new playground.

For in all cases—democratic, authoritarian, and totalitarian—the population adheres to normative symbolic codes that preserve the stability of the prevailing political system. Moreover, most governmental systems are neither one thing nor the other all the time, and populations learn to shift their politico-social behaviors according to the mood and focus of the day. These codes are vital, flexible, and only available to those who need to live within their parameters. It is such normative symbolic codes that can be discerned in cinema, as well as in other cultural spheres, and in political organization. The argument is less about whether politics or the mode of cultural production determines the content, form, or meaning of a film in the following—or any other—instance. Rather I am attempting to discern what Foucault termed the 'regime of truth', that characterizes post-Maoist China: "Each society has its regime of truth, its 'general politics' of truth: that is, the types of discourse that it accepts and makes function as true; the mechanisms and instances that enable one to distinguish true and false statements, the means by which each is sanctioned."[17]

How is this "regime of truth" enunciated in film? How is it disrupted within the narrative? Are there alternative symbolic codes that can be read off certain films at certain times? Are these perhaps the moments of publicness that prompt censors into banning a film, or cutting a large section of it before distribution?

Public Truth

Such disruption may be achieved by showing a different perspective on a 'truth' of history. This is an especially effective strategy where the truth of the past is vital to the legitimacy of a present regime, and where the meaning of the nation is mapped exactly onto that version of past events, in order to imbue that legitimacy with an aura of national authenticity. Disruption may also be achieved by an internal move. Here, the regime of truth is challenged by the representation of individual experience. The possibilities of identification, between spectator and protagonist, are exploited to undermine previously unassailable collective truths. The pathology of a national narrative is made to seem bathetic or monstrous when viewed in the microscopic person of the individual. We see such effective disruptions of history, and memory, in the films *Yellow Earth*, *In the Wild Mountains* (1984), and *In the Heat of the Sun* (1993). In these films, significant historical periods are revisited, with the wisdom of hindsight. Or, as is the case with *Wild Mountains*, the very recent past is thrown into dramatic relief with moments of touching humanity. Prevailing assumptions, or genealogies, of what these periods 'meant' and 'mean', are challenged, and the making of historical perspective is reclaimed for a contemporary public. I will discuss these films in more detail in later chapters, but the point to make here is that historical truth is subject to the conditions of its reception. Truth does not even exist apart from communication. Whatever the private conviction of the individual, the truth of history must always be tested through communication in a public space. Films offer space for such insights into the public mind, and these insights are one sort of truth. It is obviously very partial, as it is a truth made by filmmakers and audiences together. The participation of an audience makes it, like all culture, very changeable in meaning and relevance. At the point of spectatorship, the audience themselves appear in public. They are made visible by the visibility of the text.[18]

In the final sequence of *In the Heat of the Sun*, a group of men travel around Beijing in an open car. They are obviously doing well in the new market environment of China in the 1990s. They are drinking whisky, and generally showing off. These are the men whose Cultural Revolution boyhood we have been watching for the previous 130 minutes. They were louts then too, but it is this last shot that brazenly reminds the audience that loutishness can transcend political ideologies. Bad behavior responds to opportunity, and flourishes in different ways at different times. The audience is required to examine their own memories, or secondhand knowledge, of the Cultural Revolution. Was it, for example, an era of victimization, or was it just a period in which human failings were peculiarly, but not exceptionally, apparent in the public arena?

SEEING WHITE

Thinking about history is also relevant to *The White-haired Girl*. This is a film that is known by almost every mainland Chinese citizen. In talking about the film with a group of academics, none of which specialized in film, I found that every one had a clear memory of the film, its protagonists, and its importance to the Chinese revolutionary imagination. The memories were clearly and fiercely protected, but they contradicted one another at several points. Several of the younger discussants were convinced that the 1950s version was made in color—they could "remember the red flag, and the heroine's red jacket." This was a reminder that the most famous stories leave different versions imprinted in the minds of different audiences.[19] It is hard to think of an equivalent to *The White-haired Girl* in other national cinemas. In India, it might be Mehboob Khan's *Mother India* (1957), a quintessential epic of national regeneration. In America, perhaps it would be Selznick's *Gone with the Wind* (1939), or, more controversially still, D. W. Griffith's *Birth of a Nation* (1919). However, the classic status enjoyed by all these films is subject to the scrutiny of contemporary spectatorship. In new (and post-new) China, as elsewhere at the end of the twentieth century, spectatorship is influenced by two highly contentious and powerful phenomena, which are disruptive to a regime of truth. One is the concept of postmodernity in the Chinese context. The other is the nature of that context: the impact of globalization on economies of cultural analysis. Both are central to current Chinese, European, Australian, and Chinese-American debates over the meaning given both to the modern and the postmodern, in a world where even metanarratives of dissolution and reflection are questioned by the rising influence of non-Western habits of thought. This case study of cultural analysis transects these questions. Cultural difference does not necessarily preclude structural resonances that may illuminate cultural practices at home and elsewhere. This suggestion is couched in a return to Habermas, who, although not an avowed postmodernist, yet offers us conceptual paradigms within which we may negotiate our postmodern conditions.[20]

Postmodern conditions are exemplified in the characterization and representation of Mao Zedong in and out of Chinese cultural, social, and political practice. In a recent visit to Beijing I came up against Mao four times within as many hours. First, I (and everyone else there at the time) was invited in to the remembrance hall on Tiananmen Square to see a huge statue of the man, and to have my picture taken by representatives of the People's Liberation Army (PLA) (for 15 RMB—about $3 Australian). The invitation had come from a soldier shouting into a megaphone, reminding us that Mao was still the Father of the People, and that we should pay our respects to his memory. 'Pay' is the operative word: the PLA had up to twenty thousand businesses trading in 1994.[21] Second, I could not help but notice the huge picture at the far end of the square, the one famously daubed with paint during the Tiananmen demonstrations and repression in 1989, and within hours, cleaned up by the Army. This portrait now carries a dual load of representation, of power, and of the elimination of its detractors.[22] Third, once inside the gate, Tiananmen was packed with souvenirs of the Great Helmsman, from ceremonial plates to fob watches and cigarette lighters.[23] Finally, the taxi driver who drove me back to the hotel had hung a Mao talisman at the front of his cab for good luck.[24] It seems that Maoism should be reinvestigated as part of a reappraisal of modernity, and especially the cultural realization of that modernity, in twentieth-century China. So, although I will not deal directly with the figure of Mao here, I want to flag his presence as strong as we assume the presence of American academic hegemony in any arguments about cultural theory and 'pomo' (a common and unhelpful conflation of postmodernism and postmodernity).

I am also struck by Rey Chow's recent (although it is thematic in her work) demand that we reorganize our thinking away from a subaltern/hegemonic paradigm of global relationships, which seems to be based on a suspicion that Westerners will always either get there first, or attempt to persuade others that where they did get was after all the place to be. She wants Chinese scholars to look at China as Chinese and as Asian-Americans—but not necessarily within theoretical straitjackets that were developed in a non-Chinese historical context and trajectory. In a response to a collection on postmodernism in China she criticizes Terry Eagleton's ignorance of, or disinterest in, the complexity and *modernity* of Maoism in China. For Chow this is an example of the irrelevance of much West-centered discussion of things Chinese.[25] As a person of white ethnicity myself I can only partly respond to her demands, which are articulated in terms of ethnicity and subjective histories. [26]

I am interrogating the cross-cultural and, possibly, transcultural expression and usage of 'whiteness' in British and Chinese visual arts. I do so from an English speaking, acculturated British position, and as it is the gaps in my observations that will probably give the best clues as to cultural difference, this is obviously an exercise that can only be completed with input from other positions and experiences. I am also writing from the disciplinary perspective of film studies, and my emphasis is on reading visual signs in a transcultural environment more than on an exhaustive history of whiteness in either British or Chinese cultural experience. Having said that, I will make some references to other instances of whiteness where I perceive slippage across discourse of race and gender (in the British film) and class and gender (in the Chinese film). The point is to bring out possible *communicative moments* between cultures, and ultimately, to test them against the experience of those who 'see white', and understand 'white' from a different position. If the resonances that I have noticed are important, it is only insofar as they indicate the possibility of larger, more widely shared transcultural collisions. What I have seen produces a moment of publicness between the texts, myself, and possibly some others. It is small scale, but its fact is exciting in that it underlines the communication and illuminations of cultural space.

In arguing that film offers unique forms of publicness, through an acculturated narration of the political imaginary, I am also constructing an argument about female visibility—as whiteness—which transects the west/east relation, and which in itself provides an example of publicness that is not available within periodizations which ignore revolutionary history. To this end, I argue that whiteness, even if it is a discourse *rooted* in constructions of race or of class, is *mediated* within representations of gender. As well as the two films from the 1940s and 1950s, *The White-haired Girl* and *Black Narcissus*, I will look at two pieces of art from the 1990s: Jiangjie's *The Magic Flower*, 1998, and Helen Chadwick's *Piss Flower*, 1992. In these films and installations the female is characterized by a whiteness which is embedded in cultural associations, producing a public narration of the discourses of race and class which simultaneously excludes and contains the female gender. Those associations are different in the Chinese and British cases, but they are both similarly associated with loss and invisibility. It seems here that structural similarities in the use of whiteness connote a communicative action between cultures, which hints at shared public space in cultural forms.

The complication of my readings is present in these analyses—readings grounded in a whiteness of which I have only become fully aware since leaving Britain and coming to live in Australia. Simply put, the level of racist discourse *outside* the galleries, artshops, and cinemas is such that, *inside* our cultural temples, whiteness intrudes on my vision and makes me uncomfortably visible to myself. Why this should be the case in my relationship with cultural forms is not hard to decipher. Paintings, films, sculpture, even maps, are valued for their 'to-be-looked-at-ness'.[27] I look at art, and in so doing I look at the other, and find myself absent. The absence should not be a problem for me except that I know—historically and politically—that my absence is *white*. It is not a true absence, but one that crowds the piece of work, institutionally and economically. I step back trying to be unobtrusive, but not wishing the pretense of invisibility. It is impossible. The paintings and sculptures always catch me looking, and I am embarrassed.

Seeing and being seen is part and parcel of hearing and being heard in public, and it is that emphasis which the work of Jürgen Habermas brought to philosophical debates on the public sphere. The frequent description of Jürgen Habermas as a postmodernist thinker in Chinese postmodernist (*houxue*) debates has surprised me, however. I have understood his thinking as rational and optimistic (and also pessimistic in the more contemporary writings) and quite openly grounded in European history and politics. Unlike, say, Fredric Jameson, he does not make claims for 'an era' (of late capitalism), nor does he seem particularly concerned to make claims on polities and societies beyond the limits of his observation and belongingness. Furthermore, his disputes with poststructuralists, French philosophy, and the New Conservatives (which he has been wont to conflate at times), marks him as decidedly *outside* those spectra.[28] It may be that his name crops up in discussions of postmodernism because, in the context of New China, the 'search' for civil society has coincided with the exploration of new modes of thinking and 'in' the present, from which postmodernism has come. The conflation of the term 'postmodernism' with 'all theory'—even that which specifically distances itself from or interrogates the postmodern matrix as part of its project—may also be a cause of the imprecision in characterizations of Habermas's position. It may be, then, that even here, in the theoretical heartlands of Habermas's influence, we should be careful when thinking about its non-European uptake.

Habermas's version of *Öffentlichkeit* seems, as I have suggested, a dangerous sine qua non in China given its origins in European liberal-bourgeois democratics, and the history of the rise of the mercantile bourgeoisie in that region. The search for civil society in new China and 'post-new' China has been hampered by methodologies which look for a form of civil society which replicates idealized versions of state-public relations in Western Europe and America.[29] As Liu Kang has pointed out, Mao and the Chinese Communist Party (CCP) *succeeded* in revolution; their lack of attention to civil society might then be understood as a marker of their difference from Gramsci's strategic thinking at a time of *failure* for Italian revolutionary ambitions. Liu Kang's point is that political scientists who look for change in a postrevolutionary society should never forget that the constitution of change will be more strongly inflected by the revolutionary experience than by reinventions of a past that never quite happened.[30] This is why the presence of Mao Zedong is crucial to the ideas both of modernity and of postmodernity in China. Despite the fluctuations in his political career, the revolutionary experience which he fashioned (with others) was as modern as anything that has happened since his death. Furthermore, the international currency of his name—for good and ill—gives him a postmodern status within that modernity. He has been both political leader and cultural artifact, and, latterly, kitsch symptom of commercialization in China.[31] However, he has not been, before or after his death, a symbol of parliamentary democracy or of civil society.

The continuing value of Mao's image in the PRC is a reminder of the saturation of the social by the state. The search for publicness in China involves an acknowledgment that this is not an ideal Habermasian sphere of action. Nonetheless, Habermasian structures of thought can be useful. *Öffentlichkeit* is, after all, a fabulous word. It has connotations in English of *the public, publicness, publicity,* and *in public.* All these possibilities of position and subject allow wide scope for thinking through the concept of the public. Indeed, Habermas's acute choice of word seems to prefigure his admission in the late-1980s that perhaps the main differences between French poststructuralists and German rationalists were ones of rhetorical style.[32] This is a sweeping interpretation of both Habermas and Outhwaite, but it perhaps begins to explain the insistent presence of Habermas's name in debates on *houxue*.[33] Habermas never loses sight of the political in his thinking, but he pays less attention to culture. This is a drawback if we are only reading Habermas, but not if we see his work as a contribution to a larger enterprise within European philosophy. His work complements rather than contradicts other ways of thinking within postmodernity.

From this standpoint it is possible to return to Chinese experience and political history. The necessary link between culture and revolution is emphatic throughout CCP theoretical development. It seems likely that publicness pre- and post-new China will be found in the interstices of cultural expression and revolutionary experience and reflection. Hence my decision to look for signs of public distraction in cultural texts of the Maoist and post-Maoist eras, and to describe these as moments of *cultural public space*. Part of the impulse for this move is of course the suggestions of Antonio Gramsci, and the connectivity of consciousness and culture in changing times. This is not to argue that film can produce democracy, but rather that it may contain moments of publicness that give symbolic weight to the history, memories, and psychic organization of particular groups of people. I am suggesting that film can narrate the present, and the political imaginary of that present, in ways that produce forms of human association based on spectatorship.

Now, it is possible to describe these textual distractions as postmodern*ist*. They are frequently expressed through irony, parody, anachronism, or just an insouciant irreverence. More fundamentally, these textual moments exhibit a desire to understand the tensions of contemporary life. John Frow has noted the difference between postmodernism as a rather glib descriptive non sequitur and postmodernism as the search for coherence in time and culture: "That is to say the concept cannot be thought of as the representation of a given field of cultural production, or of a tendency within this field; it is rather the embattled attempt to *construct* the unity of such a field or tendency."[34]

This encapsulates many of the problems in current debates. China is modern, premodern, modernizing, and central to global patterns of consumption (over seventy percent of low-grade goods consumed in the U.S. are made in China). Can it, possibly, also be postmodern—and do not postmodern theories retreat from the real problems of the Chinese citizenry and government? As I understand Frow, the answer would be—it is postmodern insofar as it is difficult to conceptualize, and postmodern theory may be an appropriate response to the task. Such theories are not essentially apolitical—except when the postmodern is understood as a period which exceeds one version of modernity, and which eclipses the histories and present horrors of local politicking and capital intrusions. Also, to reiterate another of Frow's points, the cultural may be reduced to a derivative political status, if the epoch is prioritized over the forms of production: "For one of the driving difficulties of any attempt to think modernism and postmodernism as specific epochal structures is the temptation to *derive* the cultural from the logic of an epochal system."[35] Trinh Minh-ha suggests avoidance of epochal typologizing in a discussion with Leslie Thornton on the dynamic relationship between avant-garde film and mature visual politics:

Postmodernism, in a way, has always existed; it does not merely come after modernism, but exists before, with, and after it. This is what Jean-Francois Lyotard is probably pointing to when he affirms that a work can only be modern when it is first postmodern. These two qualifying terms do not stand in opposition to each other and postmodernism is here defined as modernism at its nascent stage—one that is always recurring. As in all 'ism' histories, however, the urge to circumscribe and unify the situation is often unavoidable, hence the tendency to turn the postmodern condition into "another version of that historical amnesia characteristic of American culture—the tyranny of the New," as Stuart Hall puts it. One can never situate oneself outside mainstream values. In challenging them, one has to go constantly back and forth between the center and the margins.[36]

So, when a film problematizes previous, or supposedly current, political, or social mores by an ironically long take—*Yellow Earth*—or through flirtations with Hollywood genres—*Stage Sisters*—there are (at least) three expectations in play. First, the texts suppose that there is a contemporary spectatorship able and ready to enjoy the irony; second, that these spectators are sufficiently intimate with convention and shared histories to appreciate the *difference* on offer; and third, that the act of spectatorship is an act of public communion with connotations for the political imaginary of the *polis*.[37]

I have already spent some time discussing how we might use Habermas in the context of new China. My basic proposition has been that the idea of the public and publicness may be taken away from the liberal-democratic history of Western Europe and reacculturated through anchors in Chinese cultural production. This, in itself, produces political and social knowledge that *may or may not* resonate with other forms of institutionalized public action. Publicness is strategically and qualitatively different from place to place, time to time, and from one ideological field to another. The resonance between institutionalized public action and cultural public space (which is really my concern here) can only be found within the terms and conditions of its emergence, and not against a foreign ideal of how people should communicate with each other and with the state. Nevertheless, communication does happen across cultural and national boundaries and one way of explaining that happy fact might be that public spaces have, simultaneously, structural and symbolic similarity and difference. But where are these spaces, and how might we recognize them across cultures and from different contemporary positions? In the cluster of examples that follows I use what is *publicly* available to me as a white British consumer of British and Chinese cultural products.

The differences strike me but so do oblique similarities. In *The White-haired Girl*, a young girl, Xi'er (played by Tian Hua), is sold into slavery to a harsh landlord.[38] He rapes her soon after her arrival. She escapes and hides in a mountain cave. Her hair turns white, as she lives on mountain berries that affect its pigment, reducing her to a caricature of an old widow left to die alone (figures 2.1 and 2.2). Meanwhile, the landlord exploits the peasants' fear of the 'mountain

Figure 2.1   White-haired Girl

demon' to maintain his power. Finally, Xi'er is recognized, and liberated by her lover, now a member of the Liberation Army forces. She returns to live in her village, and in the last sequence of the film, racing clouds and profusions of white blossom crown her renewed black hair.[39] In the archive still reproduced here, Xi'er is framed at a slight low angle. There is no one else in the shot, and the point of

Figure 2.2   White-haired Girl

view can only be that of the spectator. Xi'er, and her hair, are displayed as spectacle in this shot, but also in much of the cave sequence. There can be little doubt of her status as signifier within a larger narrative (and ideological) agenda. The white-haired girl's hair is a complex signifier that serves plot and ideology very neatly. White hair is associated with ghosts, transforming goddesses like the Lady Linshui/Whitesnake, old age, and sexual rapacity (particularly associated with the Guanyin), while whiteness on theatre masks signifies jealousy.[40] These connotations are not good, but there is an alternative signifying chain of whiteness. Whiteness of skin (white jade) is part of the discourse of feminine beauty, whereas inner goodness or chastity is 'pure white' (*qingbai*). Meng Yue has already argued very shrewdly that the story in this film and in subsequent versions desexes the girl until she is 'renewed' through the male agents of the Party.[41] Thus her song on the way up the mountain on the night of her escape: "I will not die, I will survive, and I will have revenge," is only vicariously true. The narrative takes her sexuality hostage while she waits for the men to sort out the problems of class and brutality from which she fled. Her transformation makes the villagers think she is a demon or ghost, and only the soldiers can recognize her and restore her feminine possibilities. In this way her whiteness is a marker of her ordeal, but also of her invisibility. It also emphasizes her class purity in contrast (literally) with the dimly lit landlord—a black class element (*hei*). Purity (*qingbai*) is not gender specific, men and women can be 'good', but the double signification of whiteness as good *and* ghostly seems significant in its association with a sequestered female.

In *Black Narcissus* a group of English and Irish nuns are sent up to a remote palace in the mountains of Tibet to start a hospital and school for local inhabitants. Here whiteness organizes the narrative along lines of race rather than class purity. That is not the white that we are encouraged to *see* however. Racial positioning emphasizes difference-as-blackness, and conflates that difference with other traits (wantonness, vanity, fecklessness, savagery, and so on). Meanwhile, the nuns are wearing flowing white robes. The choice of garb is clearly associated with their symbolic status as 'brides' of Christ, although the terms of their agreement are different from the marriage vows. These nuns are not in the Order for better or worse; they renew their vows annually. Much of the dramatic tension of the film's narrative focuses on Sister Ruth, who is a problem, and who does not renew her vows. She orders herself a scarlet dress from Calcutta, and on the first night of freedom shakes loose her dark red hair, applies her lipstick, and runs through the night in pursuit of the one white man available. When he turns her down she tries to murder her supposed rival, the sister superior (Sister Clodagh) played by the young Deborah Kerr, fails in the attempt, and falls down the mountain to her own death.

Julian Petley describes this film as "surely one of the most truly hysterical films ever made."[42] It is always classed as a melodrama, and Peter Wollen has noted its compositional closeness to a musical score, which aligns it with a modernist concern to bring film to music.[43] Before discussing the thematics of the two films further I want to point out that *The White-haired Girl* is also a melodrama; it is also "truly hysterical" and it is highly dependent on the score for its internal cohesion and impetus. But what is the nature of this hysteria? Is it, as Petley implies, simply that female psychodramas veer into the hysterical if the libidos in question are not quenched and married off with dispatch? Diegetically, hysteria seems well founded. The white-haired girl has been raped by her employer and flees for her life up a mountain. The nuns are sent to do good works in a place where natural beauty (cloaked in pure white snow) and very fresh air take their collective religious breaths away, tempting their minds and bodies beyond the fall of the white cloth. But more than this, the hands of the filmmakers produce a textuality that is excessive, whether it be the darkly lit scene when the crawling hand of the lecher-landlord reaches for Xi'er's neck, or the striped forest through which Sister Ruth runs in a madness of desire. This excess, which derives I would argue from the fear of desirous female bodies, is displaced into the rich melodramatic texture of the films' narration. The vanishing point of the excess is, ironically, placed on the bodies themselves. They are whitened in ways that makes it impossible to see their sexuality, but equally impossible not to look for it. In both films then, white, the metaphorical color of chastity and of absolute beauty (white jade skin/Snow White) in Chinese and Christian cultures, is coded as mask of female sexuality.[44] In both films, too, women thus coded are removed to a mountaintop until, in two very different scenarios, they return to the lowlands of civilizations. In the first there is a triumphant return to the arms of masculinity and the then-new Chinese horizon. In the second the descent is from grace to desire, and without male acquiescence it is a deathly fall. As an ex-Catholic I cannot help but read that mountaintop as a parallel to the forty days in the wilderness, and I wonder whether there are similar structural resonances between the mountain cave and the period of recuperation in the northwestern hinterlands. The second point that refers the two films is that the strategy of color coding, by which they designate female absence, transfers agency from the woman to masculine, institutional authority: the Party and the Church.

These films were made within five years of each other, two years after the end of World War II, and one year after the establishment of the People's Republic of China. One might assume these were optimistic times for Britain and China, even accounting for the hardships of rationing and postwar shortages. Yet, the marking of woman as either white or consumed by desire for the male (whether it be appropriate or not), is a reminder that the achievements of wartime women were significant but culturally problematic for the national imaginary.

The "national interest" is male and marked as such by cinematic decisions. My suggestion in relation to the films of the period is that woman is not marked, or rather she is 'disappeared' into the anonymity of whiteness. This complicates perceptions of ethnic whiteness, which is often unmarked to the subjective advantage of 'white' people. As Ruth Frankenberg argues in her work on theorizing, and thus *displacing* whiteness, whiteness can be made visible from the perspective of outside interests and experience: "communities of color frequently see and name whiteness clearly and critically, in periods when white folks have asserted their own 'color blindness' as well as in times of self-conscious white claims of superiority."[45] Or rather, I am addressing the curious phenomenon that the unmarked color of whiteness is already invisible in white culture, but is also used strategically to deny visibility to inimical forces within that same cultural group. So the whiteness of the sisterhood in *Black Narcissus* is on the one hand played off against the blackness of the Tibetan population (especially the sexy young prince whose supposed vanity attracts the nickname *black narcissus*), and on the other is used to hide the attributes of 'blackness'—secular desire in particular—where it might appear in white women. In this defensive move the strategy of whiteness is used as a secondary mask, whereby the doubling of whiteness in the nuns' robes (and perhaps in every bridal gown) hides the fear that whiteness might be 'normal' but the essence of that status is not stable and must be protected.[46]

The racial mythologies of China are different from those of Britain—although is it a coincidence that both national groups saw (and perhaps in their different ways still see) the Tibetans as targets for ideological redemption?[47] The discourse of whiteness is not as generally associated with Chinese identity, although there are arguments to suggest that within Chinese cultural production bodies are made significant along lines of ethnic difference. Visual representations of non-Han peoples tend to be differentiated by the brightness of the clothing depicted.[48] In the 1963 film about Tibet, *Serfs*, however, the emphasis is on oppression in a feudal state. Non-Han people are not figured as brightly clothed and deeply happy as they are in post-Liberation New Year television specials. The eponymous serf, Qiangba (Wang Dui), is sunburned and poorly clothed, in recognition of his need for redemption. Peasants who are not specifically 'other' are not marked by toil (and absence of *qingbai*) to the same extent.[49] Han identity thus is normalized in distinction to the assumed exoticism and sexualization of the minority and indigenous peoples in the territories of Taiwan, the People's Republic, and Hong Kong. The whiteness of the white-haired girl, however, is not, primarily, a racial statement, but rather a convolution of references to exclusion, which foregrounds whiteness as a signifier of class purity. Her class status is complicated by the association of white hair with the world of ghosts. Moreover, a connection with whiteness and racial discourses also appears when we consider that hell is shared by foreigners who are themselves ghosts (*gui*). This ghostliness also then implies a peripheral status, and an isolation from the centrality of Chineseness. As Janet Lee has argued in her work on female missionaries to China, white femininity was enhanced by its civilizing potential in *white society*, but was criticized as monstrous by *Chinese*: "Their own [women missionaries] violations of Chinese expectations for women were so profound that, rather than eliciting criticism for their breaches, they were conferred a new status as "she-tigers" or "elephants," which granted them the opportunity to do as they pleased."[50]

The elephantine whiteness of Victorian missionaries is a statement of absolute cultural difference on the part of those who named them. Yet again, further reading of *White-haired Girl* begins to suggest that the move from the feminine to the monstrous is a habitual step. One implication of the white-haired girl's ghostly seclusion seems to be that only the agency of the Party, personified in her soldier lover, can remove her from purgatory and reestablish her humanity, which is cast along gender specific lines. Or, and also, as her whiteness is a badge of class purity, it positions her between the darkness (*hei*) of class impurity, personified by the rapist-landlord, and the agents of change, the soldier-lover, who *sees* her whiteness as both pure (*qingbai*), and unfortunate.[51] She is marked out as spectral (ghostly and ghastly), in need of redemption, having been too closely penetrated by the dark. This ambiguity is reminiscent of the whiteness of pearl maidens, dragon princesses, and fox fairies who work through a deadly eroticism in Chinese literature and myth, and who are generally "tremulously white, like bleached silk, like a white lotus, like soft moonlight, like drifting snow."[52] Xi'er's release becomes a symbolic reentry into the world of men from the prison-cave of monstrous ambiguity. The penultimate shot of white blossoms comes as an ideological afterthought, reinscribing the eponymous center of the narrative within a visual discourse of political purity. In this shot the narration draws a floral curtain over the period of her nonhumanness, when she was without the custody of men, yet also an abject victim of masculine penetration from the wrong class.

I am not suggesting therefore that the two films are working from identical cultural or ethnic bases, but rather that the *strategies* of containment of the female are remarkably similar. The narrative of *White-haired Girl* is structured to remove the girl at the same time as using her to focus the plotline. As the victim of the piece she is marked twice, by her class (which operates as the normative 'goodness') and by the desexing mark of whiteness-as-death. The nuns in *Black Narcissus* are also marked as good and pure, but are simultaneously desexed by the demands of their ghostly deity-spouse. In both there is a close relation between the anonymity of the ghost and the invisibility of the woman outside socially legitimate sexuality. These disappearing acts produce a contradiction in both cases. In *Girl* this opens up between the foreignness and danger of the ghost— and the good class status of a particular female subject. In *Black Narcissus* it lies between the assumption of white racial supremacy within the film, and the danger of untrammeled white female desire. bell hooks's observation that Black Americans have known the White space as "mysterious, strange, terrible . . . a bush of ghosts" adds another dimension to the *Black Narcissus* story.[53] When the nuns finally leave a place to which they have no claim, the Tibetans might well remember them dimly as a "bush of ghosts."

These films were produced at moments of national crisis. Wars had been won, but new worlds were yet to be fully implemented. Britain had won a war but was losing an empire; China had ended a civil war but was now redescribing its borders and its relationship with neighboring states. In these contexts, the figure of the pure but monstrous woman reads like a mitigated approach towards an expression of hatred against whatever is different in race or class. Did this whitening of the female subject disappear with the access of stability and confidence as the century progressed? Did, for example, female beauty transcend the white jade/Snow White nexus? Apparently not, but the whitening has at least become conscious and critical in the hands of women artists of the 1990s. Helen Chadwick's performance sculpture *Piss Flower* shows up the transformation of desire into whiteness. To make the piece, Chadwick went out with her lover into a snowy field and peed. She then made a mold from the shape of the hole that their hot urine had burnt. This is the piss flower. It is the most exquisitely defiant, yet loving, piece of feminist art that I have seen. A flower that takes its form from lovers' pee constitutes both a homage to, and a mockery of, the passing purity of a snowfall. It reminds us that the whitening of female sexuality, in the nuns' habits and the reflecting snow on the Tibetan mountains, and perhaps also in the pearly whiteness of a T'ang dragon goddess or a peasant girl's hair, seeks to contain the tense ambiguities between the representation of gender and female sexuality, burning hot within a pall of ice.[54]

I was reminded of Chadwick's piece when I visited the In and Out installation exhibition (1998) at the John Curtin Centre in Perth, Western Australia. The exhibition was curated out of the Earl Lu gallery at LaSalle College of Arts in Singapore, by Binghui Huangfu. The title is drawn from the curator's inspiration to disrupt expectations of mainland Chinese art held by diasporic Chinese and non-Chinese communities (and vice versa—some of the artists are Australian citizens), and to "ambiguously hint at all of the variations implied by the linking of opposites. The works examine the notions of artists working in a cultural structure while at the same time not being recognized by that culture."[55] One of the intentions of the exhibition is to transect culturally specific public space, literally the gallery in this instance, with works that speak across imaginaries and discourses other than the Chinese, while addressing the experience of Chinese ethnicity in and out of China. Jiangjie is the one woman artist represented here.[56] Her work *The Magic Flower* is inspired partly by the yin/yang cycle of giving and receiving, and partly by the writings of the French feminist philosopher Simone de Beauvoir. It consists of a white plaster egg-shaped bowl, imprinted with the image of a kneeling woman (*nü*) and filled with translucent plastic. This 'magic flower' is placed on a plinth a meter away from a series of small corner-shelves, where small male dolls stand one above the other, bandaged and pierced with acupuncture needles. These men-dolls are three-dimensional convex statuettes: they are 'out'; the woman is a two-dimensional impression in the heart of the flower: she is 'in'. Jiangjie's aim is to demonstrate a relationship between men and women that acknowledges gender difference but does so within strong indications of cultural specificity, here Chinese. In an interview with the curator she explains: "her understanding of Simone was that she (Simone) saw things that made women different from men in terms of their female physiology, psychology, and language, but that these things only underpinned the need to be concerned with a much wider social and historical context."[57] For Jiangjie this context is Chinese but its address is international. Her white plaster flower displays Chinese gender relations by removing the woman's substance and filling the impression it leaves on the plaster with transparency. She takes up no space at all, although the white 'flower' into which she disappears dominates the space of the installation. The implication seems to be that woman is contained by the flower, but that the process of containment exceeds the discursive boundaries of its own production. Chadwick's flower gives substance to an impression in the snow and takes up space, actually as well as metaphorically. She gives the lie to the effectivity of the containment of woman in whiteness, through an act of active sexual presence and presentation. *The Magic Flower* is thus a complementary antithesis to *The Piss Flower*. Taken together the two pieces spark a cultural exchange on the subject of whiteness and its importance in the representation of the femaleness. This exchange produces a moment of transcultural publicness, where gender is privileged over dominant discourses of race and class.

I have, perhaps, been a little daring in suggesting transcultural resonance between People's Republic of China (PRC) and British classic texts. Interest in transculturalism, in Chinese film, usually concentrates on the relationships between Chinese-dominated imaginaries, in Taiwan, Hong Kong, the mainland, and as part of Asian America. But film is an intercultural as well as an international product. As such it may, perhaps must, be enjoyed in many contexts, and within many experiences. The color of experience is national and cultural, but also something more. The success of James Cameron's *Titanic* in China, Hong Kong, and Taiwan in the spring and summer of 1998, does not make it any less an American film, concerned with American values and American structures of feeling. In fact, when I was invited to see it with friends at Taipei's huge new Warner Brothers' cinema complex, I was warned that it was an 'American film' and 'so, a bit silly', but 'very beautiful'. Somewhere, in that cluster of scorn, prejudice, and aesthetic pleasure, lies the core of that film's address to a transnational public. This core touched the color of many people's very different experience. Watching the film I realized why it was doing so well. The cinematography and computer animation are spectacular. The moments on the prow of the ship, when shot organization and emotional climaxes come together, are irresistible. Money saturates the production values, so that even Southampton Docks look pretty. All that is likely to attract the fleeting pleasure of most audiences. There is also a rhetoric of class justice, which although anti-East Coast financiers (the poor tend to be mid-West or Irish), could also (just) be read against the grain as anti-Western exploitation. The only parts of the film that impacted on me were scenes of mothers protecting their children, and a British merchant seaman shooting himself in the head when he realized that fear had made him kill one of the passengers. These moments spoke to my own desires for publicness, one maternal and female, the other a nostalgic version of my country's honor (I admit this with some embarrassment, but affective reactions to film can be extremely strange). In the rest of this book I want to find the other cores, the other flushes of experience, that keep audiences in China going to the cinema.

3

Childhood and Public Discourse

Ning Ying's comedy, *For Fun* (1992), tells the story of a group of pensioners who meet every Sunday in the park, to play and sing old opera favorites. When Old Han, the janitor of a local opera house, retires, he joins them. His agenda, however, is bound up with notions of how things should be done, with personal influence, and with tying fun to official organizations. He moves the old men inside to a dusty hall, forces them to participate in a local talent festival, and generally ruins the atmosphere of play and experiment that characterized the original set up. His own sense of fun is iconically marked in an early scene, when we spot his little Red Guard (*hong xiao bing*) alarm clock on his bedside table. This is similar to a Mickey Mouse clock, except that the waving gloved hand of the Disney character is replaced by the waving hand of a young Red Guard clutching a copy of *The Quotations of Mao Zedong* (Mao Zedong's little red book). This anomalous reminder of the Cultural Revolution hints that this old man is living his old age through the memories of other people's childhoods. He is too old to have ever been a Red Guard himself, and too scared of youth to take a lead from the young at heart whom he meets in his retirement.

With such subtleties, the film takes the flux between what is of the State, and what is spontaneous, as its central theme, illustrating the movement between the two with great clarity and humor. These old men are not especially anti-State, but nor do they adhere to official pretensions to judgment as part of a good day's entertainment. Their antiquated insistence on *play*, in the open air, is a telling example of negotiated civility, appropriate to retirement. In terms of publicness, it's all here. Until Han gets involved, the opera group is an autonomous and informal organization. Its cohesion comes from the passion and pleasures of the participants, which is itself based on a shared cultural memory. Publicness is in this way fundamental to the narrative. The movement of publicness through the narrative is also sustained through Ning Ying's interest in a contemporary world shared by a generation, and through them with the audience. The world of the pensioners becomes a public space where we are invited to contemplate the nature of play and collaboration in a conversation between generations. The film perceives and simulates negotiation, as it occurs in the oppositions of youth and age, work and play, and state and civility. As the narrative unfolds, we are encouraged to question these oppositions. The pensioners singing in the park are both young and old, organized and casually civil, working at their craft, but playing too. It is, after all, just a bit of fun.

Why, however, do I begin a discussion of childhood and public discourse with a description of a film about pensioners? Simply, because the filmic world reveals that childhood does not just belong to the young. Adult concerns are often articulated, in cultural production, through the figures of children, and therefore, within the world of childhood. This cultural habit serves to turn childhood into a figure of public speech. It becomes one of the ways in which adults talk to each other in public, and also, one of the ways in which adults describe themselves within culture. Childhood in *For Fun* might be a barely enunciated theme, but it is vital to our understanding of the film. Old Han's Red Guard alarm clock is not just an amusing piece of kitsch. He is not a cool collector of chic Maoist paraphernalia. In fact, he possesses only two personal souvenirs: the clock and a portrait of an opera star. Put together, these objects suggest a life and personality that is childish and adolescent, but lacking the fun that goes with the first, and the passion of the second. Old Han is depressing because he cannot recollect the play of childishness nor can he relinquish the rules and disciplines imposed on the young. As an audience we need to recognize this conundrum in order to pity the man, but also to condemn his tyranny towards his peers. Ning Ying calls on a public knowledge of childhood in order to tell a story of extreme old age. She is also making a political statement about the suppression of maturity in certain political environments. The infantilized Old Han is a symptom of an era of China's history when to be truly adult was to exceed the requirements of the State.

Childhood has long provided a major theme in Chinese film. Themes are not the same, however, as target audiences. The films I describe in detail here were mostly made for adults. Some may have been available to children, but were not aimed solely at them. This is not to say there is no children's industry in Chinese filmmaking. The Children's Film Studio, started in 1981, was set up to bring together people working on films for children to give them a base and industrial profile. Before that, children's films were often used as quota fillers for the main studios. The Children's Studio produces films especially for a young audience, and the Animation Studios are also active.[1] In 1992, fifty-six reels of animation were produced, a 225 percent increase from seventeen reels in 1962. The Children's Film Studio deals with a wide range of narratives that address the topic of childhood. To what degree they investigate the *interests* of children themselves is another question, and one that informs my discussion. There are adventure stories, biographies of 'famous' childhoods, stories of patriotism and youthful heroism, magical fairy tales, and schoolroom dramas.[2] These genres are also explored by other studios, particularly Shanghai, Emei, and Beijing. Often the main protagonist is a child, as in the wartime coming-of-age dramas *A Boy in the Heat of Battle* (1975), *Little Soldier* (1963), and a female version *Hai Xia* (1975). In recent years, this genre has shrunk to make way for family dramas, dealing with divorce and childhood trauma, and in which the child generally displays a tragic desire for reconciliation. In *Don't Cry Mummy* (1990), a little boy has to deal with a mentally ill parent, deserted by her husband; in *Divorce* (1992) a toddler is an onlooker to his father's ambiguous relationship with his 'country-wife'. That one ends appropriately for wife and children, as the family returns to a rural life. The meat of the film, however, is in the husband's quandary, and this trace of family sadness is not erased by his decision to give up his job for the unlikely rural idyll.

Family life is part and parcel of Chinese cinema. The theme cropped up several times in my account of Chinese cinema history earlier in this book. It is the core of melodramatic narration, and it is an excellent framework for political storytelling. In revolutionary films, the Party often replaces families lost in war or other accidents. Indeed, whereas Xi'er, the white-haired girl of 1950, is unwittingly betrayed by her father, the servant-girl, Qionghua, in *Red Detachment of Women*, does not have a family to begin with. She is already deracinated, and ripe for inclusion in the family of the Party. A historian of children on film, Li Suyuan, summed up the importance of family structures in a recent interview:

> Now I come to think of it, images of children are always connected with the idea of family. . . . In the Chinese concept of family (*jia*), there are two kinds, internal and external. For example, a revolutionary team is a big *jia*, especially to those children who don't have an immediate family. So in society they enter a larger version, just like going into the army . . . like Little Soldier (*Xiao bing zhang ga*) . . . he joins the army and gains a family in the guise of his revolutionary team.[3]

In pre-Liberation film, politicized narratives eschew formal families for sibling relationships, or pacts of friendship between inspired young people. *Big Road* (1935) tells of a group of young men and two girls whom they meet 'on the road'. They are working as road builders, and thus doing their bit for the effort against the Japanese (and getting themselves something to eat along the way). One of the girls has a father, who runs a café, but the emphasis is on the combined strength, and eventual self-sacrifice of just one generation (figure 3.1). *Street Angel* (1937) has two sisters at the center of the story, the younger of whom is escaping prostitution, with the help of a band of young male friends (figure 3.2). The elder generation here is not just excluded, it is demonized. The China en-

Figure 3.1   White-haired Girl

visaged by these prerevolutionary, nationalist filmmakers is, above all, characterized by youth and the goodness of new generations.

The childhoods, or teenage years, that are described in all these films, from
the silent worries of the tiny boy in *Divorce*, to the kitsch memories of Old Han

Figure 3.2   Street Angel

in *For Fun*, are central to cinematic discussions of public life, and the ways in which that life is culturally conceived. Children are used in cultural production to signal how things should be. When a child is disturbed or unhappy, the audience understands that society as a whole, or a single family, is in trouble. The Children's Film Studio production, *Don't Cry Mummy*, focuses on a child and his mother living together after the break up of the parents' relationship. The story is disturbing, and surprisingly so for a film made for younger audiences. The child, Tongtong, is about eight years old, and presumably that age group is the target audience. He is portrayed as a relentlessly optimistic helper and friend to his depressed and confused mother, and he himself is supported by an elderly man who lives in the same courtyard. The mother is described as 'schizophrenic', but that condition is falsely understood within the plot as an illness caused by a single trauma (the loss of the child's father), and is therefore inadequately resolved at the end of the film. The boy has been befriended by his errant father, and is being coaxed to live with him and his new wife. However, the relationship between mother and son is strong. He rejects his fathers' material offerings and returns to be with her, with the presumption that this brings her back to 'herself' and gives us the happy ending. *Don't Cry Mummy* is an excellent example of the way in which childhood figures are portrayed in filmmaking to produce public spaces in which children are addressed by adults. Tongtong's relationship with his mother verges on the abusive (although the blame for the abuse is difficult to determine). Like many child carers he shoulders a huge practical and emotional burden that is only increased by the emergence of a father figure. The people who do assist are the older man and a single man who both live as close neighbors. In the mother's case, she receives support from her son, the guilt for which exacerbates her suffering, and at a crisis point local women help her. The point that the film makes is that the symptoms of social ills are more likely to be alleviated by public concern than within the family. Or rather, that there is no such thing as private trouble; everything is best dealt with outside in the open. One of the most visually successful sequences of the film occurs when Tongtong's mother walks through the rain searching for him (he is meanwhile with his father). Women, many of them, crowd around her telling her to go home, and shielding her from the rain with black umbrellas. Tongtong turns up, but when he admits where he has been he is attacked wildly by his mother. The older women shield him from the blows, and the shot pulls out to look down on a screen full of umbrellas. This moment encompasses the force of life in public. It also blurs the boundaries between maturity and childishness as the loss of the mother's control contrasts with the careful loyalties of the little boy. None of this, however, turns a film about adults into a film for children. It conforms to the Children's Film Studio's purpose of combining education with uplift, and with a narrational style that is detailed and conversational. Yet its overall effect is strained (*mianqiang*). Yu Lan, as director of the studio, made several statements in a recent interview in Beijing (1998) that are hard to bring together.[4] She is herself an experienced actress, whose work includes the classic *Living in the Flames of War* (1965), in which she plays a heroine of the revolution, Jiang Jie. In this film a young child is instrumental in keeping Party information in the jail where the heroine is imprisoned (figure 3.3). Here is a film with a child protagonist that is clearly not a children's film, and yet it comes from an era that Yu Lan has described as a time when audiences could watch everything together: there was nothing in these texts harmful to children. This indicates that children as composite elements of a heroic tale must be able to understand themselves as such in the process of spectatorship, for this child dies through the trickery of her captors. Yu Lan's comments on Cai Chusheng's classic, *Lost Lambs* (1936), however, are that a story of child poverty in pre-Liberation China is directed at adults: "Cai Chusheng didn't think that his film was directed at children. [He] thinks that if I let children watch his film the children would become depressed, with no hope for the future." Of course, she is correct; only with the wisdom of hindsight can one watch that film knowing that Liberation (thirteen years later) might offer a happy ending long after the closing credits. Presumably, the level of identification and empathy that the children might feel for the children, and especially the hero Little Three (Xiao San Zi), would not be helped by hypothetical happy endings.

But, in educating children about adult failings, and suggesting that a happy and steadfast child can cut through her/his traumatic syndromes, are films such as *Don't Cry Mummy* not absolutely depressing in the amount of responsibility for the narrative closure that falls on the shoulders of the child protagonist? Films aimed at preschoolers are often similar. Guang Chunlan's *Happy Angels* (1996,

Figure 3.3   Living in the Flames of War

Children's Film Studio) is the story of a tiny girl whose unhappiness brings her parents back together, and who, it turns out, thought that her request for a special toy caused the break up in the first place. The film was highly commended by the Broadcasting Bureau and the Propaganda Bureau. The director is proud of the strategies she used in maximizing the small actors' attention spans (short takes with an adult miming the words for them) and in recording their voices (holding them to the mike to get clarity as well as 'baby pitch' *naili naiqi*).[5] But, whatever the degree of apparent authenticity in the representation and presentation of children, there seems less concern with examining the relationship between adult expectations and childish problems. How many children of single parents in China can expect to bring their parents back together, and how can that be explained adequately to the children without exacerbating their worries? Is it more depressing to use film to suggest that the world is perfectible than to create a public debate between adults and children on the nature and experience of daily life? To return to pre-Liberation times, there is a distinction drawn between *Lost Lambs* and *Sanmao's Travels* (1949). It is a similar story, but Sanmao is funny. His physiognomy is based on the cartoon character that preceded the film, big nose and three hairs on his head; the adults are similarly grotesque (figures 3.4 and 3.5). Yet he is also pathetic and endearing and his story provides a

Figure 3.4   Sanmao's Travels

Figure 3.5   Sanmao's Travels

fitting reminder of the cruelties of pre-Liberation street life. The success of this film, and its continuing appeal, throws into question the boundaries between films for children and those for adults. It also introduces doubt into the certainty that film for children must be overtly educative.

This is a debate that continues among filmmakers in the children's sector in China. Are films for children those with particular educational aims, or are they simply those with children in leading roles, films 'about children'? Also, and this category was not highlighted in the thinking of film professionals, what about films that entertain children? Films like *Sanmao*? How are they devised, and what is their value? The features of this debate are not particular to the last two decades of reform, nor to a comparison between the Shanghai of the 1930s and Beijing in the 1990s. Children have been 'there' from the heroics of the 1950s war stories to the 'models' of 1960s and 1970s' production. *Shining Red Star* (1974) is the classic model-child-soldier story, produced by the August First PLA studio. From the perspective of the late-1990s it may look 'ridiculous', but it is a film that captures a brand of political society that was impossibly optimistic, and therefore cruel and finally untenable.[6] That impossibility is contained in the lack of shadows, and the colors; especially the shining red star that runs through the tale as a physical motif (a badge of honor) and a metaphorical reference to the child's place in the narrative and the national imaginary. The film's similarity with earlier, more humane pieces such as *Little Soldier* lies in the way the growth of the child into a soldier is achieved through mimetic actions that are focussed on a future adult self more than on the state of childishness. When a child is pursuing heroic deeds in the cause of revolution, spectators are encouraged by the apparent 'innocence' and wholesomeness of the political or military process. Children are, in short, extremely effective as part of the phenomena of film. The key to understanding how, and why, this might be so lies in the mimetic relationship between children and adults, adults and society, and society and its leaders.

MIMESIS AND VITA ACTIVA

The concept of activity, *vita activa*, is central to the performance of public life. Intentional and communicative activity is first seen in children's learning behaviors. These behaviors tend to be mimetic, which is more than copying, but less than total invention. Mimesis is a vital component of childhood, whether as a tool of development, or retardation. It is the means by which children learn to first 'play' at being grown up, and finally to control their dealings with the world around them, as though they had grown up. Mimesis is, in anthropological terms, the magic and ritual that members of a society employ in order to describe, understand, and manipulate the physical world, and each other. Politically, mimesis is used to produce good subjects, citizens, or, perversely, infantilized objects of political control. The processes of complicity begin with this perversion of mimetics into a method of control and transparency. Mimesis is a means by which the adult subject is created in the space between the pragmatics of the real and the symbolic structure of communicated experience. As such it is central to processes of social formation, reproduction, and of the creation of consistency or sanity among the population. Gertrud Koch describes mimesis as the "unity of separate poles, psychic content, and physical form."[7] Her definition is suggestive of contemporary art forms in which the actual is represented as itself. In anthropological and psychotherapeutic readings, mimesis is a process by which the unrepresentable, the 'real', is negotiated through pragmatics and ritual, experience and mimicry. This understanding of mimesis in development is a foundation for agonism in politics, aesthetics, and social relations. The 'unity' described by Koch tends on one level to deny the notion of the real as unrepresentable, which in turn throws into doubt a distinction between the ideal image and the imperfect human agent. It is a false unity that arguably is achieved by a complicity between image and spectator, the latter returning a gaze in order to confirm that the real is in fact knowable, controllable, and already in the sight lines of Party policy. Theodor Adorno addresses the complicity of the collective gaze as a mimetic compulsion. In "Transparencies on Film" he moves from an earlier position of total antipathy towards mass culture, and allows that filmic textuality is dense and complex in its address to the spectator. His version of film mimetics is also unitary, in that the spectator has only one possible mode of reception and response to any given text.

Such collectivity inheres in the innermost elements of the film. The movements that the film presents are mimetic impulses that, prior to all content and meaning, incite the viewers to fall into step as if in a parade. . . . As the eye is carried along, it joins the current of all those who are responding to the same appeal. The indeterminate nature of this collective 'anything', however, which is linked to the formal character of the film that facilitates the ideological misuse of the medium: the pseudo-revolutionary blurring in which the phrase 'things must change' is conveyed by the gesture of banging one's fist on the table.[8]

The arguments of Adorno and Koch indicate that mimesis can be *experienced* as a false impulse towards childishness. The aim of society is to create a framework of development in which children become attuned to the requirements of adult life, by the time that they are expected to take up adult responsibilities. In a totalitarian context, mimetics are appropriated as a means of controlling the population before it reaches a stage of development that might be described as adult. In such an instance, the mimetic impulse is channelled towards a closed set of meanings, and a single source of power that appropriates the agency of the individual and the group to its own maintenance. Here mimesis resides within the unrepresentable elements of a medium of representation. Its potential for the worst kind of collectivity is located in the uncharted relationship between gesture and intention, vision and interpretation. Furthermore, Adorno denies that the *effect* of film has any space for—possibly radical—ambiguity. As in *The Dialectic of Enlightenment* and *The Culture Industry*, he perceives an obsessional relationship between the consumer and the commodity, always fearing another manifestation of the totalizing cultural productions of German National Socialism. This position supposes that the technology of film, its mass potential, and its innate lack of any claim to authenticity, was itself a predisposition to totalization of reception.[9] In Adorno's terms, Old Han is not only an example of retarded mimetic control, he is also irredeemable by an audience, either now or in the future, who might see something progressive in his attitudes or behavior.

Adorno's scenario of obsession does not prove, however, that mimetic relationships are *necessarily* totalizing or complicit. The very idea of obsession admits an agency in the spectator, even if that agency is then frittered away on consumption, or on complicity with a restrictive symbolic order.[10] The symbolic order can be restricted by a totalitarian system, but not entirely. Ning Ying has created a character who 'shows' retardation, but whose final meaning can only come from an audience. She makes the space and they make it public.

In discussing this further, I will focus on one childhood film, *The Blue Kite*. This film, made for an adult rather than a child audience, takes childhood as its theme in several related ways. First, the main protagonist is a young boy. Second, the narrative is organized around the stages of his family life, and, in particular, by his relationship to the men in his mother's life. Third, the main object of the film, a blue kite, is a metonym for the experience of childhood. Finally, the political background to the plot is presented in tandem with an exploration of childhood itself. In this way, childhood does not lend an innocence to political action (as in those war dramas from the 1960s and 1970s). On the contrary, childhood is complicated by political experience, and at last is ended by the need for children (themselves) to enter the symbolic world of violence. The film shows that the mimetics of childhood are intimately bound up with the fashioning of adult histories.

The director of the film, Tian Zhuangzhuang is cynical about the relationship between children and adults:

> Adults do not regard children as the same, equal, as people with their own rights. Before the age of sixteen, children are basically pets for their parents. They have no right to be independent. It may sound horrible, but I think parents give their children exactly what they *don't* want. The problem is replicated in Chinese film, filmmakers seldom consider what children want to see, or indeed have any notion of what children might want to watch.[11]

For Tian, the processes of mimesis are forced to cope not just with the perceived realities of adult life, and the preparation for that, but also with unhelpful adult guidance in how to fashion the process of mimesis itself. The requirement to educate leaves out the possibility of public space that is also children's space in cultural production.

THE PUBLIC SECRET

> The thing about playing is always the precariousness of the interplay of personal psychic reality and the experience of control of actual objects.[12]

The Blue Kite was a coproduction between China and Japan, and was distributed through Longwick in Hong Kong. It collected prizes for best director, best film, and best actress in festivals in Tokyo, Singapore, and Chicago. Its international success was not matched by its domestic welcome. The Chinese delegation stormed out of the screening at the Tokyo Film Festival in protest at the use of an unauthorized print (since then China Film Co-productions have been made only if the negatives are kept in China). Subsequently, the offending production companies in Hong Kong were banned from further involvement in the Chinese film industry. Zheng Quangang, at that time the president of the China Film Co-production Corporation (CFCC), defended the move on account of China's reputation and the finances of its film industry: "Zheng accused the companies of including pornography and violence in their 'overseas versions' and causing economic losses to their Chinese partners."[13] In the piece quoted, Zheng does not explain exactly *how* these 'overseas versions' harm the domestic industry, nor are particular violent and pornographic moments specified. *The Blue Kite* is actually extraordinarily unsensationalist, despite telling a story where violence is implicit in almost every twist of the protagonists' suffering. It is a fine piece of 'conversational' (*bu mianqiang*) narration. The destruction of love by circumstance is certainly thematic, but it is presented through the gentle eroticism of shared routines, rather than through overt sexual encounters. It is likely then that Zheng's problem is with aspects of the film that he cannot, or will not, explain. I can only imagine that the film offended bureaucratic sensibilities because of modes of narration and turns in the narrative that fell outside the regime of truth as recognized by the CFCC.

In *The Blue Kite* a loving father makes and remakes a kite for his son, Tietou, replacing it with an exact replica each time it is spoilt or lost. When he dies, in a rightist camp in the early 1960s, the boy's mother forms a relationship with another man. He in turn repairs the objects of childhood. When Tietou's horse-lantern is spoilt at New Year, his 'uncle' promises to make another. Moments later, he also collapses and dies. Having worked extraordinarily hard, and been named a model worker (*mofan gongren*) for his pains (motivated as personal atonement for his guilt, at having been unwittingly responsible for Tietou's father's arrest), he dies of heart failure and malnutrition. Finally, Tietou's mother marries a Party official in an attempt to secure the boy's future. It is not a loving partnership, but becomes more tolerable after the now-older Tietou takes care of his stepfather's little niece, himself making her a blue kite, and promising to make another when it gets stuck in a tree.

The kite is a common toy in China, and a common signifier of childhood in Chinese visual representation. In *The Kite* (1958) the kite bears messages from China to France, uniting children from both places in friendship. In the Taiwanese melodrama, *Four Loves* (1965), and in Hou Hsiao-hsien's *Summer at Grandpa's* (1983), girls and boys handle kites, as they face the joys and disappointments of growing up. Children are often shown with kites in paintings dating from the T'ang, Yuan, and Song dynasties (and probably more than that).[14] The kite disappears somewhat in the political posters of the 1960s and 1970s, its place often taken by flags and handheld banners. This is partly because the didactic poster tended to show children either at work, or engaged in political ecstasy, the kind of fun that Old Han memorializes in his alarm clock. So, in the return of the kite in Tian Zhuangzhuang's film, we can deduce a cinematic appeal for a different account of childhood in revolutionary China. What, asks the film in almost every sequence, do we mean by 'play' in this particular historical place and time? Is play itself infused with the publicness that surrounds the playing children, and does it therefore politicize the most infantile of their actions? Furthermore, given Tian's own explanation of the kite being the perfect toy to use as a motif in the film because it also epitomizes a condition of "life on a string in contemporary China,"[15] the kite marks a juncture between child's play and adult socialization.

In *The Blue Kite* the kite as, rather literally, a floating signifier of childhood, is emphasized by its treatment within the frame. There are several shots where the kite is central, and framed without a human 'handler'. Kites, though, often need rescuing, usually by an older child. They are the perfect metaphor for social interdependence in childhood, and for the importance of play to a child's relationship with his world. This is brought to a sadly ironic conclusion at the very end of the film. There is a classic shot-reverse-shot sequence, where the child and kite are placed in equivalent relation one to another. As the boy stares up at the lost kite, his childhood voice returns in voice-over, singing a childhood nursery rhyme that he learned from his mother. The child's childhood-object is stuck up a tree, and out of reach. The battered kite cannot be rescued for the piping-voiced toddler (himself rather than his niece at this point in the film) by his now mature and equally battered owner. This account of a boy's childhood in the 1950s and 1960s in China begins, then, with the mimetic responses of an infant, and ends with adult loneliness as the once infinite perfectibility of life is finally perceived as fluttering tatters, stuck up a tree and out of reach.[16]

The description of internalized trauma through the placing of external objects within the frame is a tested filmic device. Alfred Hitchcock would often lay much of the burden of meaning of his plots onto an inanimate object. Sometimes, this object was only hinted at (as in the secret behind the coded tune in *The Lady Vanishes*, 1939). At other times, it was solidly conceived, and its physical presence essential to the unwinding of the narrative (as in the cigarette lighter in *Strangers on a Train*, 1951). This kind of object also features in revolutionary film, but even more abstractly. It almost always acts as a metaphor for the future, for the Party, and its successful transformation of popular consciousness.

There is a second type of object, however, that follows a different kind of logic. It is a fascinating, captivating, bewitching, spellbinding object that necessarily possesses a kind of materiality and a certain lethal quality.[17] This "lethal" object gives meaning, not just to the plot, but also to the relationships that sustain it.[18] In *The Blue Kite*, there is a tripartite relationship between adulthood, childhood, and the domain of play, in which the one learns about the other. This narrative framework is schematically held in place, and propelled forward, by the kite. The kite is the object of affection, the replacement of which guarantees the repair and continuation of childhood. The adults, the boy's female relations and a sequence of male alter egos, his father, his 'uncle' (*shu-shu*), and his second stepfather, are themselves in an uneasy relationship with the public world of adulthood. Here again, a toy serves as the object that marks the fatal proximity of the political and the domestic. When the boy Tietou is still young, and very angry that his mother has to leave him to go away to do politically motivated work, he witnesses a family argument break out over the demands of the State on its members. In an uncanny echo of the drum-beating and flag-waving marches that take place in the streets outside, he bangs implacably on a toy drum. The noise silences his family, and marks an early stage of the boy's mimetic entry into a perversely antilinguistic Symbolic: a public world of retardation.

Tian Zhuangzhuang's treatment of Tietou's youth is akin to a clinical appraisal of a child's development.[19] In particular, the problem at the heart of the boy's story seems to be that, given the pathology of the national political narrative, he may not experience conflict, except in heightened neurotic forms. His first and only beating from his father occurs after a political meeting at the father's workplace. The father has been scapegoated as a rightist, and is contemplating a dismal and dangerous future. When a childhood argument erupts outside, the boy is hit, dragged inside, and then the parents fight with each other. All this is observed by the other courtyard children, who peer in eagerly, and report the fight to anyone who wants to know. The political has, quite literally, found its way into the domestic space. The madness of a campaign to produce rightists—a certain percentage of the work force was demanded from each workplace—produces fear where before there had only been love.

Throughout the film, Tietou experiences this domestic internalization of political melodrama rather than the traumatic but ordinary confrontations of development. His oedipal experience is ruptured and fragmented by political circumstance. He loses a father, a surrogate father, an (albeit unpopular) stepfather, and he is twice separated from his mother. Domestic antagonisms are always experienced in context, but for Tietou this context is abnormally pressurized. In the domestic space, his relations and daily antipathies are made monstrous by the patterns of public life in which they happen. When the Cultural Revolution implodes against its own paternity, and the cadres of the old order are 'struggled against', the madness of a totalitarian ego moves inside the domestic space to destroy competing intimacies. The stepfather has a heart attack when he is arrested, and Tietou's mother is also taken away. It is at this moment, at the end of the film, that the relentless narrative of nation and politics is revealed as a mortal conflict between external imperatives and individual development. The violence of public life demands violence as a symbolic sign of belongingness to the body politic. However, as Tietou's bleeding body and disembodied baby voice indicate at the end of the film, this kind of symbolic maturity is fatal, and liable to produce madness. It is this unhealthy breakdown of childhood that forms the core of *The Blue Kite*. The film's secret is a public secret, shared in the memory of collective brutality and the betrayal of the young. Tietou's young life is made pathological and violent through the madness in his world. A child's compulsion to mimesis means that there is no escape without a retreat into infantile babbling.

Nonpathological conflict entails a meeting of the external and the internal realms of psychic experience. It is incompatible with the excessive interiority of narcissism. Equally, however, it is incompatible with the impositions of totalitarian politics and society. Space for conflict in the interior mind is, therefore, reliant on the availability of public space.[20] As the psychoanalyst Dominique Scarfone argues: "At one level, one could say that conflictuality is a name for the ego's capacity to work . . . at another level, it could represent the ego's capacity to love. . . . To become able to love and to work, is it not what Freud expected from analytic treatment?"[21]

Watching *The Blue Kite* is hard work. The attention of the spectator is split between the emotional point of view of the child and an ambivalent emphasis on the child as metaphor. On the one hand, Tietou's point of view is the only diegetic point of identification. Even at his parents' wedding, his presence is established through a voice-over. Identifying with the boy allows the spectator to be his contemporary, who has yet somehow escaped into the public and present world of adults. On the other hand, camera angles switch from low-angle point of views, to omniscient shots of adults, landscapes, and children playing. This doubling of effect addresses the audience both as possible children themselves *and* as adults, who feel empathy for the remembrance of rupture in their own processes of maturation, while also pitying the extreme and abrupt progress of this particular child. The viewer's position is thus one of uncomfortably complicit survival.

The Blue Kite is a film through which the history of a particular human's journey towards selfhood is plotted through the disintegration of public and social responsibility. His political environment leaves the adult population stranded, between the security of mimetic dyadics with the Party, and the satisfying, but dangerous memory of achieved maturity. Meanwhile, a new generation avoids maturity altogether or is thrust into breakdown by the impossible tragedies of continuing childhood. The filmic world demands that the audience recognize itself as product, and protagonist, of the same history of these adult children and child-adults. We are functions of Tian's cinematic world. Our presence as spectators gives it a public dimension, for that is why we went to see the film in the first place: to offer our memories and fears to its validation.

> In both instances, male and female, imagined worlds become not only theatricalized but factualized as religious axiom, and social custom. Illusions thus serve the cause of belief, if not truth, thanks to the magical series of transfers between theater and reality held in place by mimetic art and the public secret. Mimesis sutures the real to the really made up—and no society exists otherwise.[22]

In *The Blue Kite* the public secret is that the public conspires against itself to prevent the development of mature mimesis. In childhood, mimicry frees the child into the symbolic world of self-representation and communication. In maturity, this process constitutes the way in which adult society orders and understands itself. We look to *see* the world and *know* ourselves. In the world of *The Blue Kite*, there is neither history, nor nature, nor a man nor woman mature enough to bear a mind of his/her own. The perpetuation of childhood poisons the original value of infantile mimetics, which is to learn how to function autonomously in society. Instead, the careful mimetic responses of the infant become ever more grotesque patterns of irresponsible and meaningless behavior, as the child grows and learns just one thing—to fear itself and its own extraordinary place in the world. Fear of maturity and autonomy is the fear of being different, being mad. Yet is not D. M. Winnicott right in his diagnosis that the madness is already present in that fear?

> The fear is not of madness to come but of madness that has already been experienced. It is a fear of the return of madness. . . . The patient's need is to remember the original madness, but in fact the madness belongs to a very early stage before the organization in the ego of those intellectual processes which can abstract experiences that have been catalogued and can present them for use in terms of conscious memory.[23]

Winnicott was concerned as a clinician and researcher with the first years of life, but he also expected this work to foster his understanding of adult problems. The narrative of *The Blue Kite* concentrates on the susceptibility of childhood, but the film's narration is also concerned to make connections with adult traumas. The fear of the return of madness, either the loneliness of difference or the shared madness of total domination, is a theme that haunts many contemporary Chinese films. It is in all cases connected to the public status and political visibility of the protagonists.

In the scenes I have discussed so far, the boy, Tietou, has been observed to 'play' and fight with the external pressures of his political environment. There are also passages when his play—or just his presence—disrupts the logic of external reality, so that its arbitrary cruelty is represented as madness. Tietou's mother is talking to the former girlfriend of her older brother. It is evening, they are sitting on the bed, and Tietou has fallen asleep between them. The ex-girlfriend explains that she is worried that her association with the brother is dangerous for him. She has recently left the Army (PLA) in order to escape 'dancing' with senior Party cadres. The implication is that she would at some point be expected to do more than just dance. Her action has ruined her once promising political career, and she is deeply frightened of what the future might hold in store. She 'feels' that something bad is about to happen. (It does: she is arrested as a counterrevolutionary and sent to prison in the following scene). As she tries to explain her fear, a medium close-up on the women's faces emphasizes the apparent security of a domestic evening. They are framed, though, not by the walls that surround them, but by the protective gaze of the camera. There is no security beyond that of representation and memory. The picture is completed and the scene ends on a shot of the sleeping toddler. Silent, still, unconscious at this point of adult concerns, his stolid vulnerability at once embodies the target of the external regime of truth, and undermines its claims on the past, present, and future. Those very precious commodities of consciousness are the prizes of the struggles of childhood and development.

ANIMATED LIVES

Childhood is a category of publicness in Chinese film language, but it is a public of adults and a space constructed for the airing and sharing of their concerns. The strong emphasis on education above entertainment value exacerbates this situation. Perhaps the place to look for children's cultural public space would be in the world of animation, where the 'stretch and squash' of drawn narrative allows for a literally elastic approach to representation. Animation series have been didactic but they rely on fantasy for their images. *Hailibu* (1985) is a moral tale about a young Mongolian warrior who cares for animals. He saves the mountain god's daughter from hunters (she is disguised as a squirrel) and is rewarded with the fruit of the gods, which allows him to understand the language of fish, birds, and other animals, but which leads eventually to his transformation into a statue. There are several entry points to the film, for any age group. The story is exciting, and can be read straight or as a succession of colors ranging around the central character. My own child, age two, felt that the story went 'bad' when the 'boy went grey'. An older child might be better able to pick up the musical clues to Hailibu's heroic but also pathetic status at the point of transformation into stone. Many children are entertained by the animals: Disney-like large-eyed deer, squirrels, bluebirds, and gentle horses. The style is in fact very reminiscent of the forest sequences in Disney's *Snow White* (1937). Some children would notice that the film was set in Mongolia. This reinforces the mythological aspect for Han children, and allows a connection with dominant representations of minority peoples in China; it is not surprising that there should be a mountain god with a beautiful daughter who transforms from a squirrel in the opening sequence—but in animation it is not surprising anyway. There are, then, points of entry and levels of comprehension that are not necessarily available to all audiences. Whereas in live action this might serve to occlude the force of the film, here it reinvents itself through its multiple and equivalent modes of storytelling. The adult political sphere is present, but it does not dominate the formation of spectatorial communities.

Similarly in *Three Monks* (1980) the moral basis for the story is one of cooperation. The story is told in a style based on shape and color arranged to suggest character and spatial relationships between characters. Much of the time the characters are sitting on prayer mats (often with their backs to one another), or they are travelling up and down the 'landscape', a solitary green hill, fetching water to the temple. Spectators may engage with the story as a whole or with fragments of its composition. I will conclude this chapter with the suggestion that (at least young) children's public space may be abstracted from a perfect narrative form. When Benjamin wrote of the colors of a child's painting, he had already understood one of the secrets of form and space in animated film.[24] The shared laughter and pleasure of young children define them as a body of spectators. These actions are 'being' in public, and whatever the intentions of their creators, may have no moral outcome to them at all.

4

National Publicness

National and public consciousness are closely aligned in many films. This is a sine qua non of revolutionary cinema, but becomes self-conscious in the post-Maoist era, perhaps especially in the new waves of the fifth and sixth generations. Critics have been quick to pick up on this in their responses to the most accessible of these films for international audiences. Sheldon Lu's analysis of Zhang Yimou's 'Gong Li' sequence charts these responses, recognizing, as he does so, that while Zhang 'reinvents' national allegory in his work, he also panders to international, sentimental preconceptions of Chineseness. Lu's other point, however, is that a new, cinematic national imagination, as produced by Zhang, is one that takes China away from revolutionary romanticism and back to childhood. Many of his films revolve around children, and possibly, they stand for China, "a generation of 'lost children' without a father."[1] Lu's work on childhood resonates with much that I have discussed in the previous chapter. Here, I will expand on the idea of the national imaginary, emphasizing those moments where it is in conflict with a cinematic publicness.

Two films from the mid-1980s, *Yellow Earth* (1984) and *Wild Mountains* (1985), offer contrasting perspectives on the Chinese cinema in the era of economic change.[2] Both achieved international, critical success, and *Wild Mountains* also did extremely well in the domestic market.[3] Zhang acted as cinematographer on *Yellow Earth*, and the theme identified by Lu of China as the lost child is opened up in the characters of Cuiqiao and Hanhan. In *Wild Mountains*, the child is a baby, and he is used, primarily, to contrast traditional family life in rural areas with the neocapitalist ambitions of peasants in the 1980s (figure 4.1). The concern of both films with the experience of peasants, the core of the Maoist revolutionary ideal, is an indication of their overall interest in talking more generally about China's self-perceptions in the wake of Deng Xiaoping's economic

Figure 4.1　Wild Mountains

reforms. In both films, the limits and false premises of the ideal peasant-experi-
ence are exposed, either through textual inconsistency, narrative ambiguity, or in
the stark emotional disjunctures between personal development and communal
intransigence. *Yellow Earth* allows a reading of revolutionary history that admits
disruptions to the unconscious interpellations of the Party line. *Wild Mountains*
tells the stories of individuals caught up in the 1980s rush towards modernization while unravelling the subjective costs of their engagement with it.

Even before reading the arguments that raged at its release, and the discussions
that have evolved since about its layers of meaning, *Yellow Earth* seemed on first
viewing to be uncomfortably subversive. The critic Li Tuo has been quoted as
saying that the film came as a shock to the system, like an "unwelcome guest":
"For Chinese film audiences and critics alike, the arrival of *Yellow Earth* was quite
unexpected. It was like a . . . social gathering where people are awaiting the arrival of a friend: the doorbell rings, the door opens, but the person who steps in
is a stranger that no one recognizes . . . there is an awkward silence."[4]

It is at first difficult to locate the actual cause of this discomfort. Repeated
viewing led me to certain moments in the film that seem disruptive to the assumptions that underlie the narrative as a whole, the familiar story of peasant redemption through Communist illumination. In this film, the supremely non-ironic style
of socialist-realist filmmaking is subverted by attacks on its most precious tropes.
One of these is the socialist-realist gaze. The other is the prioritization of people
over place in depictions of the national landscape.

A SOCIALIST-REALIST GAZE

In film theory, the gaze has been understood as the way in which the camera, spectator, and the principal male character 'look together' at the sexualized females on screen. The problem with this idea is that it gives spectators only one way of watching the film, from a masculine perspective. This argument, and its detractions, is fundamental to feminist film theory. On the one hand, it allows the critic to show how the relationship between prevailing sexual politics and cinematic narration is maintained.[5] On the other, it provokes the critic and spectator into arguing for a more flexible approach to film consumption and its analysis. In non-Hollywood, revolutionary film, the theory of the gaze is a useful starting point for considering how audiences were, or were not, accepting of the ways in which they were invited to watch film. This is to argue that public modes of spectatorship are affected by a changing political climate. This is obvious, but nonetheless, interesting in the way it actually happens. The gaze of the audience works with that of the camera/filmmaker to reconfigure the meanings of a politically charged on-screen look.

An important element of this argument is the mutuality of gaze and fetish. A fetishistic close-up may safely 'puncture' the cinematic space constructed within the exchange of the gaze. Fragments of a female form will destroy the narrative space, or at least suspend its dynamic, but in so doing will enhance the erotic power of the narration. An early example of this in Chinese cinema is the scene in *Goddess* when Ruan Lingyu's character leaves her infant son asleep, and steps out of the house to work as a prostitute. As soon as she leaves the maternal home, the camera treats her differently. We no longer see her face, or her cradling arms around her sleeping son. Now she is cut up into shots of her ankles, legs, and the nape of her neck. In a revolutionary, totalitarian context, the gendered gaze, as a guiding concept, is still apparent. The fetishistic close-up, or *puncture*, is vital to the affirmation of meaning of cinematic space, although the emphasis is different.[6]

In socialist-realist texts, all narration is designed to reinforce the Party's version of history. Here, as always, the notion of history implies ownership of the present and the future, as well as a version of the past. In these circumstances, cinematic narration must take into account the gaze of the leader in a totalitarian regime. If there is to be a spectatorial position, it must be singular and willing to conspire in the transparency of total power. The priority, then, is the collectivization of the gaze. The gaze of the camera, the spectator, and the cinematic subject are ideally brought together in a visual logic that serves the official historical narrative. This is likely to be facilitated by the transposition of age-old gendered power structures, but arguably such reinforcement of patriarchy is, in this instance, a convenience rather than an end in itself. In the right exhibitionary climate, the socialist-realist gaze freezes the narrative while producing for the narration a sublime and completely bogus moment of completion. Present, past, and future lock together on screen and off in a moment of ecstatic communion. When the narrative introduces doubt into the narrative outcome, as occurs in *Yellow Earth*, this communion slips heavily into irony.

Yellow Earth was made in 1984, eight years after the death of Mao and four years after Deng Xiaoping had signalled wide sweeping economic reforms at the Thirteenth Plenum of the Chinese Communist party in August 1980. This breach in ideological continuity, forced by the demands of 'capitalism with a Chinese face'—as President Jiang Zemin describes marketization—and particularly marked in the loss of status of the peasantry, is a breach that informs the textual disruptions in *Yellow Earth*.[7] The director of the film, Chen Kaige (b.1952), and the cinematographer, Zhang Yimou (b.1950), were both 1982 graduates from the Beijing Film Academy, the first cohort of students to graduate since the Cultural Revolution. Chen Kaige was in his first year of high school when the Cultural Revolution began in 1966 and spent three years as a Red Guard. He then lived for two years in rural Southwest China and was for four years in the army.[8] His international reputation has grown in the years since *Yellow Earth* took the 1985 Hong King Film Festival by storm, but the delicacy of visual subversion achieved in that film has not been surpassed by his later work.

In *Yellow Earth* the conflict between tradition, revolution, and modernity underscored by the memory of resistance to external hostility and internal oppression, informs what is, on the surface, a simple narrative.[9] It is 1938, the Communist forces are holed up in Yan'an, gathering strength four years after the Long March. A soldier, Gu Qing, has been sent to Northern Shaanxi to gather songs from the peasants. These songs of bitterness (*kü ger*) are to be reworked with Communist lyrics, and then returned to the people as an appropriate cultural product for the revolution.[10] Gu Qing's project is a foretaste of Mao's dictum from the Yan'an talks for artists to find the appropriate form for the content: "Serve the Workers and Peasants, Serve the Eighth Route and New Fourth Armies, and Go Among the Masses."[11]

Gu Qing stays with a small family, a widower and his two children—the girl Cuiqiao and the boy Hanhan. Gu Qing's optimism infects the children who both express their wish to join him and his revolution. Cuiqiao is particularly impressed that the soldier has learned to sew, and that women in his movement are allowed to cut their hair short. She is also under pressure as her marriage to an older man from a neighboring village is being negotiated. She asks the soldier to take her with him when he returns to base. He refuses, as he needs permission to recruit new soldiers, but promises to return for her in the spring. During his absence, the marriage takes place, and Cuiqiao later drowns in an attempt to escape across the Yellow River. When the soldier finally returns, the region has been struck by drought. Hanhan cannot fight his way through a sea of praying peasants to the redemption offered by the Communist horizon.

In the scene, where Cuiqiao asks Gu Qing to take her back to Yan'an, there is a rather peculiar moment. Cuiqiao tells the soldier that she trusts in him, and he looks straight ahead, away from the girl, and just above the spectators' eyeline. It is uncomfortable to watch. The camera lingers on this off-screen 'look' fractionally more than is acceptable (figure 4.2). The emphasis is not a miscalculation. It makes a deliberate point about how spectators might understand Cuiqiao's trust in a Communist horizon in the year 1984. Cuiqiao has told the soldier that she trusts in his return, but when he has gone on his way, she sings a song lamenting that his return will be too late.[12] Cuiqiao's song of loss is her parting gift, a jewel of bitterness for his notebook. The optimism of Cuiqiao's trust, and the soldier's promise, is punctured by this longueur that turns the narrative into a farce, and reminds the spectator of her own gaze.

To be reminded of the gaze while watching a film is characteristically radical. The French innovator Jean-Luc Godard's *Tout Va Bien* (1973) does this time and time again, in an effort to make the spectator break away from their conventional expectations, and start thinking for themselves. Godard repeats scenes, focussing on different characters each time through. Characters speak to camera, and are often introduced facing the spectator, eliminating the gaze of the masculine position within the frame. Godard, a founder of the Dziga Vertov group, was a Maoist when he made *Tout Va Bien*. The direction of his radicalism was differ-

Figure 4.2   Yellow Earth

ent to that of Chen Kaige. Yet, both directors demonstrate that, in order to say anything new about contemporary ideologies, they have to disrupt the screen conventions of their time and place. Godard's target is Hollywood-dominant narration; Chen Kaige's is socialist realism. Godard takes up Hollywood stars (the idea of Bogart in *Breathless* (1960), the figures of Jane Fonda and Yves Montand in *Tout Va Bien*) and (almost) reduces them to his theme. Chen Kaige takes the socialist-realist gaze, as performed by the soldier Gu Qing, and evacuates it of its previous potency. The convention, in both their hands, is used to destabilize the foundations of an entire stylistic mode of address.

The socialist-realist gaze has long, international credits. Mikhail Gelovani, an actor who made a career out of playing Josef Stalin, was a past master of the off-screen promise.[13] In a scene from *The Vow* (1940) he looks soulfully at a snow-covered bench, remembering conversations he had had with the recently deceased Comrade Lenin. There is a cut to close-up, as he turns his eyes up and looks off screen right. The first shot binds the two leaders together, while the second places them in an infinite relationship with the future. In *Children* (literally 'sons and daughters') *of the Storm* (*Feng yun er nü*, 1935), Chinese patriots urge each other to rise up and fight the Japanese aggressor. The scene builds through a montage of sound and vision, as face after face is captured in an ecstasy of certainty and national strength. The repetition of actions, as close-ups show hands and forearms reaching down to grasp rough and ready weapons, and faces staring exultantly off screen, is obviously influenced by the work of Soviet filmmakers. The sequence is reminiscent of Eisenstein's use of montage in *October* (1928) and *Battleship Potemkin* (1925), where illusions of emotional consistency are cut into a collective attachment to the future. In these shots, the romanticism of socialist realism is very clear. The gaze off screen is a fixed stare out to a horizon, beyond the diegetic world, and apparently also beyond the world of the audience. This gaze is quintessentially anti-individual. It belongs to great leaders, and to representatives of collective action. As a trope of narration, it favors the romance of revolution and a heroic future over the intimacy of personal psychology. It is a gaze that cannot be returned, but needs to be shared with the audience if it is not to look ridiculous. The gaze is shared, in the sense of being understood in its context, in the films of Gelovani and in Chinese revolutionary romances. *Stage Sisters* is a film that, as Gina Marchetti has convincingly argued, is socialist-realist in structure with Hollywood and Brechtian characteristics.[14] If there is any argument as to its primary stylistic focus, one need only fast forward to the last scene. The two dialectically arranged characters, Chunhua and Yuehong, sit in a boat. They look up and forward, their revolutionary sisterhood reestablished in the sharing of the socialist-realist gaze. In *Yellow Earth*, the gaze is not shared, either by other characters or by the audience. Cuiqiao continues to look down at the ground, and we feel slightly embarrassed at what seems suddenly like anachronism. This is a gaze that if it is not shared, collectively, becomes empty of any meaning, and thus, powerfully ironic.[15]

Leaders of Children

The nature of this gaze is epitomized in Stalin. As leader, he claims knowledge of the future, as well as holding the power to create a meaning for that future, through the manipulation of the past, and control of the present.

> For a communist a great man is, hic et nunc, one who helps make History for himself—a History whose meaning is defined, without possible error, by the dialectic process and the Party. The greatness of the Hero is objectified, that is, relevant to the unfolding of the History in which he is at that moment both the means and its consciousness . . . the image of Stalin presented as "real" conforms exactly to what a myth of Stalin would have him be—to what would be useful for him to be.[16]

In writing about Stalin on film, the film theorist André Bazin is interested in the representational conundrum of Stalin the actual man and political operator, and Stalin the leader who is best personified by an actor in a film narrative. The 'unfolding of history', and the confirmation of personal greatness, is dependent on a tacit agreement between subject and spectator that the image and the real are interchangeable in the realm of the public imaginary. In order to retain control over the meaning of history, Stalin must allow his own meaning to be fixed within a tension of complicit gazes: the camera on the face of the chosen actor, the spectators in rapt acceptance of this face of power, the actor's look off screen to a commonly assumed horizon, and the gaze of Stalin himself confirming his own confirmation.

The exultant masses of *Children of the Storm* create a sense of untrammelled progress into an explosive future, a clear borrowing from Eisenstein's theory and practice.[17] The common ownership of the socialist-realist gaze, which every child of the storm possesses in this sequence, is a reminder that the assumed horizon was once clearly visible to those idealistic enough to believe in it, or those suffering enough to need it. It had not yet been appropriated into the gift of the leader and the leader's representatives. The gaze of the soldier in *Yellow Earth* ironizes only the second stage; the first is a casualty of political history. However, it is worth noting the title of this film again, *Children of the Storm*. Even here there is already a presumption that the adult presence is separated from the people, that the storm of revolution has its own impetus and presumably its own cloudy horizon and that its sons and daughters must look, exult, and have faith. They are not expected to develop beyond the horizon of a family hierarchy within which they are subordinated. The reasoning behind infantilization is shaky. As we have noted, the panoptic effect characteristic of modernity, and reinforcement by authoritarian government, is already a system of self-surveillance. Totalitarian insistence on the saturation of public space by the iconography of the leadership is an overkill that infantilizes the leadership more than it compromises the people.

Yet this infantilizing of the population, and in particular of the cultural discourse of the nation, was a Maoist strategy that affected several generations. It was structured around anti-intellectualism. When Mao brought life and art into cold alignment by the Yan'an Talks of 1942, he did so to curb the intellectual arrogance of the bourgeoisie. His long-term achievement was to deny to the public imaginary the space between internal and external experience and expression, and to refuse a passage from one to another unless by way of the ideal. It is notable that the images and cinematography of recent films often focus on the intense relationship between the sky, the horizon, and the human. In *The Blue Kite* the ideal is again visible, but tattered and out of reach. In *Yellow Earth* the political drama is played under a sky that fills two-thirds of the screen space in many shots, and it is the horizon that eventually returns to crush the soldier and his claim to a political future. Tian Zhuangzhuang, the director of *The Blue Kite*, was a young boy in 1966—the start of the Cultural Revolution. In Wu Wenguang's video documentary *1966–My Times in the Red Guards* (1992), Tian remembers his compulsion to the ideal, in fact to any available representation that did not puncture the perfect surface of his absolutely political self: "[paraphrase] We were all in Tiananmen Square, so excited that we would see Mao himself, our leader. I saw a plumpish man along with all the others far away up on the viewing platform. I thought it was Mao. I waved my red book at him frantically, it wasn't him but that didn't make any difference to the way I felt."

The memory of the good old, bad old days is visualized in terms of distance, of doubtful visibility. The horizon is finally seen for what it is: the source of sunlight and the beginning of darkness. Wu Wenguang, who was only ten years old in 1966, described the making of the documentary (within the script of the film itself) as "an exploration into the tunnel of history. I often had the feeling that I was inside an enormous black hole."

Although in *Yellow Earth* the past is recalled in the light and space of the northern plains, Chen also accuses history of darkness. The bitter emptiness of his camera's gaze on Gu Qing paints a shrinking horizon in a boundless sky. It reprimands the spectators for placing their childish trust in that tiny horizon, for not demanding to continue to see it for themselves. After all, it is only by watching the horizon that its fluctuations between the place of darkness and the place of light are visible. It is only through this fluctuation that there is such a phenomenon.

EROTICISM AND HISTORY

Socialist realism is the primary aesthetic of Soviet and Chinese revolution in the twentieth century. Although, after 1958, the term 'socialist realism' was dropped in favor of cultural nationalism, exemplified in revolutionary romanticism. Indeed, the influence of peasant painting does mark a difference between the development of the Soviet aesthetic and the work of Chinese artists in the (national[ist] art) *guohua* school. Bold use of color and a strong peasant theme are typical. Socialist realism is still an appropriate term, because the work of the revolutionary romantics is as dependent on a socialist ideology for the organization of its aesthetic as it is on a tradition of national culture. The realism of the image after 1958 derives its claim to reality, as well as its romanticism, from a belief in the socialist future. In this way realism implies an acknowledgment of the inevitable brightness (sometimes quite literally in terms of paint and cinematographic palettes) of the achieved socialist future and narrative prioritization of the ideological means to that end.[18]

In his history of Chinese cinema, Paul Clark divides socialist realism into six genres: minority film; proletarian heroics; the joy of hard work; musicals; reworkings of May Fourth narratives (in which the original ironies were overwritten with popularized optimism); and history films. Although all of these genres can be traced back to pre-Liberation genres, the ideological emphasis makes the ascendancy of socialist realism quite clear. This emphasis was overwhelming in the years of the Cultural Revolution when few films were made. Those that were made combined the Maoist tropes of revolutionary realism and revolutionary romanticism so that all genres collapsed into a single narrative pattern. Clark describes it through the stock character list: Hero (Initiator/Fount of knowledge/Fighter), Young woman (Eager to learn and join the struggle), Old woman (on hand with a tearful story of the *ku* bitter—pre-Liberation—years), and Old man (who waivers but is kept on track by Hero).[19]

If the gaze originated as a description of a patriarchal impulse and set of techniques in classic Hollywood filmmaking, it is also useful for thinking about socialist-realist film, which has both a patriarchal impulse and an ideological motivation. Socialist erotics pin down the narratives described by Paul Clark—the revolutionary romantic fervors between girl acolyte and male Communist hero in films such as *Red Detachment of Women*.[20] In *Yellow Earth*, the romance of revolution lies in the relationship between the soldier and the peasant girl. Although itself not entirely free of patriarchal narrative and narration, *Yellow Earth* succeeds in exposing the mendacity of this central technique, the erotic socialist-realist gaze.

The erotic gaze is refused in *Yellow Earth* insofar as a sexual encounter between man and girl is avoided. The intimacy of Cuiqiao and Gu Qing's conversations carries an erotic edge despite her extreme youth—she looks a young fourteen. Gu Qing's ability to sew draws a wondering gasp from Cuiqiao, and her desire is deflected onto the cloth as she examines his handiwork. Their conversations tend to be shot in the darkness of the family's cave dwelling, and are followed by shots of Cuiqiao alone with her thoughts, which are transmitted to us in her songs of mourning. The songs that the soldier has come to collect are inspired by the longings that he himself conjures up, and which bear such a harsh contrast to the life that the girl knows. They are sung in his absence, and partly *because* of his absence. This love story is essential to the development of the political rapport that builds up between the two characters.

At climactic moments of the narrative, when Gu Qing is leaving and when Cuiqiao asks in vain to accompany him, the expected romance is unfulfilled. The two are kept apart by the gendered tropes of socialist-realist storytelling, which the film ironizes, but does not displace. Cuiqiao displays herself only to the viewer, when she sings and speaks of her suffering as she works alone at night, or by the river. The third point of the gaze, the on-screen male, is always absent at these most touching moments. Even when she sings a plaintive and un-ashamedly romantic farewell—much of which was cut from the Beijing approved version of the film—his back is turned. He trudges resolutely away from her bitter song, her parting gift—which is no less than herself.

Even her little betrothal of trust, *wo xin ni* (I believe you), is ambiguous. In Confucian literature *xin* (very loosely translatable as 'trust') is a loaded term. At the beginning of *Yellow Earth* there is a wedding feast which Cuiqiao observes. The bride is dressed in traditional red suit and veil. Cuiqiao also wears a red-patterned jacket. The bride is a girl as young as herself. The implication, that her turn is coming next, is very clear. During the scene, Cuiqiao slips off screen left to get closer to the action. In so doing she also appears to try and escape the gaze of the camera. To no avail, she is recaptured and framed by Confucian quotations that hang on the villagers' doorframes to mark the occasion. Cuiqiao even decorates her own home with simulations of Confucian writing; she cannot read or write, so she draws circles on red paper. This attempt to signify in a language that damns her warns of the imminent betrayal of her *xin*.

The philosophers David Hall and Roger Ames explain *xin* as requiring "the articulation, disclosure, and realization of personal significance. If a person is true to his word, he has made himself a source of meaning in the world, meaning that can be realized and transmitted by others."[21] One might add that the person thereby articulates herself within a regime of truth that is subjective and legible to those around her. Cuiqiao, as a woman in a Confucian environment, has meaning only in her passage from dutiful daughter to object of exchange. She can bestow *xin*, as she does on Gu Qing after he promises to return for her in the spring, but she cannot articulate her own position through it. The exceptional way in which she might succeed in this articulation of "personal significance" would be through escape to a different symbolic order, or through suicide. The first possibility, joining the Eighth Route Army, is initially refused to her. When she later attempts her *escape* by river, presumably to find the army for herself, she dies. This escape route is revealed to be just another way of dying.

Despite his apparent autonomy, the bestowal of Cuiqiao's *xin* shows that Gu Qing is also bound to a narrative that prevents him from 'realizing and transmit-ting' trust in any form other than that determined by his historical position. He is a Yan'anite, a soldier in the narrative of revolution and Maoist ethics. He may not be true to his word, but only to the revolutionary narrative, in which he is embedded. When Cuiqiao says that she trusts Gu Qing she is, in a sense, talking to someone whom she has never met. The lack of the erotic gaze, and the bogus completion offered by Gu Qing's aping of the socialist-realist gaze, undermine both Cuiqiao and Gu Qing's personal agency, but also their historical significance. They are two characters in search of a legitimate history. This fundamental disruption to the filmic text, which betrays to biting political effect the status of its own characters, is achieved through the revelation of absence. Where the past is always already condensed in the present, which is in turn only meaningful in the terms of a future perfect, a chronological narrative of liberation is impossible. The absence may be described as an absence of autonomous agency, or as a reductio ad absurdum of agency in certain key characterizations. The gaze as a technique of patriarchal suture is an effective tool in the direction of audience identification. The failure of the technique opens up a moment of contemporary consciousness through which the originator and recipient of the gaze are revealed as—putting it in the kindest terms—out of date.

LANDSCAPE AND AGENCY: *YELLOW EARTH* AND THE DEMON LOVER

Space can be a surprisingly literal phenomenon, in terms of politics and publicness on film. Imaginary space should be distinguished from space per se, but there is a noticeable change from the use of rural and landscape in Chinese filmmaking before 1984 to that of *Yellow Earth*. Revolutionary drama is lacking in empty space. There are shots of natural beauty, but they are infrequent, and almost always peopled, or in a shot-reverse-shot relationship with an intentional human look. Human endeavors and agendas are prioritized in most frames. This can be illustrated with a comparison between *Yellow Earth* and the painting *Fighting in Northern Shaanxi* (Shi Lu, 1959). These works can both be analyzed in terms of a symbolic politics of nationhood. Both texts offer a sense of the contemporary nation, which is communicated visually.

Yellow Earth is another film made by survivors of the Cultural Revolution. It critiques the past, but it is not a conventional 'scar' or 'wound' (*shang hen*) film. It may even be seen as the film that signalled the end of the genre. It returns to history but it is not nostalgic. It questions the conventions of both the scar film genre and of the entrenched aesthetic form of socialist realism. In particular, the film undermines the notions of a larger narrative frame and of faith in the communal. It is the film's unsentimental return, to the signs and stories of nostalgic politics, which renders it such a powerful document of past failure and contemporary unease.

In *Yellow Earth*, points of disruption within the text are dependent on the preexistence of a public imaginary that can be subverted. The familiar is made strange, and the strangeness is recognizable on its own contemporary terms. And so, in a society where criticism of past and future is led and constrained by the Party, such disruptions allow us to glimpse the structure of that public imaginary space. Although here I am looking primarily at the disjunctural representation of *space*, and especially landscape, this cannot be altogether detached from the question of *time*. Space is invested with national and historical meanings. Space and time are thus mutually supportive in an address to an audience, in a seamless exchange of signifiers of the nation and the national. Breaks in this circle can only be recognized by those who share a common sense, a contemporary vision that can substitute the national for something else. Those who do not buy into this 'something else', will experience those same breaks as narrational mistakes, as flaws, or as simply meaning*less*. The structure of public space that is created in the text through these disruptions is thus both powerful as a mark of the new and invisible to those whose spectatorship does not recognize its provenance.

The use of topography in *Yellow Earth* is a case in point. The film is concerned with landscape, shanshui, not countryside, *fengjing*. The difference is important in both Chinese and English. Landscape "is a cultural image, a pictorial way of representing, structuring, or symbolizing surroundings."[22] Landscape is not countryside, it cannot be entered, worked, or in any way made ordinary. It is visible only on the level of icon, and those that do enter it themselves become icons, elements of the cultural imaginary, and their meaning is in fixed relation to the meaning of the landscape.

The landscape of *Yellow Earth* is the mountainous regions of Shaanbei, the northern part of Shaanxi province. Its symbolic resonance can be amplified through a comparison with Shi Lu's *Fighting in Northern Shaanxi*. In Shi Lu's painting the intention is quite clearly the inscription of China, a post-1949 Maoist China, into a certain landscape. In Chen's film, the same place is represented, and figures of the same historical period are present. In the painting, the figures are recognizable representations of the present transposed onto the past. In the film, the figures seem to fit into the past they occupy, but here the landscape itself devours their meaning. The landscape in *Yellow Earth* reasserts itself, and the meaning of China and its history across fifty years of revolutionary control is up for negotiation and change.

Thus landscape provides not just a backdrop for the drama of history, but becomes part of a process of rewriting, or reinscribing, history. Ann Anagnost has described how the rewriting, or more accurately the re*saying*, of personal history was of central importance to the restructuring of national memory before and during the establishment of the Communist state in 1949. Cadres worked with peasants to help them articulate the bitterness of their experience as part of a national narrative of oppression and class difference. The random cruelty of fate, *ming*, was replaced in their speech by the selective crimes of the class enemy, usually the landlord. She notes, however, that the authenticity of the peasant voice, the voice of the subaltern, is not the whole point in this strategy.

If China of imperial times was indeed graphocentric, in preferring the written word as more transparently 'truthful', then what does the privileging of oral performance in the context of revolution suggest? . . . Might it not have reflected a metaphysics of presence already inherent in Marxism itself, as one of the master narratives of Western modernity? Might it not have had something to do with the importance of these narratives in the actual process of constituting the class subject — not just in terms of inscribing the subjectivities of the one telling and those listening, but also in terms of creating a socialist realism, in which the different classes cease to be theoretical, but take on an embodied form as the subjects of history in the eyes of the party itself?[23]

The very aesthetic of the new age, socialist realism, is defined through the resaying of history, and the subjects of that history are themselves defined by the emergent aesthetic. This circularity depends on the metanarrative of Marxist class analysis. So class subjects are always aesthetic, as well as political. Political legitimacy that relies on a particular configuration of class subjects will be dependent on an aesthetic that can bear the symbolic weight of a complete national self-image. The obvious link between the representation of landscape, "a pictorial way of representing, structuring, or symbolising surroundings," and the dominant aesthetic may then be understood as a determining factor in the symbolic structure of a national imaginary.

The centrality of discourse to the establishment and maintenance of a Maoist state has been thoroughly argued in David Apter and Tony Saich's account of the symbolic importance of Yan'an, the revolutionary base of the Communist Party during the struggle against the Japanese and the Guomindang in the 1930s and 1940s.[24] They describe the systematic taking apart and remaking of individuals through the appropriation of their stories. It is the formation of a genealogy, built as a regime of truth through which to stabilize meaning and history in a new order. The narratives of past suffering and present rebirth into the Party project were used to feed a general narrative that was the new truth of universal Chinese experience. This was linked exegetically to Mao's personal history. Mao's life story was told as a progress across China to Yan'an, marking it as his own. Yan'an was Mao, Mao was Yan'an, and the same principle of borrowed meaning would be stretched across the entire territory of the Chinese state so that Mao and Mao's line were the imagined ideal of the new China. "In Yan'an, storytelling was transformed into something quite different when in the space formed between lapsarian doctrines and dialectical truth the Rectification Campaign began. Its consequences went far beyond ideology or pragmatics to the formation of symbolic capital, with exegetical bonding as a form of discipline, a way of internalizing bonds." Mao was able to draw on this symbolic power of narrative, this historical aesthetic, to undermine those who dissented from his line. Apter and Saich cite the instance of the so-called 'twenty eight Bolsheviks':

He pooh-poohed their knowledge by drawing from public experience events that could be converted into metonymies for his own 'universal' truths. These he elevated to the position of dialectical breaks in historical consciousness, 'levelling down', he then manipulated these into metaphorical narratives. This mass line enabled Mao to recast time from history to situation, situation into the particular space of the border areas, and border areas into the simulacrum of Yan'an as a utopic community. Yan'an was made to serve as a moral template, rather than a model, of the China yet to be born.[25]

TAKING TIME AND MAKING SPACE

Apter and Saich's notion of a moral template is close to what I call a *national imaginary*. In the Chinese case particularly, this template or imaginary has been indelibly marked by the nature and legitimating requirements of ruling groups, whether those of the imperial dynasties or those of a totalitarian Communist regime. It is the essence of a moral template, or national imaginary, to be so deeply ingrained in the social and psychological structures that constitute normality, or even reality, as to be invisible. Nevertheless, their features can be glimpsed at moments of disjuncture, whether textual or historical. It is therefore interesting to look at the transitions between dynasties. The transfer of dynastic power in China has traditionally been marked by the beginning of a new era. Although the sixty-year cycle of year names continues, the age in which that cycle turns is regarded as pristine and graced by the Mandate of Heaven. The emphasis on a new beginning relates to what Joseph Needham called the contradictions of "human society in time."[26] He is referring to the conception of a golden age that haunts Chinese myth-history. It was an explicit article of faith for Mohists and Taoists, and implicit in the Confucian model of developmental progress as that was read as an exhortation to return to the standards of the golden past. The neo-Confucian pull between regression and development is pertinent to an understanding of both Mao's manipulation of Chinese history and of post-Maoist negotiations with the recent past and with tradition. The word for time, *shi*, means only the specific happening, the moment when something happened; the frame in which *shi* is placed is entirely a matter for human, official and power-holding. Hindsight.

The rootedness of this sense of rupture, change, and renewal can be seen in the extended transfer of legitimacy and authority from the Ming dynasty (1368-1644) to that of the Qing (1644-1911). The art historian Jonathan Hay uses this historical remaking of the national imaginary to analyze the work of what were called *remnant painters*, those artists loyal to the old Ming Mandate.[27] Hay describes how their paintings suspended the establishment of dynastic time. The moment at which Qing rule becomes legitimate could only be truly established in retrospect, after the 'remnants' had died. Hay refers to two artists in particular, Zhang Feng (d.1662) and Gong Xian (1619-1689). Zhang worked allusively. Images of peace and tranquillity were visually and verbally coded to hint at disquiet and division within the landscape. In one album leaf a man looks towards the bright (Ming) moon and away from the lucid (Qing) stream. In Hay's reading, the landscape is split, its space constituted in two contradictory times. Gong's work went further towards the creation of a symbolic space through which new time, Qing time, was absented. For example, Hay describes the 1689 painting, *The Grain Rains*, as a landscape that was actually a reconstruction of the Ming Imperial Tomb, the Zhongshan Mausoleum, at Nanjing. In the painting the Ming is mourned, but there is no space for the Qing to occupy. Time is held still by vacancy.

Hay's work highlights two notions of the *symbolic*. At one point, the symbolic is presented as dependent on allusion and intended action, as when the scholar-artist faces south, the geographical seat of Ming loyalty. The symbolic is here a relationship between represented action and meaning that operates as a shared code between artist and informed viewer. It is a habit of the oppressed to use a symbolic code to communicate their experience to themselves and to their imagined community of fellow sufferers. In Zizek's terms, an open identification with the world is impossible for the oppressed without betraying the *real* that silently informs their experience.[28] Such an allusion then hints at an entire symbolic structure of meaning that is emphasized to prevent its disappearance, but which could not be represented except through icon and metonymic signifier. Emphasis is also present in a dominant symbolic.

In his account of Gong Xian's work, Hay uses a rather different conception of the symbolic. Here he draws out a symbolic *structure* whereby allusion is unnecessary. His approach to visual discourse, like Apter and Saich's work on text and speech, assumes a Foucauldian understanding of discursive power. In Hay's reading, Gong's landscape is indeed an attempt to represent the *real*. Of course, it cannot be done. Instead, Gong presents a landscape in which the *real* is present but hidden from view. It is a composition where the lines and tensions are excluding, lonely, and inviolably struck in grief. Here the landscape bears its meaning in a temporal and spatial logic that is either recognized in complicity or misunderstood as a poetic abstraction. The possibility that landscapes were actual places, places with particular historical and political relevance, is avoided. Yet, many painters worked for patrons who would doubtless have wished for representations of favorite places, *as well as* a connoisseur's regard for style and tradition. Although a landscape must be pictorial, represented, and inviolate, the work of artists in the late Ming and in the Maoist era suggest that it can also hold particular topographic and political significance in the sight of its contemporary consumers.

It is this second conception of the symbolic that creates space for a certain kind of public. The different narrative structures of the paintings discussed by Hay function historically to politicize space. The official, retrospective 'beginning' of the Qing, 1644, is a moment of transition from one time to another that must be struggled over in the politics of the symbolic. History is the context for this struggle as well as the reward of victory. Once the victory is won the landscape is fixed, petrified in a static narrative that will endure until history, time, and aesthetics are again contested in the national imagination. It is in periods of flux that the emphases within the actual elements of landscape will change. It is the points of change that map the nation. Just as in the transition from Ming to Qing, the landscapes of socialist realism after Liberation in 1949 were marked by change, new configurations of older styles. Once the new realism was central to the national imagination, however, the point was to keep newness firmly on the pictorial horizon.

MOVING THE MOUNTAIN

Shi Lu (1919-1982) (born Feng Yaheng) was an artist who had joined the Communist Party before Liberation and became a leading figure in the Xian *guohua* (nation(al)(ist)-art) school. He was therefore prominent in the creation and dissemination of the new realism. As chief of the *North West Pictorial*, popularization of art was part of his official remit. His work, which included woodcuts, cartoons, New Year pictures, serial story books, as well as larger oils, was often exhibited in public spaces.[29]

In 1959 he was commissioned to paint *Fighting in Northern Shaanxi* by the Museum of Revolutionary History in Beijing. The painting shows the mountains in the region north of Yan'an, rugged, massive, and tinged with red. On the mountain's top (it is hardly a peak, more a blunt ledge) Mao Zedong stands in profile, looking out of frame right. Given his visibility in leadership terms, this gaze, of the Leader himself, is slightly different to the socialist-realist gaze of agents of power such as Gu Qing in *Yellow Earth*. The red massif to his left thrusts up as a satellite in comradely alignment with the Leader. The scale and composition of the painting are quite outrageously anthropomorphic. The sky is a thin strip along the top. Sky is after all too ambiguous for this moment. It is an emptiness that cannot be easily filled by the weight of human concerns. Instead the background is crammed with distant ranges that snake towards the foreground block. This block is in turn defined by the standing figure whose gaze steadies the mountain in the frame, pins it down to a specific historical and political meaning, and owns it. The horizon is inverted. The meeting of land and sky at the top of the painting is here a barely observed convention. The horizon is in the power of Mao's gaze off frame. It is also contained in the future that is already perfect, the reddened foreground that is a mirror in form and thought of the figure of Mao.

Mao's size, a tenth of the height of the painting, bestows it with a heightened reality, a revolutionary romanticism.[30] It also suggests age and weight. He is, quite literally, a big man; big enough, in this image, to span the time claimed by the Revolution. It may be titled *Fighting in Northern Shaanxi*, but for Mao the battle is retrospective. He is not the young fighter of the mid-1930s. He is already victorious, the national figurehead who declared Liberation in Tiananmen in 1949. Why then the need to return here, to the battleground? The answer again lies in the necessity of hindsight. When the painting was commissioned in 1959, the battle for authority had been won. The legitimacy of the new regime depended on an absolute hold on historical narrative, which was to be visualized for common consumption across China. So in this painting there is a double claim. The landscape, chosen allusively as the place of revolutionary resurgence, is claimed figuratively by the presence of the Great Helmsman. Mao gives authority to the mountain, and allows it to *be* China. But, in the same gesture, the political legitimacy of Mao's Liberation is fixed by the provision of a national landscape.

This is no ordinary dynasty, however. It is the dynasty of the *People's* Republic, and it cannot lay open claim to the traditional Mandate of *Heaven*. In this dynasty Heaven offered less legitimacy for power than could the promise of a future that power would bring about. It needed to be signalled to the people, to be constantly figured for them. The landscape is therefore markedly different from the multiplicity of landscapes in the scholar-painter and in commercial traditions. Perhaps its surface unfamiliarity is due to the figure of Mao that features so hugely. The mountains no longer reveal man to be a tiny dependent creature. On the contrary, these mountains need him to give them a meaning, to dub them Chinese. Mao wrote admiringly of the old man who moved the mountain. Shi Lu has used the tense perpendicular presence of a political man as a compositional device that holds the mountain together.

QI

In his historical blockbuster *Landscape and Memory*, Simon Schama too considers variations on humanity's relationship with mountains in Chinese art. Focusing on a tenth-century painting, *Dreaming of Immortality in the Mountains*, he remarks of the Taoist Immortals: "Such was their success at transcendence, in dissolving themselves into the vital breath of *ch'i* (*qi*), that they could materialize on the backs of stalks or, as in one spectacular Taoist mountain painting, travel through the thin vaporous air."[31] Schama is wrong about *qi*. Transcendence is *not* necessarily a feature of *qi*. Transformation, the ability of man to become mountain, or mountain to become man, is closer to the mark.

Qi is an exceptionally difficult word, and concept, to render in English. It is in everyday use, and yet it carries a great deal of philosophical weight. Although John Hay translates it as *energy*, he still feels the need to provide a long footnote on the unease surrounding the use of a word that simply does not have an English equivalent. *Qi* connotes energy, breath, life spirit, and circulation, but its overall sense is more than the sum of these parts. It is, for instance, central to medical discourse on the harmony, or not, between the human body and its environment.[32]

Mencius, *Meng Zi*, a philosopher of the fourth century BC, used *qi* to capture in a word the driving force of Man as a courageous and sentient creature. D. C. Lau describes fourth-century BC thinking on *qi* (*ch'i*) as an explanation of life itself.

> It was believed that the universe was made up of *ch'i* but this *ch'i* varied in consistency. The grosser *ch'i*, being heavy, settled to become the earth, while the refined *ch'i*, being light, rose to become the sky. Man, being half way between the two, is a harmonious mixture of the two kinds of *ch'i*. His body consists of grosser *ch'i* while his heart is the seat of the refined *ch'i*. Hence the term, *hsueh ch'i* (blood and *ch'i*). It is in virtue of the refined *ch'i* that a man is alive and his faculties can function properly.[33]

Mencius turns this *qi* into the property that "will unite rightness and the way" (*ren* and *dao*). In a world dominated by the politics of the secular, *qi* is the breath of the sublime. It is what makes a man a man, and it is also what determines his place between Heaven and Earth. Without this tripartite relationship, man is not of his time or his place. He has no weight. In Confucian cosmology the primary elements—heaven, earth, and man—are "mutually immanent." The key word is correlativity and not, despite Schama, transcendence. It is thus *qi* that, for example, allows ideas of the personal and the public to be perceived as complementary, not antagonistic.[34] *Qi* is also implicated in the movement of time. For Taoists life is a spontaneous and uncreated circulation of the whole of nature. "The whole of nature *tian* . . . could be analogized with the life cycles of living organisms. 'A time to be born and a time to die, a time for the founding of a dynasty and a time for its supersession.' "[35] From these uses of the word I extrapolate a sense of immanent subjectivity, an ontology of what it is to be a person who is inseparable from the transformations and samenesses of time, space, and the unspeakable presence of Heaven.

This underlines the extent of Schama's error: Taoism neither has, nor needs, any concept of transcendence. The natural world is a natural (*ziran*) circulation of energy. There is no need for transcendence where transformation across an equal plane of being is available to the Immortal. To repeat, and to return to the landscape in Shi Lu's painting, a man may indeed become a mountain, and a mountain may be the man, and then also the nation, without exceeding the philosophical or physiological boundaries of *qi*, at least as I understand it. Shi Lu's socialist realism was still, in 1959, a symbolic structure under construction. Even so, it was hardly innocent of previous dynastic modes. The relocation of *qi* is the strategy of address to the moral template that is embedded in the viewing of

Chinese landscape painting. The space of *qi* is emptied but not vacated. It is open to colonization, and it is the figure of Mao and thus the presence of the Party that fills the gap.

In looking at the symbolic landscapes of Chinese films since the Cultural Revolution, the concept of *qi* makes it possible to grasp the passion that is a part of human correspondence with an equivalent circulation of the natural world. *Qi* is also referred to in the revolutionary history film genre as a deliberate appropriation of the circulation of the natural world in favor of the dominant agency of the Party. This politicized *qi* is a bastardization of the concept, but one that should be understood as typical of the ways in which a genre uses traditional structures of feeling in order to engage and convince its audience.

And so I return to the landscape and cosmology of Yellow Earth, and the way in which they both demarcate and rework the symbolic public space of a national imaginary. The film is set in Shaanbei, part of Shaanxi, the national landscape of the Maoist dynasty. Should it not then be absolutely familiar to the Chinese audience, at least those born in the 1950s? Apparently not. Yuejin Wang has commented that the terrain of *Yellow Earth* is as unfamiliar to a Chinese audience as it might be perversely glamorous—as perhaps Mao himself was glamorous to the enthusiasts of *Tel Quel*—to the Western eye. Only the fetishized snapshots of the work of Shi Lu and his contemporaries have entered the popular political imaginary.

> To the average urban Chinese, these landscapes are equally alien, remote and 'other-looking', as they presumably appear to a Western gaze—and urban Chinese may well be struck by their ethnic difference and otherness while the Western mind might immediately 'recognize' their ethnic distinction as a presumably unified Chineseness. They are a cinematic representation of a cultural other both to the Western eye and the Chinese eye.[36]

This seems strange. But, on reflection, might it not be an entirely predictable clue to the way in which the yellow earth of *Yellow Earth* has been reaesteticized? The distanciation of art, *ostraniye*, has defamiliarized the nation and its landscape so that it is literally strange, even unrecognizable. I am not sure that it is a matter of the 'other', as Yuejin Wang describes it. Or if it is, that may have emerged as a later development within the life of the text. Rather, the landscape is quoted in the context of a national myth, ironized by the undercutting of that myth in the telling, and thus stripped of national status as we watch — or rather as *some* people watched shortly after the film was released in 1984.[37] The resaying of the landscape is achieved through an inversion of the familiar revolutionary history film, in which standard reference points, premised on Mao's analysis of contradictions between the enemy and the people, map personal narratives.[38]

In such stories, as in *The White-haired Girl* and *Red Detachment of Women*, a young woman's redemption is marked by an event that is a materialization of Party power or spirit—*qi*. This is often a battle, or a symbolic killing, in which the national (Japanese), political Kuomintang (KMT), or class enemy is dispatched. Afterwards she and her young male mentor are brought together in the presence of the Party, symbolized by a flag, a military victory, or just a mutual ecstatic gaze off screen; here the classic socialist-realist gaze culminated in an impossible but nonetheless expected outcome. Their togetherness is not consummated, and in some films (*The Red Detachment of Women*) the young man dies in the course of his heroic duty. The female revolutionary is always sutured into a discourse of male supremacy, which is fixed by the power of the patriarchal enemy, and the agency of the Party representative. The enemy is a demon, whose demonic nature arises from the contradictions of his class or his politics. The lover is similarly determined by the spirit of the Party. He can never consummate the woman's passion because his *qi* is not his own to give. The demon and the lover exchange the woman as a vital signifier of their alternate ascendancy on behalf of their respective driving forces. At the core of these films is a battle for control over life itself. Hero and villains scuffle over the mind/body, the two are undifferentiated, of a young woman in order to demonstrate their agency, which for them is authority over living matter.

Revolutionary history films offer one model of this logic. They tell the story of a struggle for the imaginary place of Heaven from the narrative standpoint of the secular victor. The narration of these films is slanted, so that the winner is signalled from the beginning. What is absent is the sense that the scuffle is meaningless. If meaning is understood as the result of a connection and unity across space and time, the nature of Heavenly authority, the authority to make meaning possible, is of paramount political necessity. In the late twentieth century, the Heaven of the dynastic regime has given way to a *worldly* authority. The future perfect of Maoist belief completes the narrative logic of existence. Yet the concept of a holistic life force, a circulation of *qi*, allows this model to be irrupted from within its own generic structures. In victory, the tension point of *qi* is always relocated in the focus of the socialist-realist gaze and in the unconsummated passion of the new recruit. The pattern and order (*li*) of the worldly is reimposed on the passion (*qi*) of the spirit.

In *Yellow Earth* this duality of passion and order is again invoked to organize the narrative, and is used as a template for its own destruction. The three points of the model are Cuiqiao, the girl who misses her mother and is frightened of the rest of her life:

> In the sixth month the ice in the river hasn't thawed
> It's my own father who is dragging me to the wedding board
> Of all the five grains the bean is the roundest,

> Of all the people the daughter is the saddest
> Up in the sky, pigeons fly, one with the other,
> The only dear one that I long for is my mother.[39]

There is the yellow earth, which, if Lu is right, and Cuiqiao is a daughter of China, must be China itself. Thirdly there is the lover, Gu Qing. He is supposedly the agent of the Party, and like the model lovers his *qi* is not his own. Yet he has no cathartic moment of heroism, there is no visible enemy, and he fails to redeem Cuiqiao from her misery. If there are enemies they cannot be vanquished. The peasant culture that condemns Cuiqiao is the object of Gu Qing's attention. It is necessary for his agency to have a legitimate focus. The hindsight of history, in the model narrative, tells us that the peasant class will be extolled in Mao's Yan'an Talks. In anticipation of Mao's exhortation to go among the people, Gu Qing is doing fieldwork with his notebook, collecting his 'bitter' songs. The film exploits the technical potentialities of representation and reproduction to debunk history. It does so while depicting Gu Qing's attempt to *achieve* that same history through a very basic method of record and appropriation. The resaying of history is at stake in both the narrative and narration of the text.

The other enemy is the yellow earth itself. But again, Gu Qing can have only an ambiguous relationship with this landscape. It is the site and source of his mission. The Communist Revolution had set out to harness the dispersed strength of rural China by taking hold of its hardships and transforming them. This is not simply to state the obvious, that communism promised to reorganize national life so that the peasantry would have an easier time of it. Rather, it is to say that they sought to transform the meaning of the place in which this suffering occurred, and thereby to effect change on an imaginary level in order to create a space in which real reform could literally *take place*. Land reform was a rhetoric of freedom; it did not make the ground softer nor the rain wetter. The achievement was perhaps to persuade peasants that government-sponsored irrigation works would be more reliable than the Dragon King.

In the film's final scene hundreds of farmers are praying to the Dragon King for rain. Gu Qing appears on the horizon. He rises from the meeting of land and sky and walks against the tide of human folly. Is he then the perfect manifestation of manly *qi*? He has found his place between heaven and earth, and he occupies it with courage and sentience. Yet the audience knows that his return is already too late. Cuiqiao has fled her marriage and disappeared over, or into, the river. Furthermore, his progress seems so slow that it might be a mirage. The camera holds him in a relentless and repetitive long shot (in perspective and duration). The political logic of the filmmakers draws to a conclusion of brilliant anomaly. If Gu Qing occupies a harmonious position in the circulation of the natural world, he cannot move forward as a successful agent of the Party. The Party stakes its legitimacy on a perfected future, a horizon that is only visible through the medium of its gaze, its agency. In the final scene of *Yellow Earth* Gu Qing's gaze has been recaptured from him by the landscape. He has himself become part of the horizon. His agency, which has been ironized throughout the film, is finally removed and handed to the audience on a visual plate. In this moment the Party disappears from the text and the landscape. The struggle for dynastic time is again suspended as the audience, in the now of watching the film, holds the horizon in its gaze. The disassembly of history through the restatement of the place itself estranges the audience from the national landscape and the public imaginary that has been contained in it. Nation, public, and landscape are freed to start again.

The film, originally titled *Silent Is the Ancient Plain*, was retitled *Yellow Earth* after the filmmakers had viewed the rushes and had seen the color of the film on screen. But in this reworking of the revolutionary history film, *Yellow Earth* is an eponymous title. The landscape is a central player in the drama that reveals itself as a drama over who may act, and on whose behalf. The landscape takes on generic demands and turns them inside out. The landscape is both demon and lover. Its moment of consummation is not however deflected by a nonsexual trinity of Man, Woman, and Party Spirit. It enjoys a double consummation. Cuiqiao is consumed beneath the waters of the river, and the Party song goes down with her. Gu Qing, who misses this moment entirely, is himself taken by the earth as he trudges endlessly forward with no prospect of progress or escape. A national landscape has become the demon lover, capable of devouring both the object of its passion and the agency of its rivals.

In the foregoing discussion of *Yellow Earth* I have made two suggestions. First, disrupting the audience's expectations of a film's visual or narrative mode produces an ironic comment that may be political. Those expectations may be based on a particular genre, or on representational habits that are likely to be closely linked to a general public, political imaginary. The possibility of comment, and especially *ironic* comment, is inherent in cultural public space. Second, *Yellow Earth* demonstrates the scope of this irony. The meaning of contemporary history is shaken by the exposure of a visual trope, the socialist-realist gaze, to contemporary ridicule. Through the manipulation of narrative space, agency is passed from Party to China-as-landscape in the story of Gu Qing's mission and failure. Although the use of narration produces public space within the text, the *narrative* bypasses the human agent in favor of institutional and mythical powers. The form is optimistic in its address to the audience, but the content is deeply pessimistic.

IN THE WILD MOUNTAINS

In the subsequent default of a particular phase of a dominant culture there is then a reaching back to those meanings and values that were created in real societies in the past, and which still seem to have some significance because they represent areas of human experience, aspiration, and achievement, which the dominant culture undervalues, or opposes, or cannot even recognize.[40]

Raymond Williams observes that a dominant mode, or culture, or perhaps political system, should watch out for signs that the contemporary mood is turbulent. Turbulence is a sign of conflict in daily life, and therefore, in the symbolic structure of the public imaginations. *In the Wild Mountains* opens up just such a public space in its disturbing account of subjective construction in China in the 1980s. It does so by describing the choices available to peasants at that time as absolute and mutually incompatible. If the idea of the national plays a central role in the symbolisms of *Yellow Earth*, by contrast, *Wild Mountains* is a pragmatic film. It is not impressed by landscape, but is deeply concerned with the rigors of the rural poor. *In the Wild Mountains* was directed by a Fourth Generation director, Yan Xueshu in 1985. Yan trained at the Beijing Film Academy from 1958-1962. He was assigned to the Xi'an Film Studio immediately, but during the Cultural Revolution he was expected to 'dive into life' and spent several years in Yunnan collecting material from 'real life', a latter-day Gu Qing. He did not complete his first feature *Ayung* until 1975. He was still working at Xi'an when he made *Ye Shan* ten years later.[41]

The film presents a conflict between two synchronous, but antagonistic, virtue systems. On the one side lie traditional peasant habits of hard manual labor, gender-specific division of time, and family loyalty. On the other is the stirring of the rural entrepreneur, the investment of money in dodgy schemes, seasonal journeys to the nearest township to earn cash capital, and an inevitable erosion of the family unit. The central protagonists are each locked into one or another path, and cannot be civil across the divide. The film sets up a double love story that feeds off a dualistic model of China. The traditional-rural element is portrayed as a ritualistic and performative society, where rules are internal to the ontology of those that conform to them, while the market-urban element develops through individual ambition, which must eventually be monitored by externally imposed laws.[42] The secrets of performance in town and country are not mutually legible, and the drama and publicness of the narrative lies in the tension between adaptation and confusion for new urban peasants.

TOWN AND COUNTRY

In the Wild Mountains tells the story of two peasant couples. One couple seems reasonably content with each other and with their grinding routine of manual labor and subsistence farming. There are tensions between them, however. The wife, Guilan, has not borne a child, and shows a deepening interest in the town and the new market initiatives. The other couple has already separated acrimoniously.

The wife, Qiurong, who has a small son to care for, continues to work on the farm while her husband, Hehe, tries to set up business ventures according to the new entrepreneurial atmosphere. She objects, partly to his long absences as he works in the town to earn capital, and partly to his many failures.

When he returns to the village with yet another project in mind—this time the rearing of silkworms—it is Guilan who supports his initiative. As this entrepreneurial friendship deepens, her husband and the forsaken wife grow close as he helps her out with the heavy farm work. He also grows attached to the little boy, disappointed that his own marriage is childless. Inevitably suspicions grow, although they are centered around the entrepreneurial couple, whose reputation is sealed in the eyes of the village when they spend a couple of days together in the nearest town. They are in fact innocent of adultery but the damage is done and the second marriage breaks down. Meanwhile the silkworm project has been destroyed by a flock of hungry crows. Hehe is undeterred, and after another spell of work in the town, and having received a development loan from the local finance department, he sets up a squirrel farm to produce squirrel dung, a valuable substance in Chinese medicine. After the scandal he runs away but the now divorced Guilan stays and cares for his enterprise. Her husband marries Hehe's wife. Hehe finally returns having bought his own tractor, and the new couple is soon seen by the village as exemplars of the new ways. The film ends with their purchase of a generator to help in the grinding of the grain. They promise to lend it out, for a fee. The other couple watches and takes turns in the arduous job of grinding the grain manually.

The decollectivization of rural labor and the introduction of the rural production responsibility system were introduced in 1978. The seemingly 'traditional' farming lifestyle of Qiurong is actually a recent return to household-based labor and *baogan daohu* (concentrating everything within the peasant household). Elisabeth Croll has described the policies and their local implementations in depth in her account of the peasant experience of market reforms, *From Heaven to Earth*. She notes that:

> After five years of rural reform, the majority of peasant households had begun to diversify their activities so that it was estimated that some eighty-five percent both cultivated responsibility lands allocated to them by the village government and undertook a variety of domestic sidelines ranging from vegetable production . . . to the provision of services for their local community.[43]

Whereas Hehe tries to implement state policy in its entirety and initiate household enterprises alongside their agricultural work, Qiurong only sees that she has a small family—herself, her husband, and a baby—and land that needs cultivation. To Qiurong, Hehe's absences are an abdication of his responsibility within a modern peasant household. To Guilan they indicate his coherence with the contemporary mood that she recognizes and of which she struggles to become part. For Hehe himself, the opposing perspectives of the women are also experienced as trauma. In Hall and Ames's words his subjectivity is configured both by the 'external ordering principles' of modernity and by the 'constitutive and immanent' rules of traditional culture.[44]

In one sequence Hehe is in town, working on a building site to gather capital for his squirrel dung project. He has been offered a pack of prerolled cigarettes to replace the 'grass' that he has brought from home. As throughout the film his reaction is explicit and physical. He hurls the pack away as though rejecting both the urban product *and* his fellow work mates' implicit condemnation of his peasant background. A few scenes later Hehe is getting drunk in a café in town. He interrupts other men who are trying to watch a soccer game and finds himself thrown out for brawling. In a public sequence that is echoed in the previously discussed umbrella scene in *Don't Cry Mummy*, he staggers pathetically around the street accusing the onlookers of being 'a bunch of crows'—eating his money rather than his silkworms. He shows them the cash that he has earned and throws it down as a challenge. If his money is good enough for town life then so must he be. The onlookers' reaction is a mixture of sympathy, bewilderment, and amusement at the peasant's distress. Hehe's losses of control and self-respect in the city epitomize the ambiguity of his condition. He has been formed in one configuration of virtue, interest, and action, but he seeks to reconstruct his life within another promised modality. *Wild Mountains* contains a potent and radical public space in which the gap between two models of contemporary peasant subjectivity is exposed and described as uncoordinated and potentially violent.

Andrew Kipnis's anthropological research in Fengjia emphasizes the changing relationship between urban and rural China. He notes how the split—made very explicit by the issue of separate passports (*hukou—nongmin, fei nongmin* the nonpeasant not even graced with a positive title) has been encouraged by central government policy since 1949. The class label 'poor peasant' has, until recently, been an asset. Although probably not a guarantee of material advantage, the label linked the individual into a structure of social relations that affirmed the virtue of the peasant and that stressed the political interests of the peasant class. This was especially important at times of ideological quickening, the Cultural Revolution being the obvious case. Yet, post-Cultural Revolution there has been a decided shift in emphasis. Peasants are exculpated as feudal and backward. The poverty of the peasant (depending on the depth of that poverty), once an identification of goodness, is now a sore on the face of new China. It has to be confronted through market-oriented initiatives or through escape from the land by education. Kipnis records for example that in Fengjia ten to fifteen percent of the population are reregistered as urban dwellers by achieving senior education status. There is also an increasing number of people leaving the land without an official change of status. They enter cities and towns as unregistered temporary workers and are becoming an insistent reality on the margins of Chinese society.

In *Wild Mountains* Hehe straddles two groups. He takes the risk of working without registration and therefore without welfare provision and to some extent outside the reach of the law, its protection as well as its harshness, and yet he does return to his home village to invest his money and ideas according to government priorities. Kipnis concludes his study with a definition of his understanding of the processes of subjectification. His purpose is to emphasize that a cross-cultural reading of particular signifiers must not be reduced to the concerns of current critical fashion in another context. Hence the importance of reiterating the difference between individual identity and the construction of the subject through a collective and social process.

> Subjectification is always a temporal process. Though a villager's *hukou* may be changed from nonpeasant to peasant or, in the case of marriage, moved instantly from one family and village to another, subjectification takes time. Subjectification is not merely a matter of institutional classification but the creation of a subject within and against that classification. It is only after adapting to one's classification, and creating something positive within it, that people can make themselves and be made into specific kinds of acting subjects.[45]

Kipnis's definition tends towards a conflation of identity and subjectification; that is, he suggests that the classification and naming of a subject (his/her identification) is part of his/her ontological construction. In *Wild Mountains* the process seems to be more one of disruption than construction. The meanings of habitual identifications—peasant, nonpeasant; farmer, entrepreneur—have been changed by the economic policies of the state. The disturbance in the subject—epitomized in Hehe's drunken but passionate meandering—is caused by its lost access to recognizable patterns of identification. To use the terms of Zizek and Lacan, the *real* has lost sight of its ideal self in the mirror.

Wild Mountains addresses the mid-1980s contemporary Chinese audience with a direct appeal to those who have observed or experienced rural dislocation in the wake of economic reform. History is invoked insofar as the memory of the political ascendancy of the peasant after 1949 is necessary to understand the pathos of Qiurong's stubborn allegiance to the land and Hehe's confused series of escapes and returns. In *Yellow Earth* history itself is at stake. The narration of transfers of historical meaning and agency from one player to another makes that clear. In *Wild Mountains* it is the subject of contemporary history that is scrutinized. Whereas disruptions in the text of *Yellow Earth* can be read as provocative fissures in the audience's historical memory, in *Wild Mountains* the radical, contemporary power of the film lies in those textual moments where the subject of the contemporary is visibly disturbed. In particular there is the profound disturbance of Hehe. His and Guilan's final triumphal return to the village, complete with tractor and generator, suggests a satisfactory resolution to his earlier moments of panic. It is however, the moments of fascination in the film, when we, with the camera, look on—with the onlookers in the frame—at the distress of Hehe. Here are public spaces in a country-first account of the early years of rural reform.

5

Authenticity and Silence

> Authenticity as a need to rely on 'undisputed origin' is prey to an obsessive fear: that of losing a connection. Everything must hold together . . . a clear origin will give me a connection back through time, and I shall, by all means, search for that genuine layer of myself to which I can always cling.[1]

Julia Kristeva's visit to China in the early 1970s inspired a meditation on the tropes of the primeval Mother and the silence of difference. Kristeva takes at face value the advances made for Chinese women by the Revolution, and concentrates instead on the traces of maternity in the myths of the Chinese nation. Her Chinese women are a world away from the pre–Liberation victim of patriarchy (figure 5.1). Kristeva does not question Han leadership, but rather takes as her theme the eternity of Chinese being. In her account there is pre-patriarchal myth, and post–Liberation invigoration, but no history. Without history there can be no experience, and so 'Chinese women' are presented as natural, essential echoes of their maternal origins:

> One can watch these relaxed feminine bodies floating lightly along the streets of Peking, among the tufts of willow moss . . . one can listen to these women's voices, which don't stick in the throat, but rather vibrate, rhythmic and melodious, with the whole body, down to the tiniest cell, free of guilt or provocation.[2]

Kristeva's impression of Beijing in the early 1970s is conditioned by her own notion of the female semiotic as presymbolic. If female signification is found in sound not in language, then for Kristeva the lack of history in her account is inevitable. Despite this, she does give a short account of the history of socialism and feminism, in the Chinese context. This moves swiftly, from two pages on the early suffragettes, to a version of Mao Zedong's psychological and political in-

Figure 5.1   Street Angel

volvement with women's liberation. In writing about China, Kristeva abandons the female voice to the silence of the presymbolic, and delivers history through the medium of male hindsight. Yet, in her conclusions, she cites the Chinese woman as the oppressed who may still function as the symbolic male in society, given her matriarchal inheritance:

> However, a *power* (what I called 'a paternal function' above) assumed (and not *represented*) by a woman is already a power with a body, and a body that knows about power: symbolic contract, economic limits, but also impulse, desire, and contradiction. A power in infinite process: *a power that cannot be represented.*
>
> Thus, when Mao launches women, on the heels of students, into the Cultural Revolution . . . when women today are placed in posts of command—mightn't it be to proclaim that *power* in a society is not to be abolished . . . —but rather, that it must not be represented—and, in fact, cannot be?[3]

Here power takes the place of the real. It becomes unaccountable: "no one can appropriate it for himself if no one, not even women, can be excluded from it."

At the time of which Kristeva writes, women were far from either position that she claims for them. Feminine bodies on the streets of Beijing were experiencing a crisis of estrangement from their female bodies. There was an imperative to be seen as a good citizen, and Communist first, and woman after.

> The conflict between the law of the Party and the law of the father [the author, Meng Yue, does not share the notion that the law of the Father is somehow ungendered],

or between the socialist and sexist standards of behavior, did not originate in a struggle against the derogation of women. Rather, it emerged out of the Party's desire to dominate all distracting forces, including sexism, since as a minor dictatorship, a local authority, the localized sexist tradition held the potential to splinter or complicate the Party's total control over society and ideology.[4]

The disembodiment and silencing of the sexualized female is more graphically related in Anchee Min's autobiographical account of life in a commune during the Cultural Revolution. A major event (and spectacle) of the narrative occurs when a fellow work mate has been caught having sex with another student-worker. The man is tried and executed for 'rape'. The girl is then supposed to deny her desire and return to her work.

No one talked about the man after the execution, although he was on everyone's mind. But Shao Ching had changed. She stopped washing. Months passed. Still she hadn't washed. There were complaints about her smell. When I tried to persuade her to wash her underwear at least, she took a pair of scissors and cut it into strips. She chopped off her long braids and stopped combing her hair. Mucus dripped from her lips. At night she sang songs off key. . . . The doctors referred her to a hospital in Shanghai where she was diagnosed as having had a nervous breakdown.[5]

Anchee Min's account is emotive, and is in part designed to prepare the reader for her own homosexual awakening of desire, but it is also a riposte to Kristeva's poetics on the subjectivity of willow-like women. Min never denies that the male/female divide has been effectively blurred in Mao's China; she even cites a friend of a friend who does not know whether Chairman Mao is a man or a woman. The process of desexualization takes Shao Ching's sexual core, her smell, and her saliva, and deposits it as a symptom of madness on the outside of her body. It is again her madness that removes her from the realm of language, and a share in the symbolic, and replaces her in the presymbolic world of burbled sound making. Shao Ching's madness is exacerbated by the bodily and social denial of her desire, and presumably, by the death of her lover. Accounts of the Cultural Revolution are not unrelated, however, to the audiences they serve. The propensity of memoirs of the Cultural Revolution to feed Western appetites for Chinese degradation and female spectacle has been noted before.[6] Anchee Min's adept translation of her time in the countryside to the currency of erotic suffering is a powerful case in point. Her work does rebut one 'Kristevan' version of 'Chinese women'. She is sexually active, although still caught in the revolutionary androgyny that Kristeva so enjoys. She is also transgressive, but in the direction of the audiences' literary desires rather than in a way that really describes her relationship to the system in which she matures. Meng Yue's analysis of the politics of androgyny is more persuasive; her reading of desexualization as a by-product policy to derail the development of gender politics would not, however, fit into the memoir genre. These books require individual victims more than political constituencies of complaint.

Min suggests that female bodies were dressed down in an attempt to dissolve their femininity. Dressed *down* rather than dressed *up* to avoid the possibility of fetishization through masquerade?[7] This may have been the intention, but in a cultural climate built around political cults and fashions, it seems more likely that any kind of fashion would have been well 'worked over' by its wearers, as part of its entry into publicness. Masquerade, dressing the phallus, is as much a staple of cultural representation in China, and Chinese film in particular, as it is in mainstream Hollywood. It was there in the extravaganzas of the revolutionary operas, but also in the personal dress games of individual women. The return of overt masquerade in the post–Mao era seems to be a self-conscious response to the experiences described by Anchee Min, and is in the long run less interesting than the figures that emerge in earlier films. It is central to He Ping's film *Red Firecracker, Green Firecracker* (1995). A young woman masquerades as a man in order to preserve her right to her inheritance. She is known to be a woman, but is forbidden to perform her femininity. She falls in love with a tutor hired to teach her/him art, and the most erotic moments in the film occur when he recognizes her desire *through the mask of masculinity* that she is forced to wear in his presence. The rest of the film is more Freudian than Freud. The woman changes into female clothing as soon as she enters into a sexual relationship. When her lover is refused permission to marry her, as this would give him control of her wealth, he enters a strange fireworks competition, in which he literally blows his balls off. He loses his masculinity, and access to the woman, at which point she is found to be pregnant. The phallus whisks around this film with strict adherence to possession and taboo. The film takes pains to exemplify the problems facing Chinese women, looking for a way through the ambiguities of *funü* (woman-citizen) and *nüxing* (female-subject), and parades its facility with the discourse of phallocentric power relations. Yet, through the return to classic masquerade, it further confuses and conflates femininity and female difference, let alone allowing the completion of a homoerotic trajectory. In the space of this film, woman may not be both powerful and sexual, and survive socially.

The problem of women's articulation of their subjectivity was so severe that the very word for 'woman' became a focus for struggle in the years after the end of the Cultural Revolution. The Maoist woman/subject of the Revolution *funü* was represented by the Government-sponsored *Fulian*, National Women's Federation, which was relaunched at its conference in 1978.[8] Meanwhile, scholars and feminists who doubt that *Fulian's* close alliance with Party authority can ever do much for women, beyond deploy them as agents of other people's power structures, have returned to the word *nüren*. This represents an emerging modern usage of an ancient term reestablished as a composite of *funü*, the modern woman citizen, and *nüxing*, the sexualized female subject.[9] Wherever the discussion leads, its power is first in its indication of the plethora of female opinions on the nature of female subjectivity in contemporary China.

Kristeva's emphasis on the natural and uncomplicated essence of Chinese womanhood may have been due to her own desire to present an authentic experience of China. Unfortunately, in seeking to represent the authentic, her description becomes tied to the language of race and difference, as constituted, unchanging and inactive. It is a conundrum well noted by the Vietnamese filmmaker and critic Trinh Minh-ha:

> Silence as a refusal to partake in the story does sometimes provide us with the means to gain a hearing. It is a voice, a mode of uttering, and a response in its own right. Without other silences, however, my own silence goes unheard, unnoticed. . . .[10]
>
> Today planned authenticity is rife: as a product of hegemony and a remarkable counterpart of hegemony and standardization, it constitutes as efficacious means of silencing the cry of racial oppression.[11]

As Trinh Minh-ha points out, authenticity cuts both ways. It may allow legitimacy for the speaker, but it may also be a "planned authenticity," born of another's narcissism. In which case the authentic is silenced. In *Yellow Earth*, the narcissism of socialist realism, as wielded by a monolithic Party-State, is used ironically to reveal the inauthentic center of its own history. Narcissism is a central plank of personality cults, cultural nationalisms, and imperial histories. The strategy is also activated in racial and gendered exclusions within society. In thinking about female publicness, one needs, therefore, to also think about narcissism, and the kinds of authenticity it produces for its own ends. "Planned authenticity" does not merely configure an ideal, from the outside; it also denies its subject the right to change. In that sense, we can argue that cultural authenticity denies access to the articulation of experience in time.

The filmmakers of the 1980s and 1990s have shown a concern with the feminine in three major ways. First, an existing genre that deals with structures of gender oppression in pre–Liberation China has continued. Zhang Yimou's adaptations of Mo Yan's *Red Sorghum* and Su Tong's *Raise the Red Lantern* are the better known of this type.[12] While justly famous for their injections of sexual energy and cinematographic bravura, Zhang's films tell a familiar story, albeit from a point of view that is both gendered and sexualized. Within this mode, there is 'mini-genre' dealing with the worst case, the marriage of a grown woman or teenage girl, to a toddler. *A Good Woman* (1985) and *Girl from Hunan* (*Girl Married to a Toddler*) (1986) tell similar stories. The eponymous Good Woman is Xingxian, a teenage village girl, is set up in the opening credits as one in a long line of suffering women. She finally elopes with her mature aged lover, having gained a new 'goodness' under the influence of a land reform work team. The most interesting part of the film is outside the rhetoric of suffering and liberation, however. When Xingxian declares her intention to divorce her tiny husband, the film does not forget the ramifications of change. The child's pain, and her own, at the loss of this maternal and possessive relationship is registered as the cruellest necessity of her freedom. In *Girl from Hunan*, the sting comes when the teenage girl grows up, bears an illegitimate son whom she can keep (because he *is* a son). Now it is the young, student-husband who is embarrassed by his older wife, and it is she who arranges a similar marriage for her own little boy. These films explore the predicaments of women, but are more ethnographic than experiential in the narration. There have also been 'wound' films that focus on women's struggles under particular phases of recent history. These are conventional melodramas, but with an anti-Cultural Revolution motivation. Xie Jin's *Hibiscus Town* and *The Legend of Tianyun Mountain* are models of the type. The third kind of film moves closer in, offering a feminist phenomenology as well as a female narrative. These tend to be made by women directors, who use different styles in an attempt to hear the woman, and make the female public.

Sacrifice of Youth (1985) is on one level a feminist and an antiracist film. Its main protagonist is a girl, and its main interest is in a non-Han people, the Dai. It is, also, deeply implicated in racist and sexist discourses on film. The story of *Sacrifice of Youth* concerns an urbling, Li Chun, a teenage girl, sent to the countryside during the second phase of the Cultural Revolution. She goes to a Dai village, the Dai being one of the minority peoples living on the southwestern peripheries of Chinese territory. Li Chun is a Han, the dominant ethnic population in China. The script is based on *Such a Beautiful Place*, and the film slips rather easily into voyeuristic meditations on the endearing beauty of the place itself, but also of the Dai themselves. They are apparently all kind and gentle (except her adoptive Dai brother and admirer, who gets violent when drunk and rejected). They work hard, sing, and dance and never offer an opinion on their contemporary situation. Commentary is always given by Li Chun, the Han visitor, or by Ren Ju, her Han boyfriend, who is posted in a neighboring village. Indeed, any comments from Dai characters are rare. Two exceptions are when her Dai "Father" advises her to "*make yourself pretty*," and when Ya Li, the prettiest of the Dai girls, who is in love with Li Chun's Dai "brother," snaps at her to "*go away, you don't know how to love him, you are not one of us*." These remarks are motivated within the plot, but their origin is the same. They voice an eternal 'Dai-ness', from which Li Chun can come, or go, but which is represented as internally immutable.

In some respects, the film is a valiant attempt to reform a particular genre of post–Liberation Chinese cinema. Narrational practices in the film attempt to undercut the ethnographic treatment of non-Han in the heyday of socialist realism.[13] *Serfs* (1963), *Red Flower of Mount Tan* (1964), and *Red Sun over the Ke Mountains* (1960) are representative of the revolutionary treatment of the minority theme.[14] In these films, non-Han characters are played by Han actors and actresses. There is very little, if any, dialogue in the regional language, and the characters are valorized according to how completely they assimilate themselves into the Party project of national identity. In *Sacrifice of Youth*, the players are found amateurs, rather than actors portraying a typical 'Dai type'. Zhang Nuanxin's work subverts the genre by her casting, although the dialogue is in standard Chinese (Mandarin).

Zhang's subversive struggles with another mark of ethnographic film produce ambiguous results. Sexuality in these films is coded through the minority woman's body. Han women are far less likely to be shown naked, sexually active, or available to men. One of the appeals of Zhang Yimou's films in the mid-1980s was his rejection of this puritanism in his films with Gong Li. Dru Gladney has described the significance of minority women's bodies in Han culture as a visual displacement of sexual desire. She argues that they provide a "national style" and "metaphorical resource" for cultural production that would otherwise struggle to represent the Han to themselves. One of the most common settings for this national resource is the nude bathing scene, which has been repeated across China in many unlikely settings, including murals at the Beijing International Airport, which were removed after outraged complaints from minority representatives.[15]

"The image of Dai (Thai) and other minority women bathing in the river has become a leitmotiv for ethnic sexuality and often appears in stylized images throughout China, particularly on large murals in restaurants and public spaces."[16]

Zhang's own bathing scene, of Dai girls slipping their dresses off and gliding out into the river, is transgressive, insofar as a Han girl spectates on screen, and regrets that she cannot participate in the swimming. By the end of the scene, her voice-over has informed us that she will soon learn to swim naked herself, but that is not filmed. Sexual potential is firmly located in minority spectacle. Here a kind of mimicry in reverse is at work. The Han girl imitates the dress and habits of the Dai, but can finally only seek a return to her former social identity. She leaves her on-screen sexual potential back in the river. Zhang's cinematography also veers away from established practices of socialist realism. "She makes a number of experiments new for Chinese film practices, including shooting in sync sound, setting up elaborate long takes, filming in extremely low light situations, and handling in an unusually sensitive way what can be a monotonous green color in that subtropical environment."[17]

Certainly, the cinematographic style is painterly rather than paint box. The marks of socialist realism have been rubbed hard, not quite erased, but blurred. No one looks into a socialist-realist horizon, and there is no version of the future beyond the unravelling of the day to day. The script is an adaptation of a written text, but the spoken text does not dominate the visual narration. Despite these innovations, Zhang still relies on a Han voice-over to perpetuate the power of the Han perspective in film narration. She also allows the details to amount to authenticity. This is particularly problematic for a film dealing with a non-Han and a feminine subject.

AUTHENTIC PUBLICS

Sacrifice of Youth invokes authenticity, to combat the invisibility of non-Han experience, but in privileging a female voice, cannot help condemning its Dai subjects to silence. Perhaps Zhang tries to do too much in one film. There are quite a number of conflicts at work in the narrative. There is the tension between rural and urban lifestyles, and the underlying inequalities of the two populations. There are competing versions of the feminine and the sexual between the Han and the Dai. There is also the complicated nostalgia for home experienced by Li Chun, which translates into a filmic nostalgia for the place where she has been sent. Finally, the overarching conflict is a temporal dispute between the immediacy of youth and beauty, and long-term educational aims. It is in the working out of this dispute that the problems of authenticity as a mark of value becomes clear. The authenticity of the Dai is insisted upon—their purity, political transparency, natural decency, collective consciousness inspired not by an external ideal—but grounded in the details of daily life. Yet part of that daily life is the awarding of work points in the collective and the acceptance of city youth into their communities. Why do we hear nothing from the characters on those central experiences? It is the Dai traditions that are held up for criticism within the text. When a child is ill with fever, the mother's prayers are represented as shrill and worse than useless. It is the visitor, Li Chun, who cures him with hurriedly learned medical skills, cribbed from a Party textbook for barefoot doctors.

Esther Ching-mei Yau has quoted Zhang saying that the "Dai civilization [is] that which is primitive, sincere, befitting to human nature while the Han [is] that modern, partly hypocritical, and distorting to human nature."[18] Zhang claims that this tension is what turns Li Chun's life into tragedy. She does not acknowledge that her Han reading, of both Han and Dai essential characteristics, is also responsible for Li Chun's reading of her own situation. She is from the dominant culture, but she has no home. Her relationships, with the other Han in the area, are informed by political awareness and by the drive to return to the public arena of political life that lies in the urban heartland. Any desire to remain in the seeming paradise of *Such a Beautiful Place* is tempered by their understanding of the difference between the present and the future—and of course the determinations of the past. Despite the insistence on Dai continuity, we do not see her village again after Li Chun's last visit, for the burial of Ya, her adoptive Dai grandmother. It is as though the continued paradise of that 'beautiful place' might start speaking for itself. Without Li Chun's perspective, the paradise might well peel away into just another contemporary tale of contemporary confusion and discontent.

The narrative in the film that demonstrates this most clearly is not that of Li Chun but that of the Dai grandmother, Ya. Ya's narrative falls within the "main" narrative but also holds the narration together. She signifies timelessness, in that she marks place, rather than plot development. Yet, as she spins or clacks her prayer beads, or rolls rice with her ancient spindled arms, she is also the signifier of the relentless motion of domestic time, the inexorable passage from youth to age, and from nurture to death. Ya is the authentic center of *Sacrifice of Youth*. She hardly speaks, and yet it is her presence in the house that ensures the continuity of the Dai life. She functions as the grounding signifier of *ziran*—naturalness.[19]

Naturalness is the desired objective of cultural production, and yet its status is in its unrepresentability. It is real, in the Lacanian sense of being yearned for, but unobtainable. Nevertheless, Taoist poets sought to create works that provided the form in which nature and authenticity might lodge themselves, without being forced into the script, or into the consciousness of the reader. Scholar-painters were taught to observe nature with their mind's eye and then take their *knowingness* back into the studio . . . not their sketch pad, as 'the function of art is convey the Dao' (*wenyi zaidao*). All they needed to do was look, and practice their brush strokes. Once the form was perfected, and once their human spirit had made room for nature, their inner eye could see the true essence of the tree, the mountain, and the water. Nature had to arrive *naturally*. This approach to cultural production is in some senses appropriated by the doctrine of *minzu*. This truly untranslatable term refers to a practice and theory of filmmaking and criticism that is tied to a particular tincture of nationhood, aesthetic form, and traditional emphasis. It connotes smoothness and a unity of expression, is epitomized as a single brush stroke, and translates into a filmic style that privileges symbolic unity over narrative drive. As a political term, generally applied, it "is equivalent to the concept of nation that refers to political communities established during the colonial-capitalist expansions of the nineteenth century."[20] In the particular Chinese case, it includes Taiwanese and Hong Kong cinemas as though 'Chineseness', here understood as a politico-ethnic concept and as an ethnically defined experience, is indissoluble by alternative imagined identities. In film criticism this produces a desire for unadulterated Chineseness, which is detectable in an inverse relationship to non-Han Chinese in films about non-Chinese culture in Chinese political territory. The inversion is informed by a narcissistic imagining of the Other. The projected beauty of the Dai is controlled by the gaze of China, whose greater power and legitimacy is expressed in the ability to see, and to be heard. In the context of Kristeva's writing on Chinese women, the symmetry of narcissistic control through a perception of another's beauty is quite striking.

Ya has to appear in the text as though the director is innocent of her presence, as though her representation has not been as carefully constructed as that of the main Han protagonist. After all, Li Chun's memories are just a selective representation of the internal recollections of Zhang and the writer of the original story. Ya is playing herself, but she must do so within the boundaries of this narrated selection. Her part is not to recount her own life, but to provide a quiet spectacle of a purity and completeness that is here accounted as authenticity. Ya's youth is shown in the singing and lovemaking of the Dai girls; her 'typically Dai' fondness for beauty is apparent in her pleasure at Li Chun's self-transformation into a Dai. The girl makes herself a skirt, and piles her hair up on her head, to simulate the Dai look. Ya smiles and fetches a silver belt that she fastens around Li Chun's waist. It is a maternal moment, and a rite of female transference. It is an acknowledgment of Ya's past youth. It also intimates that women in this film, as much as in a Marlene Dietrich or Joan Crawford movie, suffer the restrictions of the necessity of a feminized masquerade.

Ya's beauty is noticed in the film's first shot of her, when the camera travels up her arms to her bare shoulders and fragile gaze. Ya is not Chinese, and therefore watchable, and is yet within the territory of the Empire, and so fairly appropriated. This hardly disguised voyeurism works through a discourse of nature and authenticity to complete the narcissistic self-image of dominant Chineseness. It is through this relationship between narcissism and authenticity that a hierarchical discourse of time is constructed. Ya's time is, quite literally, not her own. As she fastens Li Chun's belt, or prays as Li Chun's Dai brother and Han boyfriend fight over her beloved adoptive granddaughter, it is Li Chun's experience that is marked and charted. Even at her cremation, Ya signifies a conflagration that is neither hers nor her people's.

SILENT PUBLICS

If *Sacrifice of Youth* fails to recognize the power of time in filmmaking, it is mainly because it gives some characters a greater voice than others. The possession of time is tantamount to the right to a narrative and to access to history itself. When postcolonial time, and unequal access to modernity and tradition are thematic, this is all the more pertinent. There are many alternative histories that may be simultaneous, geographically contingent, and yet still chronologically discrete. Urban and rural, Han and non-Han, China exemplifies these conditions economically, politically, and culturally. Economic market expansion is concentrated on the eastern seaboard, whereas most non-Han live in the western, peripheral underdeveloped rural areas. Political power is limited even in semiautonomous regions, and religious and cultural freedoms are subject to the limitations of Han Chinese and Communist hegemonies. The opportunities for filmmakers should be great, but I have not yet seen a convincing example of micronational cinema in these contexts.[21]

Film *could* articulate opposition within such situations of chronic inconsistency, but only if it becomes a symbolic arena where narration may be shared, or made partial. Of course, a filmmaker's own partiality and historical positioning, may be read, and disputed, by a differently interested audience. Zhang taught at the Beijing Film Academy, and it was her writing in the late 1970s that called for a new film language.[22] Her article of 1979, written in collaboration with her husband, the film critic Li Tuo, asked that film language be modernized, so that the most modern and precocious of art forms, film, could achieve its potential in aesthetic form as well as in ideologically dictated reality, *xianshi*. The vision of reform has, in Zhang and Tuo's article at least, settled on the contrast between Chinese reality and Western form. For them *re*form is not to be found in the silent voices of the Dai women, but in the absorption of cultural others into the Han vocabulary. It is easier to exploit the writings and productions of Western critics and filmmakers than it is to allow the irruption of another traumatized illiteracy into the home territories.[23]

If silencing, as opposed to the silence of dissent that Trinh Minh-ha advocates as an option, is a problem for racialized constituencies, it is also always an issue for female publics. Theories and practices of power tend to look over women's conditions, failing to hear or see them. A central cause of criticism of Habermas's notion of *Öffentlichkeit*, even by sympathetic feminists like Nancy Fraser and Seyla Benhabib, is its tendency to bleach out questions of gender and race from the formal identity of the citizen.[24] Female publicness is indebted to female agency, and the latter is often unrealized in civil practice and political conceptualization. Habermas assumes agency, on the part of the communicating public person, and ignores those who have no equivalent agency. The politically visible speak loud and clearly, and as speech is linked to their identity, they are heard. Women, speaking from outside public realms, cannot be heard in certain political and cultural constellations.

Nonetheless, the airing of these voices in cultural forms, and postcolonial feminisms, is a striking example of such giving voice. These voices make publicness possible. These public feminisms demonstrate a public sphere that is oppositional but which is nonetheless an accountable part of political, social, and cultural experience. In her critique of Habermas's theory of communicative action, Nancy Fraser concentrates her attack on the blind spots in his theory of modernity. In her account, Habermas describes modernity as a period marked by the division between material and symbolic action, production, and reproduction. Very crudely, material production is predicated on systemic, social labor, whereas symbolic reproduction is achieved through cultural tradition and socially integrated activity. Fraser's central concern is that child rearing is counted as symbolic reproduction, and is therefore excluded from the sphere and rewards of social labor. She believes that by allowing such a major proportion of (generally) female activity to be passed as a normative function of social reproduction, rather than a systemically organized, intentional, linguistically influenced function of social ideology, Habermas allows his own work to become deflated by its association with ideology. She also presents Habermas's divisions of the modern as problematic. Fraser characterizes Habermas's reading of modernity as a divide between the family, as private sphere, and the capital-led official economy; and between the public sphere of civil society and autonomous organization and the state-led administrative state. The links between the private and public spheres, as opposed to the administrative, functional, and systemic spheres of the bureaucracy and the economy, are such that Habermas presents modernity as defined by two complementary but discrete institutional modes, the splitting off from the material of the symbolic.

The problem with this is that, although Habermas acknowledges that mutual interests and dependencies mean that the spheres are not in fact perfectly discrete, he does not say that money and power, as social media, are absolutely transferable, from one sphere to the other, and across institutional modes. Power and political influence flow from the economic advantages and symbolic capital that is available to those with time enough to engage in public activity in the material world. This 'time' is not available to many women as they are involved in the time consuming but unremunerated activity of child rearing, or, in Ya's case, of feeding men and children, weaving clothes, and keeping the peace.

> The separation of the official economic sphere from the domestic sphere and the enclaving of childrearing from the rest of social labor . . . amounts to a defense of an institutional arrangement which is widely held to be one, if not the, linchpin of modern women's subordination. And it should be noted that the fact that Habermas is a socialist does not alter the matter. For the (undeniably desirable) elimination of private ownership, profit orientation, and hierarchical command in paid work would not in itself affect the official-economic/domestic separation.[25]

Seyla Benhabib makes the same point in her own critique of Habermas. She asks how exactly civil society differs from society itself. What is it, if it is not the way in which power forms and affects the reproduction of political and social meaning in our daily lives? Benhabib refers us back to Arendt's reading of modernity as the occlusion of the political by the social. But if public life is structured to still exclude these symbolic, but also very material, functions of privacy, then the problem remains. It is exacerbated by ideologies, of capital and socialism, which render them functionally invisible in both civil and official areas of power.

The conditions of modernity in China have different foundations, and a different pattern of development. I have already mentioned the temporal disparities between rural and urban, and by extension Han and non-Han experience. Modernity does not arrive everywhere at the same time, and in the same sequence of forms. Chris Berry and Mary-Ann Farquhar describe the arrival of late modern*ism* in China and its results very perceptively. Modern aesthetics, however differentiated in the Western context, in China "is more like one object . . . they all arrived at the same time."[26] Likewise, the political, social, and domestic effects of modernity are made manifest according to how and when they are experienced within the sum, and differences, of twentieth-century Chinese history. Zhang Nuanxin's later film *Good Morning Beijing* (1990) is more successful than *Sacrifice of Youth* in that the temporal scope is manageable, and so the concerns of gender do not override competing claims for publicness that she cannot answer. *Good Morning Beijing* is set in urban Beijing in the late 1980s. It tells a story of three young people working on the same bus route. Their time is bound by their shared urbanity, their youth, and even the bus timetable when they go to work. The proximity of space and time is also beautifully illustrated by the theme of bus workers living out drama on the same route, at the same time, in the same city. The onset of market opportunities disrupts their work pattern and eventually their relationships. The security of the bus route is destroyed, and the female character, Ai Qing, ends up pregnant by a fourth protagonist. This interloper is a con man who pretends to be a student from Singapore, using the cover of another, more glamorous Chineseness to inveigle his way into the girl's affections. Zhang's first point is that old time can be shattered by new time, and that there are human casualties in the process. Her second observation is that new time reinvokes a predation on femaleness, which is both 'old' and new. The forlorn pregnant girl-as-victim is desperately familiar. The sexual predator being an unemployed Beijinger, masquerading as an overseas student, is only comprehensible within the late 1980s' preoccupations with globalization.

Zhang's film is particularly interesting in its reading of contemporaneity. She clearly recognizes that the contemporary is a state of mind, shared by those who understand the present, past, and future as synchronically meaningful. She goes way beyond the authentic detailing of feminized 'Dai-ness' in *Sacrifice of Youth*, in the character of Ai Qing. Qing's only authenticity lies in her contemporary status.[27] It is an authenticity that fluctuates according to the conditions under which she lives, the fantasies within which she articulates her desires, and the power of others to determine her self-perceptions. She is a microcosm of the necessary failure that Dirlik records in his comments on the political State's attempts at authenticating itself as the nation. "In spite of stubborn conviction, and nearly two decades of effort, Marxist historiography failed to discover an all-embracing model with which to explain China's historical development without distorting the data of Chinese history, the concepts of historical materialism, or, more commonly, both."[28]

POSTCOLONIAL AUTHENTICITY

Good Morning Beijing complements Trinh Minh-ha's discussion of authenticity, as both texts unravel a scene of manipulation, within a postmodern global cynicism. Trinh's category of "planned authenticity" describes a strategic arm of postcolonial discourse. The immutable, seemingly self-descriptions, are used on a commercial basis, or as a comforting, but reductive, bolthole in a global political economy. Thus "planned authenticity" offers an alternative to naked oppression. It preys on the fears of those who have lived through the postmodernity of colonialism and patriarchy, and is ordered in a narcissistic relation to a Western/developed globalizing economy.[29] In *Good Morning Beijing*, Ai Qing's small tragedy comes in part from a perverse willingness to buy in emotionally to the myth of the authentic. Her 'Singaporean' boyfriend is a fraud based on a fraudulent idea: the myth of the ideal postmodern mate. This is a planned authenticity that feeds directly off the glamour of the new, rather than the nostalgia of the past, with disastrous effects.

Blush (1994) also works to disrupt authentic histories. The film is a triangular love story set in the 1940s and 1950s in Suzhou. It concerns two women, liberated from prostitution by the new authorities. Both are sent to a reform camp to be re-educated through speaking bitterness, cultural practice (bracing songs), manual (industrial) work, and the company of better women. The women, Qiu Yi and Xiao'e, are parted as Qiu Yi escapes to live with a former client and lover, Lao Pu, and Xiao'e completes her course of rehabilitation. Qiu Yi is rejected by Lao Pu's mother on the grounds of her former profession. The climactic scene in her stay occurs when the small nephew of Lao Pu asks if she will paint his face as she paints her own. She does so but his family reacts furiously to the child's makeup, but also, by implication, to his attraction to Qiu Yi. She stands framed in the doorway, dressed to perfection in a blue robe, realizing that her status is as a child's but without the promise of future happiness. Later in the film, Qiu Yi has become a nun and shaved her hair off. She hears that Xiao'e and Lao Pu have become lovers and are going to be married. Qiu's wedding gift to her old friend is a yellow umbrella, a sign of renunciation and farewell.

These scenes would not be so significant were it not for a dominant mise-en-scène of grey and green in the rest of the film. Li uses color to direct the audience to those moments in Qiu Yi's life when her personal tragedy is made public, by her gestures or by the open cruelty of others. The film ends after the death of Lao Pu. Xiao'e leaves her baby son to Qiu Yi, who renames him "New China," and claims in voice-over that she will now live happily ever after. The color of the film remains a steadfast green as she assures us of the promise of the baby and its future.

Peng Xiaolian's film, *The Story of Women*, the story of three rural women using a trip to the local city to sell yarn, ends on a freeze shot of the women's faces, three abreast and ready for confrontation (figure 5.2). The film is narrated in a female voice throughout, and it is significant that the aggressor is a male, and is mute. Peng introduces gender in the female voice, and uses her power as filmmaker to give agency to her female protagonists. The women negotiate their way through urban modernity, and return to their rural lives with a gloss of urban contemporary self-awareness, ready to engage in battle. Their narrative is prioritized in the publicness of film, although their actual battles are all to do with the cultural and social dismemberment of female agency.[30]

The film avoids orientalism and the lure of authenticity. The women are not represented as sexy, embroidered victims of a distant patriarchy. Their daily lives are believably 'realistic' but the stark and tacky modernity of the urban scenes are nothing like the careful authentication via detail of such films as *Raise the*

Figure 5.2   A Story of Women

Red Lantern, Red Firecracker, Green Firecracker, Farewell My Concubine, or even *Sacrifice of Youth.* Peng's film slots with Trinh Minh-ha's contention that women represent themselves according to a Western or non-Western mode. Western women tend towards 'simulation, textual performances, double displacements', whereas non-Western women turn to realism. This divergence becomes more complicated in the light of Peng's own remarks on the reception of her film in country areas: "Men said it portrayed women as too strong, women said it did not flatter them. City people said it was not modern enough, country people said they had enough hardships without needing to have it rubbed in by seeing a film."[31] Peasant women were especially certain that the film was too close to their real lives to be pleasurable. Their reaction is another cut in the attack on authenticity. Trinh Minh-ha's Western/non-Western divide leaves out the internal divisions between urban and rural women. City people said the film was not modern enough, for their modernity is experienced on a different chronological scale to that of Peng's three women. Western women use "textual performances, double displacements"; they abstract their reality and make a play of fantasy, theory, and 'Other' women, which scrapes a passageway to the real, not the reality, of gendered existence. Peng based her film on her own experience of being in the countryside, but that is the authenticity of the visitor, not entirely dissimilar to the hovering of the scholar in and out of other people's real lives. How is Peng, urbling, and cosmopolitan filmmaker, to do more than place the 'reality' of peasant women into the terms of her own fantasy, and perhaps also attract the narcissistic pleasure of the Western feminist audience (including my own)? Is her realism actually also a "double displacement" that brilliantly captures another time frame, and recreates a particular nonmodern aspect of modern China, but which does so at the expense of the inexpressible real that makes any kind of realism or authenticity unimportant? And, to reiterate Tian Zhuangzhuang's point about children's films, can any of us make art for each other? Should we not always accept that we offer each other fantasies in our films, and that the question of representation is only useful when it unearths public conflicts between the artist, the audience, and the subject of representation? It is not so much a matter of 'getting it right': Peng probably did to a great degree. It is more a matter of what constitutes a public imaginary; it may not be anything that looks 'real' at all. What a world of representations might be unleashed if a Chinese peasant woman were approached as a subject of her own fantasy and within the pleasures and desires formed by her own chronology.

CONTEMPORARY IN PUBLIC

The problem that Peng faced when her rural audience politely declined to enjoy *Three Women* was a mixture of taste and timing. For Peng, it seemed about time that people talked, made films, and were concerned with the modern rural woman. It is easy to agree with her, but in doing so not to make the mistake that a film that needs to be made for one audience—international feminists, Chinese urban populations, men in positions of power in rural townships—is not necessarily contemporary to the desires of the subject matter, the women themselves. Being contemporary is not a state that we can always assume to be our own, nor a state that we necessarily share with those around us. To live in the present demands that we are aware of our present and our past as negotiable constructs of memory. This undermines the notion of a homogeneous society with an equalized, common mode of address between members. Here again, authenticity can be a false trail. Inauthenticity is a sign that the subject is flexible and comfortable in the contemporary mode. The inauthentic subject must engage in dialogue within herself to achieve fleeting reconciliation between the material and the symbolic elements of her experience. Artists and critics function as mediators, prizing their way into the social imaginary with aesthetic tricks and barbed wit. Therefore, they must be silenced in a different nexus of exclusion, which is the discourse of the authentic. As inauthentic they have neither the confidence of the narcissistic Self, nor the doubtful honor of necessary Otherness. They hover between one subjectivity and another, seeing both and inhabiting neither.

Rey Chow has argued that the reversion to a discourse of authenticity is a symptom of the reflex colonialism of the Western critic. When trying to confront the internal problems of critical subjectivity, the critic is wont to give up and reflect instead on the authenticity that they perceive in others, and wish for themselves. In particular, she has cited *On Chinese Women* as an example of an internal argument being projected onto an international metaphor—here, China, the feminine, the oriental: "Even though Kristeva sees China in an interesting, and indeed, 'sympathetic' way, there is nothing in her arguments as such that cannot be said without 'China'. What she proposes is not so much learning a lesson from a different culture, as a different method of reading from within the West."[32]

Homi Bhabha also offers this reading of Kristeva's 'colonial discourse', quoting her work on China as an example of:

> An inevitable sliding from the semiotic activity to the unproblematic reading of other cultural and discursive systems. There is in such readings a will to power and knowledge that, in failing to specify the limits of their own field of enunciation and effectivity, proceeds to individualize otherness as the discovery of their own assumptions.[33]

Chow and Bhabha differ in the form of their conclusions although they move in the same direction. They both link the practice of the Western critic to that of the colonial formation of the subject. Bhabha then embraces hybridity, while Chow perceives that the authentication of the Other is meretricious. It is a way of dissolving the psychic link between the postcolonial subject—and she cites herself, Hong Kong Chinese, as an example—and the imagined Authentic Other. The narcissistic need of the colonizer leads to the dismissal of one as a modern travesty, and the use of the other as a fully determined projection of its missing entrails. In a world of hegemony and actual power, both groups are thus severely disadvantaged.

Chow further conceives of "the postmodernity of the colonized," whereby it is only in the West that modernity and postmodernity can be conceptualized as chronological. She argues that, for all people who have been colonized, postmodernity came before modernity, insofar as the fragmentation of an authentic self was necessitated by the narcissistic demands of the colonizer. The native had to be recognizably native and traditional, in order to satisfy the Westerners' modernist self-justification for invasion. The colonizers had to believe themselves engaged in the Enlightenment project of spreading the light of rationality in the realms of darkness, and they had to show signs of the success of this civilizing project.[34]

> The native had therefore to be seen to be educated into Western habits of thought and belief. S/he could not however expect to form any part of the structure of that system except to remain as the reflective Other—that was perpetually in the place of a subaltern in the need of further civilization. Chow claims that hence the colonized develop a self-awareness necessary to exist within the dual environments of the invader's culture and their own, as well as contributing to the hybridity that forms between the two norms.[35]

For someone with my educational background, which is British Colonial and American, the moralistic charge of my being "too Westernized" is devastating; it signals an attempt on the part of those who are specialists in "my" culture to demolish the only premises on which I can speak.[36]

Here Chow seems to both bewail and disavow her postmodern identity. For surely she has many premises on which she *must* speak. She is claiming that within the symbolic order of Western academia she is silenced by her positioning as 'Oriental' woman with an inappropriately Western voice. Yet she claims that her voice is specifically that of the postmodern postcolonial, and therefore speaks between the monolithic voices of imperial cultures. She risks constructing another monolith as her account of colonial postmodernity suggests that these conditions of existence will always produce an ideal type that is always forced into silence or compliance.

Moreover, despite Chow's stated aversion to Bhabha's notion of hybridity, his work is very useful in understanding in more positive terms her own expressions of the postmodern/colonial predicament. In his essay "Of Mimicry and Man," Bhabha explores:

The comic turn from the high ideals of the colonial imagination to its low mimetic literary effects whereby mimicry emerges as one of the most elusive and effective strategies of colonial power and knowledge. . . . Within that conflictual economy of colonial discourse which Edward Said describes as the tension between the synchronic panoptical vision of domination . . . and the counter pressure of the diachrony of history . . . mimicry represents an ironic compromise.[37]

Bhabha constructs his 'mimic man' as a presence in the colonial and postcolonial worlds that comments on the identity of the colonizer through its imperfect reproduction of the behavior and moral reactions of that party. The point is not that the mimicry creates a simplified stereotype of the invasive culture, nor that exclusion from the underlying symbolic structure of colonial culture finally renders the mimic subject powerless within that structure. From the colonizer's perspective the mimicry is induced so that the desire for difference may be contained in powerless signifiers. For the colonized, entry into a symbolic order that is only completed through the reduction of Other peoples to fixers of desire could only ever be harmful.

Chow is resistant to the idea that the postmodern-colonized form a homogeneous group within the bounds of their externally dictated fragmentation. Resisting a hostile symbolic order does not simply mean that a single oppositional structure will form as a result. She points out that the tendency for women in the developing world to be either spoken for through the liberator voices of the indigenous male culture or to be tied into national feminism prevents women, and groups of women, from challenging the very particular and very familiar source of their disadvantage, patriarchy thinly disguised as tradition and authenticity.

Fighting over one's own or someone else's authenticity emerges from this argument, and in the films I have discussed, as a fight for the control of history, for the relationship between one moment and another, that determines a *planned authenticity* for the losers. In *Sacrifice of Youth* this produces a feminized account of minority experience from within a Han phenomenology. In *Good Morning Beijing*, the battle shifts to one over time itself inside the Chinese capital. The synchronous time of perpetual revolution has not been replaced, or at least not in the minds and political will of the Chinese Communist Party government, but it is now in competition with the shifting authentications of global time frames. In *Blush*, the color of the film is indeed the color of experience. Memories of histories, past loves, and future hopes are dim, and greened with age. Moments of brightness come with the poignancies of passion; the yellow of renunciation and farewell, the clear blue of pain, and always the red of a woman's lipstick. The redness is poignant as it marks the woman as stubbornly sexual and therefore distinct from the redness of New China. These are the authentic moments in Li's film, the moments where the intensely personal is transformed by dint of visual selection into a public space for emotional affect.

The women in the films of the 1980s and 1990s in Chinese cinema are very different from Kristeva's fantasy of "Chinese women." The films negotiate the problem of womanhood as a category in various ways. Women directors explore, with their characters, the extent to which there is an authentic woman's public voice in contemporary Chinese culture. In some films it is achieved at the expense of others' interests. In others, men are silenced by female voice-overs, in order perhaps to circumvent the antagonisms of competing articulation. In a film like *Blush*, the voice is supplemented by the colors of experience to underline the areas of life that can only be understood as significant in retrospect. Li Shaohong understands best of all that it is significance rather than authenticity that commends the story to its audience. Yet, grasping for authenticity is common in the Chinese context of post-ideological culture. Perhaps it must be that reaching a public version of modernity on film involves the invention of the authentic.

6

Transnational Publics and Radical Chic

In this chapter I return to the question of female subjectivity within my overall concern with cinematic or cultural public space. In the discussion of *Sacrifice of Youth*, I followed Nancy Fraser's argument that the public space of the female tends to be hampered by the ideology of male labor. Domestic labor, and the work of reproduction, is submerged within a rhetoric of the symbolic, which refuses to acknowledge the actual effects of such work in the material world governed by the media of money and power. This process of political and economic silencing is also a feature of many films in which women often appear as an articulation of male desire. In the discussion of *Sacrifice of Youth*, I addressed the problems that filmmakers face when trying to combat this pattern, especially the likelihood of relegating women to a sphere of 'otherness' and nostalgic authenticity, and possibly a stifling obsession with a presymbolic biological essentialism: "These relaxed feminine bodies . . . down to the tiniest cell, free of guilt or provocation."[1]

In the radical films and videos of the 1990s, the female subject has been again submerged into male narrative. In these narratives of young male angst, female characters appear as ghosts of a man's relationship with his own past, present, and future. The woman signals, and to an extent articulates, male alienation at the price of her own narrative coherence. This is particularly blatant in *The Days* (1993) and in *Beijing Bastards* (1993). In terms of cinematic public space it is also possible to read these films as inadvertent examples of (to quote Hill Gates) "the mutual constitution of the two Chinese genders."[2]

SYMPTOMS OF ALIENATION

> Women's bodies may have offered unique possibilities for the expression of
> the canonical virtues, but they could not escape being *women's* bodies . . . in
> the long run even the exaltation of women's virtue operated to keep women
> in their cultural place.[3]

The position of women in traditional Chinese society has rightly or wrongly become a conceptual paradigm for bad practice in relations between the sexes.
Meanwhile, for feminist theoreticians in the century of cinema it is commonplace
to notice the gendering of bodies on screen. In this chapter I will divert from
neither of these commonplaces but I will argue that, taken together, they reveal
a developing aesthetic of transnational spectatorship that revels in sexism in
Chinese cinema. I will make this argument through readings of films made outside the Chinese State Studio system, and which have been marketed internationally as countercinema. My argument draws on theoretical understandings that
have been developed in feminist psychoanalytic work outside China. The application of such theory to recent Chinese cinema is appropriate given the aesthetic
and gender-specific resonances between these films and the construction of
gendered bodies in cinematic space of other cinema practice. There are self-conscious references to such theory in the films discussed, which confuse but do not
mitigate the overall impression of female subordination within the text. These
references locate the films within a contemporary global cinematic imaginary,
but they are subject to strong local inflection from their position within the
Chinese cinema and its historical development.

A film's contemporaneity, its genealogical place, is marked at moments of
recognition between spectator and text when the symbolic structure of the film
matches the spectators' conception of how life is—the criss-crossing imaginar-
ies of the everyday. This moment of recognition may also be described as an articulation of cinematic space through the process of reception. This needs to be
understood in tandem with the idea of transnational imaginaries: discernible overlaps in the imaginary structures of experience across the cinema-going, video-
watching global population. Such overlaps are made possible through symbolic
continuities between one cultural construction and another. The focus here is the
symbolic organization of the gendered body.

I concentrate on two films of Zhang Yuan and Wang Xiaoshuai, *Beijing Bastards* and *The Days*. Both films are valuable pieces of independent filmmaking.
They eschew formulaic plots, and rely neither on revolutionary heroism, nor on
Hollywood happy endings (nor even postclassic, neoart Hollywood *un*happy endings). They focus on the story rather than on the plot. That is, both films try to
create a sense of the moment, constructing a realism of disorder. People play
'themselves' or approximations of themselves. This produces a performative mode
that is already potentially anxious. Actors provide an illusion of subjective whole-

ness for the spectators' comfort. Amateurs-as-themselves cannot do this. They know neither themselves nor the art of being themselves, and the result is oddly affecting. The spectators find that their job is not to identify with those on screen, but to contribute a sense of contemporary recognition to that presence, to legitimate the film as fiction and document. The plot seems haphazard and is structured only by a vague chronology of the various characters' problems. Thus far, these films are very different from revolutionary texts of the 1950s and 1960s. In pursuit of the Four Modernizations, the Party-state has reorganized the political high ground to accommodate the principles of hired labor, large and small-scale capital accumulation, individualistic consumerism, and entrepreneurial and State economic enterprise.[4] It has done so without relinquishing its will to control the population. In film, the tension between the freedom to fail, inherent in market politics, and the necessity to conform, central to the politics of the one-party state, is made visible through the everyday lives of urban players at the limits of conformity.

This has produced a tendency to reduce femininity to a corporeal overtly sexualized marginal position, and this is as true of the radical films of the Sixth Generation as it is of television soaps and popular police and gangster thrillers. The imaginary spaces, created and occupied by disaffected young, male bohemians in Beijing in the 1990s, are indicative of the clashing contemporaneities of socialism and marketization. The publicness offered in these films offers a disturbing glimpse into the social imaginary of modern China. "Everything happens as if the terrain where the creativity of society is manifested in the most tangible manner, the terrain where it makes, makes be, and makes itself in making be, must be covered over by an imaginary creation ordered in such a way that the society can conceal from itself what it is."[5]

The central figure of *Beijing Bastards*, Cui Jian, is one of East Asia's biggest stars, and a fine rock performer. He is also a postsocialist hero.[6] He sings of politics as though he were singing of love against the odds. ADO, his band, was formed in 1986, and Cui Jian sang with them until 1989-90. However, it was Cui Jian as a solo name who achieved immediate success among urban youth in Beijing and beyond, after performing his song 'Nothing to My Name' (*Yi wu suoyou*) on a nationally broadcast concert.[7] Cui was banned in 1987 during the 'struggle against bourgeois liberalism', but continued to 'party'—party being the borrowed term for a secret rock concert/festival; as with British raves, locations were kept secret from the police to prevent preemptive closure.[8] A rather more public rock concert took place in China on January 28, 1990 in the Beijing Workers' Stadium.[9] It was initiated by Cui Jian, who offered to open a series of charity concerts to mark the occasion of the Asian Games and help to fund it. The authorities were persuaded to accept the proposal by the intervention of the deputy mayor of Beijing, who also attended the concert. According to one account of the concert and a subsequent national tour, rock music provoked a cathartic reaction in its audience: "As he [Cui Jian] was able to discover by himself, the central problem in Chinese culture is the artificial complication of human relations. Instead of open and honest speaking, vague demands for morality and decency are seen as more important."[10]

Cui Jian's "open and honest" singing was apparently also noted by the authorities, as the tour was cancelled halfway through, and the band returned to playing underground venues, including the 'Diplomatic Restaurant' that features in *Beijing Bastards*. The quotation from the account of the Cui Jian tour is interesting in how it expresses the difference between social normalcy and the discourse of rock. Life without rock is "artificial," it is policed by a "morality," and a "decency," which are to be seen rather than spoken. The implication that speaking is a closer indicator of intention than seen behavior is clear. The interstices of community, those that do not sit well with the demands of public order, are driven outside the discourse of morality and decency. Voices carrying discourses that fall outside the regime of truth are criminalized. The response from the criminals and their sympathizers is to see virtuous society as artificial and to encourage a rhetoric of authenticity for the outsider. Knowing that Cui Jian's secret performances are 'party(s)'—some of which are shown on film—leads a British audience to thoughts of rave and criminal justice. The Criminal Justice and Public Order Act 1994 was the Tory government's rabid response to free raves in the English countryside, travellers, and the rhythmic dancing of alienated youth.[11] It has left a cultural association that aligns some with dance as positive antipolitics, and others with dance as the epicenter of national disorder. Dancing without a license is now a criminal offense in the United Kingdom. As Jeremy Gilbert and Tara Brabazon have both explained at greater length and depth, the dancing body of the late 1980s in Britain has been seen as an aggressively apolitical and dangerously unbounded subject.[12] "What is clear enough is that dancing, the crowd, and music with repetitive beats have been things that the dominant culture has tried to suppress and to regulate for at least the whole of modernity, and that the philosophers and would-be legislators have wanted to get rid of since Plato."[13]

What is also clear is that the dancing body, 'partying' in *Beijing Bastards* to the applause of European and North American art houses, is not entirely apolitical, at least not once the politics of gender are taken into consideration. A description of the film's origins suggests its status as an underground film. The protagonists are singers, artists, roadies, and undecided bohemians, although not quite the hooligans (*liumang*) of Wang Shuo's fictions, that John Minford has described elsewhere as those that cruise "the inner city streets on [a] Flying Pigeon Bicycle, looking (somewhat lethargically) for the action, reflective sunglasses flashing a sinister warning."[14] I offer this account of the film as a radical and politically innovative text to indicate how it has been understood by international audiences. This should also underline how hegemonic versions of statehood and modernity can be replicated in gender relations, even among the very groups that feel themselves excluded from the organizing principles of their political environment.

A PUBLIC SPECTACLE

Beijing Bastards was introduced on its 1995 UK Channel Four screening as "China's first rock and roll movie . . . banned by the Chinese Authorities."[15] And so the British late night television audience settled down at midnight to ninety minutes of "right on" radical rock and roll. They had been primed to enjoy familiar music (albeit—they suspected—less subtle than the mature Western varieties of rock), and an anti-Communist, subcultural feel-good factor, laced with the peculiarly English self-satisfaction of having sat through a foreign film on a Tuesday night. Their expectancy was based on the assumption that Western rock and Western youth have been there before—and that the China factor simply reaffirmed the importance of the Western dominant and subversive relation. The audience expected to be impressed by Chinese temerity in an 'authentically' repressive climate—while patting themselves on the back that their youth, imagined, vicarious, or actual, provided the template for this musical courage. The *actual* point of contact in the symbolic imaginaries articulated by film and in a Western audience's assumptions is rather less heroic. This, submerged but essential, additional feel-good factor in the film, not, like the film's 'banned' status, openly offered to the audience by the link man at Channel Four, was its comfortable dependency on a construction of alienated youth as male.

Seeing the film in an English sitting room—or even in the Institute of Contemporary Art's newly refurbished cinema in London—gives the music, the grey streets, the scruffy dance cellars, the dour-faced policemen leading a drunk home through thin Beijing streets, the bicycles wheeling through traffic in persistent rain, and the late night cafés where men drink until they fall over, a sense of exotic orientalism turned upside down. This is all so ordinary, it must be interesting, and it cannot help but seem authentic. And if cross-cultural reception of the film might be confused, a 'banned' film, the 'first rock 'n roll movie' but that actually looks more like a skillful portrait of nothing more than the everyday, the film itself harbors contradiction. A story about young men and women trying to get by as musicians, as artists, or simply trying to be young and self-obsessed in a big city, the film offers an alternative version of life in the interstices of Party-State control systems in the People's Republic. At the same time the text relies on normative, gendered processes of identification and complicity between spectator and text to produce a romance of male alienation that squeezes female subjectivity—rendered almost entirely corporeal—into its margins.

The film opens with a sequence that cuts between a rock band's rehearsal and a confrontation between a young man and a young woman under an urban roadway. It is raining. The woman, Maomao, has told the man, Kazi, that she is pregnant. He wants her to 'get rid of it'. She is unhappy and frightened at the prospect. His response is an attempt to seduce her. This makes the situation impossible, and she runs off into the rain. The scene between the two is in medium shot, with no particular emphasis on one character or the other. It is only after Maomao has left and there is an extended medium close-up on the surprised and pensively sullen Kazi, intercut with an equivalent shot of the rock singer, Cui Jian, that the film begins to demonstrate its interests. The invitation to identify with Kazi is compounded by the association of the young man's misery with the dominant soundtrack, Cui Jian's songs of politics and love, "walking with your head against the wind." Cui's sings, "My eyes shine like a victim's [a rabbit caught in the head lamps?] . . . but I can get along without you," as Kazi runs his hand through his hair, and wipes the rain from his eyes, glistening in the lights of the road and the traffic.

There are other narrative strands in the film, but Kazi and Cui Jian hold the center in a juxtaposition of existential angst and heroic articulation of the pain of living in a modern dictatorship (or the dictatorship of modernization?). Kazi's search for Maomao runs parallel to Cui Jian's search for rehearsal space and a performance venue. Both searches express frustration at a lack of control over their private and public lives. The film is indeed about the everyday, but in particular about how the daily experience of city life, modern capitalism, in this case 'socialism with Chinese characteristics', together with a creative will to push against the boundaries of self- and social-expression, turn the everyday into a struggle between helplessness and anger.

This dual-portrait of alienation, suffered by Kazi and sung by Cui Jian, is undoubtedly male. Or at least the main male protagonists are prioritized in the camera work and on the sound track. That is easily observed. Their symbolic construction within the text is more complicated, however. Male alienation is characterized in the film as sexy, bohemian, and a walk on the wild side of the contemporary scene. To sustain this interpretation of young masculinity it is important that the symptoms of real subjective distress are made invisible. The ideal image of the male subject is symptomatically anatomized in the female body. As Elizabeth Grosz argues, in her work on the European imaginary anatomy, the human body has been reduced to a discursive shorthand of fit, white, male bodily presence. "Lacan develops his understanding of the *imaginary anatomy* largely in his account of the mirror stage . . . this too is a psychical map of the body, a mirror of the subject's lived experiences, not as an anatomical and physiological object, but as a social and psychical entity."[16]

Grosz describes the way in which the psyche conceives of the body and depends on that conception for its own coherence. A disturbed psyche acts out trauma through parallel, symbolic disturbances wreaked upon the body. The saddest image to drive this point home is that of lonely or disturbed children banging their heads on the end of their cots. In filmic terms, male and female figures share a *cinematic* anatomy. The separation of spiritual need and bodily suffering is played out as an unconscious symbolic tic, and also as a strategy to invigorate male status. The imaginary ideal is the mirror image of masculinity, the face that the male subject presents to the camera.

The question that arises, in the context of *Beijing Bastards* and *The Days*, is whether or not the anatomy of the male, and, by analogy, the female, in Chinese cultural structures is equivalent to the psychic organization of body space that Grosz refers to in a Western context. On the level of the medical science of anatomy in the two cultures, the answer is clearly no. Traditional Chinese anatomy is a holistic discourse, with an emphasis on pattern, energy, and connectivity between all the systems of the body, mental as well as physiological. As Judith Farquhar has argued, although also noting the hybridity of Chinese and Western medicine in recent years, "For patients too, the multiple body involves a certain subjectivity. . . . Medical care for many Chinese patients is continuous with their own individual and family strategies for maintaining health."[17] This is in contrast to Western anatomy that has concentrated on dissection, in the philosophical context of the Cartesian split between the ego and the corporeal self. This medical paradigm is not necessarily repeated in the symbolic world of gender. As Harriet Evans has argued, the concept of gender in Chinese *political* discourse is a noxious tincture of subordination and sexual disappearance disguised as collectivist, and latterly marketized, equality: "If under collectivist ideology, as Li Xiaojiang argues, the rhetoric of male-female equality prevented women from asserting themselves, then under the reprivatization of love and sexuality the continuing attachment to sociobiological constructions effectively legitimizes women's lack of autonomy."[18]

The medicalized body in these films is, in any case, quite specifically under the knife of nontraditional medicine, as two women succumb to hospitalized abortion procedures. The Chinese medical body, and the anatomical differences that are posed there, may be both discrete from current symbolic practices, but also implicated in the construction and performance of gender. In her work on sexuality and reproduction in Chinese medicine in the sixteenth century, Charlotte Furth notes that while Chinese medicine did not lump sexuality and reproduction unproblematically together, thus essentializing the female body, it did associate sexuality and longevity. There is, therefore, a discursive separation of the male and female anatomy, insofar as the female is the source of a dangerous pleasure, while the male is a body that must enjoy the erotic while protecting itself from female corporeal rapacity. "Orthodox Chinese medical discourse did not understand such pleasures as constituting an independent domain of 'sexuality', but rather positioned the erotic at the fulcrum of body experiences implicating human longevity and even spiritual regeneration on one side and generativity and reproduction on the other." [19]

In *Beijing Bastards* we get a casual glimpse of the painter, Liu Xiaodong. He is identifiable by the large figurative painting on which he works, while a young hopeful hangs around hoping to get accepted into the studio's set. Liu comes across as having 'made it' as a Beijing bohemian. He, and his very large canvas, inhabit the studio space and the artistic space of the scene, while the female wannabe hovers at the door asking for advice. We are also aware, from the credits, that he is responsible for the art direction of the film. In *The [Winter] Days* Liu Xiaodong and his partner, Yu Hong, also a painter, are the main protagonists. Here, however, they are seen working together in a cramped apartment above an art school, although Yu's creative output is only implied. Liu dominates the narrative and his art informs the visual narration of the film, although his persona is less confident than in the brief scene in *Beijing Bastards*, and he no longer appears as a central figure of a glamorous set. He is struggling to sell his pictures to overseas buyers, in particular an American who showed interest, but fails to come up with an actual sale. Liu's winter days are desperate forays into the commercial art world while his relationship with his partner collapses until it is she— rather than one of his canvasses—who goes to New York.

Liu Xiaodong was born in Liaoning in 1963. He graduated in 1988 from the Beijing Central Academy of Fine Arts and stayed on as a lecturer. Yu Hong was born in 1966 in Beijing. She also graduated in 1988 from the Central Academy, and has since worked there as a lecturer. She has exhibited in Monte Carlo, Macao, Pasadena, Calif., Berlin, and Venice, as well as appearing in the major Mainland avant-garde shows in the past eight years. An autobiographical pointer to where the 'buyer' might have seen Liu's work would be that both Liu and Yu exhibited as 'realists' in the 1991 *New Generation* exhibition in the History Museum in Beijing. Despite the fact that Yu Hong's oeuvre and career are arguably at least as interesting as Liu's, the work is not filmed.[20] This is a first indicator that the narrative will prioritize Liu as artist, and Yu as female counterpart. The second is a motif of sight, and mirroring, in the film that seems to make conscious reference to psychoanalytic theory, while working the narration through the paradigmatic gender structure that such theory describes.

The opening sequence of the film shows Liu alone in his studio/apartment, still working on a large portrait of a woman. The woman is Yu. She is portrayed standing at the Great Wall, facing the viewer, but with her eyes hidden behind binoculars as she scans the landscape beyond the border. In the final scene, Yu has departed for the United States. Liu has a breakdown as he tries to survive alone. He does endless push-ups, dresses himself in a Mao suit, and finally rampages through the school breaking mirrors. In the last moments of the film, he puts on his spectacles and peers in the—as yet unbroken—mirror. Where has he gone? We, the spectators, see his reflection, his imaginary self. But what does Liu himself see? Behind him there is still the unfinished portrait of Yu, eyes blinded by the binoculars. This canvas frames him and imprisons him. It is a reminder of his imaginary anatomy, the body of Yu. This sequence is peculiarly reminiscent of the Lacanian notion of the mirror stage, and the splitting of the adult subject. The loss of the *complementary* anatomy, which is perhaps an inflection of Grosz's language through Chinese medical discourse, is visualized through psychic blinding in front of the mirror. The film admits to the permanent infantilism of the single male. When Yu terminated their relationship, and left for the United States, Liu lost his access to his subjective coherence, to the present, the past, and the future. A male voice-over informs us that at the psychiatric hospital a doctor had opined that there was nothing to worry about, Liu was suffering from personality, and half the population had the same problem.

Perhaps, his condition could be diagnosed as disembodiment. He looks into the mirror for the imaginary anatomy, the wholeness that will reassure him of his symbolic articulation. He sees nothing. He clothes himself in a mnemonic of the past, the Mao suit, but even with his specs on and peering hard, he seems confused. The fixed image of Yu on the canvas behind him is now out of shot. Her absence is a reminder that his access to the contemporary, to sanity, has emigrated.

In scenes like this, male anxiety is displaced. It is articulated in the text as a loss of control over 'his' female body. This is significant in terms of the loss of agency for female characters, who are allowed neither corporeal autonomy, nor the illusion of an ideal projection of their experience. It also presents a depressing account of young Chinese urban masculinity. The depths of alienation, wherein the male subject cannot account for his own anatomy either in imaginary or in symbolic terms, is extraordinary. Although the strategy of displacement, which operates within the symbolic world of the text, is an exercise in male power over female corporeality, it is also an admission of incoherence. In these films, without the female body as a symbolic mode of articulation, the male cannot speak. The unrepresentable core—the place of anxiety—is present in this symbolic world of the text, but it is distanced from the ideal image of the male and transposed to the vehicle of anxiety, the female.[21] The male characters play out the ideal version of their unease, while the female characters bear its narrative brunt. Male anxiety, which is arguably one of the causes of male alienation, is visible only through the suffering of women.

A MUTUAL CONSTITUTION

The neglect of female subjectivity—or rather, female psychic coherence—is particularly noticeable when the female *body* is so important to the plots. In both *Beijing Bastards* and *The Days* there is a sequence concerning an abortion. In neither film is this operation presented as an experience belonging to the woman in question. The abortion sequence serves as a metaphor for other deaths, as a catalyst for narrative development, and crucially, as a narrational device for disguising the empty anarchy of male subjectivity. The association between *his* imaginary anatomy and *her* image, a conundrum of dependency and denial, reveals a fast bond between the two bodies. In *The Days* the major narrative leap comes when Liu and Yu return home to his parents. This is occasioned by her abortion, and their futile attempt to have a vacation to refresh their relationship. The main problem with the question of the abortion is the way in which it is used for the progression of *his* story and not as a factor in the development of *hers*.

At the beginning of *Beijing Bastards* Kazi has a good head of hair; by the end it has been shaved off. The last image of the film is a still of the shaven Kazi walking along a crowded street, after two conflicting fantasies, one in which Maomao has a termination, and one in which he has heard his baby cry. His shaven head has meanwhile been explained by another character as just something he does from time to time, or it could indicate that he has spent time in prison, but in the context of his narrative, he seems to be trying to look like a baby. Maomao's disappearance and apparent preoccupation with the fetus undermines Kazi's image of himself as central player in his own narrative. He admits to the camera that he would rather his girlfriend were dead than that she should disappear without needing to tell him her movements. The cinematic effect of his fantasies of control over Maomao's body is a confusion of the fate of the fetus, the distressed narrative of its mother, and his own aimless confrontation with life.

The abortion sequence begins with a close-ups of doctor's hands pulling on white gloves, of surgical instruments, and finally a shot of Maomao—her legs up and splayed and the back of her head towards the camera. The emphasis, however, stays on Kazi. He is shown pacing down a corridor, a full body shot. He reaches an open window and gazes, troubled, out over the city. At the window Kazi's perspective is shared by the spectator in a lingering point of view shot. Again intercut with Cui Jian's rehearsal and performance, Kazi's thoughts are intimated by Cui Jian's lyrics—"The pain of this city goes on, but gives me hope for a better tomorrow." Both men are shown in medium close-up, eyes to the camera.

Maomao is also shot once in medium close-up. She is lying on the hospital bed. Cui Jian's voice continues on the sound track. Her eyes are averted from the camera and she bites her lip in anticipation of the operation. The next shot—and final appearance—of Maomao's face is in the corridor where Kazi 'finds' her, and hears a baby cry. Their conversation is brief, and as with the opening scene of the film, the framing gives no real clues to their relationship. The only disruption is at the sound of the child. Maomao keeps her eyes on Kazi as he looks sharply around. The scene is inconclusive. It is impossible to say whether the meeting is another fantasy or not. What is clear is that the filmmaker constructs the scene around Kazi's reaction to the possibility of the child's birth, rather than to the state of either Maomao or the baby itself. In a final freeze shot, Kazi's hairless incorporation of this possibility reiterates the profound disregard for anything but the female reproductive capacity in this narrative strand.

In these radical films of the 1990s the female body, exemplified in its (thwarted) reproductive mode, is used more or less graphically in the narration to direct the development of a male-centered narrative. This is obviously prioritized over the woman's own story in both cases. In *Beijing Bastards*, the woman is hardly seen except in the fantasy scenarios of the young man. She is not heard except in two brief conversations with him at either end of the film. By choosing to abandon him as her central point of identification she has 'disappeared' from the screen. He meanwhile speaks directly to the camera as well as being involved in other narrative strands, implying a multiplicity of points of identification. He also of course holds narrational control over her reappearance on screen, which implies a control over her body. In *The Days*, the suffering of the woman is narrated as catalyst, a device for a descent into madness of the man. Even her image is also in his control. He does not finish painting her, but he blinds her image before abandoning the work. These very facts however are indicators of his own dependency on her anatomy for his own subjective completion. In different ways both Yu and Liu remain unfinished. The male ego does not speak through its own sex in these films. It needs a mirror image that seems discrete—female—in order to articulate its bewilderment with contemporary experience, without betraying its panic. The performance of masculinity on screen is belied by a narrative and a narration that produce the male as feminine.

So far in this analysis I have dwelt on Liu, Kazi, and Cui Jian, with references to Yu Hong and Maomao. I want to elaborate this argument by picking up on an economic and political reading of construction of gender in 1990s China. Hill Gates's description of the 'mutual constitution' of the sexes in China (and arguably everywhere else) forms part of her work on economic interdependency in town and village enterprises.[22] That does not mean that there is a conscious and positive equivalence between the sexes in China. On the contrary, research suggests that the representation of women in China, as in many societies, continues to subordinate their cultural presence to the interests and priorities of masculinity.[23] This subordination has nevertheless figured the constitution of the female subject as fundamental to that of the male. The woman's physicality supports his subjective inadequacy in the post-Maoist era of the market and modernization. The body of the woman not only obscures an engagement with any other dimension of her subjectivity but is substituted for it. When this focus is juxtaposed with the central narrative focus on the spiritual and intellectual traumas of the alienated contemporary male, the "mutual constitution" appears as a representational strategy of his survival. This mutuality is unhappy and destructive.

A third line of inquiry is historical and genre specific. Despite their radical edge, independent filmmakers of the 1990s are working within the same representational constraints as their predecessors. Thinking of the contemporary as a *symptom* of the present produces recognition of unexpected forms of publicity and civility in the symbolic narration of these formations. Post-socialist heroisms rise out of the politics of translation rather than transformation.

REVOLUTIONARY HEROISM AND CONTEMPORARY UNEASE

In revolutionary genres the woman is represented as an accessory to male success—that is itself a metaphor for the Party and the Revolution.[24] *He* leads the struggle and *she* is his acolyte. She is also the point of identification through which the spectator may observe *his* achievements. In *The Red Detachment of Women* (1961), despite the apparently female-centered narrative, the film is constructed around the agency of the male hero. *He* sets *her* free in the first place, and for the rest of the film *his* presence is *her* guarantee against a return to slavery. His supremacy, clearly narrativized in the plot, is underscored by a number of shots in which she literally *gazes up* at him. His death in the final battle ends her dependence on him but also precludes any sexual relationship that would fatally impair her relationship to the paternity of the Party itself. His surrogacy over, the hero may not survive to create a more equal relationship with his successful pupil.

The White-haired Girl follows a similar pattern. The very different representations in the film, of the heroine's and hero's (Xi'er's fiancé) flight from pre–Liberation slavery, is highly suggestive of patterns of "symbolic anatomy" and "mutual constitution." While her escape might be seen as a visual articulation of the horrors of pre–Liberation China, his escape is already evocative of the bright promises of a new future. The two escape sequences are mutual in that both are necessary to convey, visually, the rhetoric of revolution. Xi'er's escape from the landlord is framed in darkness, the only lights on screen are lanterns carried by her pursuers. The darkness of the sequence is mitigated a little by the intercut shots of the night sky and a crescent moon. This links her journey up the mountain to the earlier sequence of Dachun's escape when the sky is similarly intercut, but the space of which is eventually occupied by the fluttering flag of the hammer and sickle. Dachun ascends a mountain in full light, accompanied by a choir of nondiegetic female voices. He is greeted at the summit by brothers in arms, members of the revolutionary forces. The three male bodies move together, there is a dissolve to the red flag (a nondiegetic image as neither of the soldiers is carrying it in the establishing shot), and another dissolve to a medium close-up of one of the soldiers' faces. In a way very similar to the opening of *Beijing Bastards*, the link between a central male character, a legitimate hero, and the overarching narrative of the film is made quite explicit. Once more male agency is linked to that of the Party project, with all the power and optimism which that entails.

So there are continuities between revolutionary genres and the independent postrevolutionary, or 'sixth generation', films. The major discontinuity is that the earlier films are tied to an optimistic and closed view of the future while the recent films express fear of the present and consequently disavow the future. The central theme of revolutionary films is optimism embodied in representatives of the Party. The constitution of the male subject through the suffering and/or dependency of the female serves the interests of a gendered constitution of revolutionary success. In *Beijing Bastards* and *The Days* the main theme is alienation, or less dramatically, uneasy survival in the face of continuous disappointment. The representation of the woman is the means by which male inadequacy (Kazi's peripheral relationship to the Beijing bohemian scene, Liu's struggles on public telephones to reach the international art market) is represented as interesting rather than catastrophic. However, even in this central thematic divergence the strategy seems similar. The constitution of the male subject—and particularly the *narration* of that subjectivity—is not simply dependent on the female. It is female itself.

VICARIOUS MORALITY

> Female suicide is shown to be evidently related to male anxiety through a psychological mechanism of vicarious morality.[25]

The circulation of the ideas, images, and of the social and political imaginaries, with which and within which these films resonate, is limited. Both *Beijing Bastards* and *The Days* deal with the bohemian elite of Beijing. The films were made by directors, Zhang Yuan and Wang Xiaoshuai, who have emerged, in the late-1980s and early 1990s, as major independent filmmakers in China. Their work is not widely distributed and does not benefit from state studio subsidy. They are perhaps as well known on the Western art house cinema circuit as they are to the movie-going audiences in the People's Republic. Nevertheless, the gender implications of the films' narration suggest that their relationship to mainstream, or politically acceptable, films in China and elsewhere is closer than the Channel Four link man would have us believe.

In counterpoint to my discussion of the transnational association between rock and radical chic I would just add a referent internal to Chinese cultural memory. In this chapter I have made claims on the imaginary. This psychoanalytic term refers to the realm of articulation in social life: language, culture, and mimetic practice. I am arguing throughout that the contemporary imaginary is tied to the moment of experience, and that that moment may be reconstructed in a transnational publicness, which deepens regressive structures in the text. This moment of reception occurs in a space that I describe as the contemporary. The following account of Tien Ju-k'ang's work on female suicide in the Ming Dynasty (1368-1644) should make it clear, however, that cultural resonance may be present in the contemporary, which is not constrained by the demands of chronology.

Tian's conclusions are startlingly apposite to the present discussion and at least support my claim that historical contingencies are better understood within a complex association of continuities and revisions than as contributing to distinct cultural breaks.

The author argues that the explanation for a sharp rise in female suicides following the death of their spouse or fiancé was not—as was traditionally presumed—due to an excess of Confucian female virtue, but rather was attributable to the needs of men at periods of instability to have access to virtue, without actually behaving virtuously themselves. Women's suicides were allowed to happen because it made the male survivors feel better. Furthermore, this access had to be guaranteed by an inscription of male power onto the female body. A woman could reclaim her own virtue but not if her body had died in its construction. T'ien notes that many suicides were by starvation, which he understands as a cry for help, "a fantasy of rescue."[26] The death is slow, painful, and *stoppable* if anyone would care to offer the woman a virtuous alternative (he suggests that care for in-laws and ancestor worship would both have fallen within the scope of virtue). The fact that this call was not answered seems to indicate that virtue was not enough. Male anxiety could be placated only by absolute control over a body, which was not their own, but which became their own through its suffering and subordination.

The choice of starvation might also be understood in the light of Western experiences of anorexia, which Grosz reminds us is the modern corporeal disturbance of the incoherent female subject. In this phenomenon the woman starves herself in order to assert a fantasy of *control* over her own body. In the Western case it is an image of womanhood as a sexualized child's body masquerading as youthful beauty that is at stake; in the case of the late Ming widow it is virtue. In both cases the stake is determined by male-oriented social and sexual interest.

This analogy does not lend itself neatly to T'ian's theory of starvation as a cry for help. It does however suggest that the fantasy of control in the female is overridden by the actual effects of the controlling images of female sociability—vulnerable childish 'beauty'/vulnerable devoted 'virtue'—images that may be characterized as a feature of the dominant male imaginary in both societies. The common thread—vulnerability—is accounted for in T'ian's perceptive link to male anxiety, and the need for the female—the figurative woman—to be controlled, and even destroyed, to assuage and obscure that anxiety.

In these films about rock, the woman does not dance—she suffers. The man suffers too but he does not know it: he is too busy dancing. The spectators can both dance and know, and in fact are required to do both by the text, which needs their recognition to bestow its status as contemporary and radical. Yet this knowledge is submerged by the dancing and the spectator comes out as complicit. The subjectivity of the female is reduced to a physicality based on her reproductive capacity and the reduction is compounded by a strategy of representation by absorption. The female subject emerges in moments of the text only to disappear into the narration of the male subject's story. It is doubly disappointing that this strategy of presenting a split subject disguised by a gendered discourse of identity seems to translate so easily from one spectatorial group to another. *Beijing Bastards,* the radical film 'banned' by the Chinese Authorities, is shown on Channel Four. *The Days,* 'No.100 of the best films ever', is shown on BBC 2. These are deserved epithets or accolades, and timely screenings, but they also point to transnational continuities of the violent constructions of gender in our cultural imaginar(ies).

7

Urban Spaces and Alternative Publics

A HOUSE IS A CHICKEN, A TELEVISION IS AN EGG

As a film like *Wild Mountains* illustrates, the demands of urban living do not always sit well with country values. When the two systems are thrown together, or rather, when a character like Hehe tries to operate in both systems at once, the relativity of 'virtue' becomes painfully clear. The life of an urban worker does not suit the responsibilities of a rural peasant farmer with a young family. It is a narrative that repeats itself in various guises throughout 1980s' and 1990s' film in China. The relevance to contemporary life is easily grasped. China has been going through a fast-paced process of urbanization that will see the (official) urban population rise to 34.49 percent in the year 2000, from 17.25 percent in 1975. The relation of this process to an ideological downgrading of the peasantry in favor of socialist-capitalism and national entrepreneurship produces the kind of traumas that are played out in these films. In *Ermo* (1994) the trauma is physically realized as a television. This object of signification moves the lead female character, Ermo, to sacrifice first her health—and finally her ability to work, her living space, and her self-esteem. For Ermo, the sign of virtue is financial success, and the sign of success is a television, the biggest available in the local county town. In order to purchase it, she commutes to the town to sell her twisted noodles at a higher price, to off-load a quantity of baskets that she has made for a local fruit crop that failed, and eventually, to sell her blood. In the course of her moneymaking, she has an affair with her neighbor, which ends when she discovers he has had other affairs with 'city women'. Ermo buys her television, and the whole village crowds into her one-room house to watch it. The television is perched on the bed, her noodle sieve is turned into an aerial, and the family home becomes a communal meetinghouse. The television brings a lot of prestige to Ermo's husband, but at the expense of a place to sleep.

All narratives require filmic spaces in which to unfold. These spaces may also have a function as a *place* with status additional to the running of the plot. It may be mythological, historical, spectacular, or—as in the urban-rural films—social-realist. Although *Ermo* and *Wild Mountains* do not deal with the wide open spaces of a powerful and mythologically charged landscape as in *Yellow Earth*, their attention to social-realist topics requires the legitimation of topographical detail. The narrative of *Ermo* is filmed in a series of claustrophobic places, which lend the space of the narrative a sense of desperation and inevitability. Much of the action is filmed in tightly framed interior sequences: the village home, the boardinghouse, the hotel room where the sexual liaison is consummated, and the kitchen where Ermo earns extra money. External shots are similarly framed to stifle any illusion of urban freedom. Ermo's 'spot' on the sidewalk, where she sells her noodles, and the cab of the truck that she shares with her lover on the way to town are crowded with the competition of other vendors, and lust. The exception to this is the first shot of the television shop. The shot is in deep focus, with the foreground crowded with people watching the television, which is offscreen. Ermo enters the shop in a tilted shot that emphasizes her singularity and her exceptionally determined relationship with the television. As she moves forward and pushes to the front of the impromptu audience, the shot tightens around her and then cuts to the object of her attention—a huge television set. The space of this sequence is shown to be shared (public) but also intensely private. The moment encapsulates the intensity of Ermo's privacy. Despite 'seeing' her relationships with her husband, son, neighbor, and lover in some detail, it becomes clear in the intimacy of the shot exchange with the television that Ermo is committed only to visions of something different from the present she inhabits. Her story is concluded with a slow pan between herself crumpled in the corner of her one-room house with her husband and son and the new, huge, television broadcasting its urban irrelevancies from the pride of place on the family bed. The shot rests on the television screen as the transmitter closes down into static. The switch to meaningless buzz is an appropriate coda to the self-generating follies of Ermo's journey into urban modernity. Earlier in the film, her husband's insistence that they build a new house rather than purchase a 'window on the world' may have seemed a regressive reliance on old-style certainty. At the close, as the 'window' fuzzes up with white lines, and the family snatches an uncomfortable sleep, we realize that maybe he has a good idea of the infrastructure of life in rural China, and what it may or may not withstand. A house is a chicken, and a television is an egg.

The affective power of the city is not a new theme in Chinese or international cinema and literature. The transnational cliché of a feminized, erotic city is familiar from *Sunrise* (1927, U.S. Fox) to *Wild Flower* (1930). In such films the negotiation between sex and urbanity, and nature and virtue, assumes that the city produces evil (adulterers, uncommitted relationships, and so on) but can be reimagined in rural terms. So, a woman's love in *Sunrise* turns the city into a double-exposed pleasure garden, while a young woman's voice in *Wild Flower* allows the image of the flower to be slipped into representations of city life. These strategies make the city innocent in 'rural' terms. In recent Chinese films on the urban-rural negotiation the plot is organized around the presumption that virtue is not easily transferable from one setting to the other. The superimpositions of the 1920s' filmmakers give the impression that anything can be dreamed into anything else. Filmmakers of the 1980s largely resist that temptation and deal instead with the subjective impossibility of transition for their characters in rural and urban China.

Any attempt to cross the boundaries is painful for the characters concerned. There is always a price to pay, in the short or long term, for wanting to live in two worlds. It is a price determined according to the strategic importance of normative virtue in social, political, or civil organization. In rural/urban confrontations the individual tends to lose personal integrity—conceived of in rural terms, in order to gain material benefits—as determined in urban value systems. The films can picture this rather literally, the journey from village to town is an important trope in *Wild Mountains* and *Ermo*, as it exemplifies the passage from one civil space to another. The journey is in both cases associated with adulterous sexual encounters, and the physical dangers of motorized travel. The objects that come back from the city are immensely significant as markers of an individual's movement from one civil sphere to another. The object—a television or a new generator—affects the entire village, but particularly the person/people who have brought it back with them. They are changed forever, and occupy an unstable position between virtue and its alternatives.

In purely urban films, there is a similar emphasis on renegotiated civility. Crime dramas, hooligan comedies, and apartment block soaps are all concerned with the question of what it means to be civil in urban China, now. The 'hooligan' (*liumang*) stories, particularly those based on the immensely popular, and populist writer Wang Shuo's novellas, suggest that it is sometimes necessary for an oppositional public sphere to work within a nonvirtuous, or differently civil, framework. The necessity is framed in the narrative as a fantasy of 'real life', but also as a demand made on the spectator in the act of watching the film. These characters in these situations live close to the margins of the law, but their relationships are based on discrete civilities, and their actions evaluated according to different criteria. To participate in the fantasy structure of the film, the spectator must accept these differences, and take her/his pleasures within an alternative public space. It is necessary for the spectator to engage in a process of translation in order to recognize a coherence and a civility in the virtue of the unvirtuous.

In a discussion of the varying domestic and international reception of recent high-profile Chinese films, Rey Chow writes that translation should always involve two languages working on a level of shared priority. She defends the director Zhang Yimou against charges of Orientalism, suggesting that the translated culture will inevitably be disquieted by the translation. The act of translation and the eye of reception must produce differences and thus work against the claim of ethnography to represent the unchanging truth of another culture. Chow uses Walter Benjamin's arcades projects as a visual metaphor and argues for the process of translation—walking through the arcade from one thoroughfare to the next—itself as a bearer of meaning, particularly of accessible popular meaning. "Transmissibility is that aspect of the work that, unlike the weight of philosophical depth and interiority, is literal, transparent, and thus capable of offering itself to a popular or naive *handling*. What is transmissible is that which, *in addition to* having meaning or 'sense', is accessible."[1]

In the following discussion, it is not the popular versus the esoteric, nor the popular as opposed to the chains of ethnographic authenticity, which is foregrounded, but the popular as the *space of experience*, which is not necessarily representative of normative and approved patterns of virtuous society. Geremie Barmé has quoted the literary critic Wang Zheng who notes the connections between modern street life, the friends (*gemenr*) of Wang Shuo's hooligan fictions, and the anarchists of the bamboo groves and scholarly enclaves of myth and premodern historical romance.[2] To extend Chow's analogy, I would say that Wang Shuo's work is an arcade that traverses time from prehistory to a romance of criminality and modern urban survival. Barmé's article has explored the ways in which Wang Shuo's narratives allow the reader to inhabit the "landscape of Chinese cultural upheaval." The popularity of the texts reveals a general unease at the growth of *liumang* mentality in daily life. "Acting as though one's workplace is a piece of turf in some mafia network, doing what you please, and ignoring all laws and principles are all part of the *liumang* mentality."[3] The popular strength of Wang's narratives lies in his willingness to ignore the rather dull facts of corruption, and to concentrate on extremes. His characters are outsiders, excepted from virtuous society, who are yet witty and interesting enough to engage the more mundanely disaffected reader-citizen.

The protagonist of *Black Snow* (1989) is also an outsider. The film is concerned with his perspective, which combines criminality and a naive, youthful alienation. Li Huiquan (Quanzi) is recently out of prison, and the first shot is a track of his journey home, down through the narrow alleys (*hutong*) of his childhood, to an empty house and the ministrations of neighbors. Claustrophobic nostalgia is conveyed in this first image. The camera follows him relentlessly along the path of the alley and into his dark house, until he stops in front of a photograph of his dead mother. It never relaxes its close crop of the large man, in a small space. He is represented to us as a child who has outgrown his childhood spaces, but who cannot escape their demands on his identity. The film explores the degree to which friendship, the private self, and the public operator are mutually dependent definitions of social and political visibility.

On the one hand *Black Snow* presents depressed, social alienation. On the other it suggests a lively, if not always happy, salubrious, or virtuous public space that seems to run parallel to the social organization of official China. The legitimate and autonomous, and therefore spontaneous, organization in the public sphere that characterizes western liberal notions of civil society is not an adequate measure in this context. As Victor Falkenheim has noted "the mechanisms provided by the state to accommodate or channel citizen interests . . . are almost universally seen as preempting rather than facilitating autonomous interest articulation."[4] The spontaneous groupings based on mutual interest that are explored in this film are often illegitimate. Yet, given that the plotting depends on a notion of relationship and dependency, the state and officialdom must also be assumed to be effectively present. This narrative explores spaces in the supposedly closed, virtual circles of state and society in China. It discovers the narrow alleyway, and the messy intimacy of small apartments and houses built on top of one another. The State, in the person of a neighborhood policeman, is seen in these locations as well as in the police station. He is present in and across both the public and the private that are, finally, rather difficult to disarticulate (figure 7.1). The camerawork emphasizes the suffocation of private life, but then describes a sense of loss in the largeness of public parks and modern hotels. There is always too much space, or too little. One way in which this is accentuated in the plot is through the exploitation of the concept of social links, *guanxi*.[5] Quanzi is linked to his past and present in ways that are not always helpful, and that do not coun-

Figure 7.1   Black Snow

teract his great loneliness. The relevance of *guanxi* extends from the ordinary connections of kinship, through the loyalties of friendship and shared locality (figure 7.2), to the corruption of the modern state by habits of informal politics. Ambrose Yeo-chi King has described *guanxi* as a web of personal relationships from which, once entered, it is impossible to free oneself. People use *guanxi* as a basis for business favors, and as a general networking system across a wide range of social relations. King cites "locality (native place), kinship, coworker, classmate, sworn brotherhood, surname, and teacher student." He also points out that the demands of *guanxi* are very great and that some people will actively avoid personal links for this reason, although some association is inevitable in order to survive in the Chinese life system.[6]

The centrality of *guanxi* as a distinctive characteristic of Chinese life—or life for those who claim Chineseness as their principal point of identification—has been questioned by Andrew Nathan. He cites positivistic research that does not find a marked difference between Chinese networking and the practices of other people, "other than to say that the Chinese on the average have somewhat larger *guanxi* networks."[7] He does, however, admit that sociological research should not be allowed to immediately override hermeneutic insight. Nathan's general point is that social characteristics are a partial and unsatisfactory—easily racist or supremacist—way of delineating the identity of ethnicity. Nonetheless difference is manifested in imaginative tropes and structures of the symbolic, and is apparent in the way in which a culture communicates to and beyond itself. The concept of *guanxi* offers an effective symbolic model of practices that are notable and current in China.

Figure 7.2　Black Snow

Research into networking in local business transactions in southwest China indicates that the Chinese Communist Party officials use gifts to pull *guanxi* and to establish commercial links.[8] Nancy N. Chen's work on unofficial forms of civil society, semi- and fully autonomous activity in the public sphere, refers to the political capital of *qigong* masters who are accompanied by "lineages and networks of followers to reveal accumulation of . . . *guanxi*."[9] Andrew Kipnis has researched peasant ritual in the late-1980s in Fengjia and finds that the *ketou* (a deep kneeling bow used to acknowledge a relationship of respect although not necessarily subservience) had lost some of its meaning in relation to the worship of ancestors but had gained significance in the creation and maintenance of contemporary *guanxi*. Kipnis's analysis of respect (*jingyi*) suggests that ritualized feelings and the adherence to *guanxi* pose a real threat to Party loyalty and ideological clarity: "respect implies a concrete relationship, and the expansion of it in *ketou* helps constitute that relationship. The Chinese Communist Party's (CCP) ban on landlord *ketou* at poor peasants' funerals was an attempt to prevent the formation of cross-class relationships."[10]

Guanxi has in the past been declared a conceptual enemy of the revolution, but the anarchy caused by partial attempts to disfigure its structure further revealed its centrality to the cohesion of both state and society. The CCP may have intended to establish the Party as the single focus of private and public loyalty, and indeed to further erase the distinction between the two. In practice it reinforces habits of local, individualistic identification and the promotion of interests of those able to *la* (pull) *guanxi* over those who cannot. In his study of village leaders Duan concludes:

> Short term prospects for political democratiziation in the village . . . [depend on] an institutional realignment of the bonding between state and civil society whereby village leaders would not be required to act primarily as middlemen between government and village people and would be barred from access to and use of community-owned economic resources for political purposes.[11]

Party workers undermined the notion of central loyalty by their own methods of control and accumulation while the Party project of unassailable legitimacy simultaneously reinforced the notion of normative virtue in state and society. Arguably this conundrum produces reliance on personal links and family ties. It also defines the areas of traditional and post-1949 virtue that are mutually valid in defining the limits and requirements of these ties. With so little room for moral maneuver the need for the security of personal connections becomes very great. In *Black Snow*, *guanxi* is evident in the relations between characters, between characters and virtuous society, and between characters and the State. It is also visible in the topography of urban life, in the claustrophobia of residential streets, and in the insistent power of public spaces. The idea of *guanxi* can also work as an arcade, a visual metaphor that helps in imagining the transmittable secrets of cinematic space and time. And the relationship between experience and narration is itself an important indicator of the nature of contemporary life.

GIVE RISE TO EVENTS THROUGH WRITING

Andrew Plaks's work on Chinese narrative is a useful precedent in thinking about film and event.[12] He shows that Chinese narrative prioritizes history to such a degree that even the obviously fictional becomes history in the telling:

> Because both history and fiction are engaged in the mimesis of action, it is often difficult to draw the line neatly between the two. This is particularly true when one notes that in traditional China it is frequently the same group of literati who have indulged in both official historiography and more fictional (or at least less historical) forms of narrative.[13]

It is not a new idea but it does not hurt to rediscover it in different cultural and discursive configurations. Plaks's analysis uses older examples of historiographical writings and fiction but its conclusions give a literary resonance to Michael Taussig's inquiry into mimesis and alterity. One of Taussig's conceptual tools is the idea of a *public secret*. This refers to the areas of shared experience that are lodged in the imaginary of a group or society, but which is not openly referred to, described, or acknowledged. It is symbolically invisible but it is that which makes the group, the society, or whatever point of identification is being used, recognizable to itself. The key to Taussig's "public secret" lies somewhere between the output of the imaginary and sociological fact, among ritual, mimesis, and the pragmatics of physical survival. Therefore the act of symbolically exposing the public secret, of making visible some truth of contemporary experience or shared memory, offers a radical challenge to the dominant status quo.[14] The relevance of Taussig's idea here is that the keeping, or the exposing, of a public secret is one of the effects of historiography, and throws light on the necessary relationship between fact and fiction, or between narrative and narration that Plaks identifies so astutely. Plaks's theory of Chinese narrative reminds us of the two-way street between the determination to historicize and the desire to tell a story, which is then validated by acquiring the status of history, or myth.

> In both the historical and fictional branches of the Chinese tradition, the final justification for the enterprise of narrative may be said to lie in the transmission of known facts . . . the necessary assumption of such transmission is that every given narrative is in some sense a faithful representation of what did, or what typically does, happen in human experience. . . . The sense that what is recorded is ultimately true— either true to fact or true to life . . . despite the obvious untruths of hyperbole, supernatural detail, or ideological distortion.[15]

In film, directors and audience discover truths about how and why they live. Some of these discoveries are intended for presentation by the filmmakers, others are not. Although not all films can be read against the grain, the elements of screen language may combine to exceed the scope of the filmmakers' agenda. Thus the crucial revelations of the public secret are not exactly "obvious," but they are both hidden and visible. Their power is in the oxymoron, in the peculiarities of content and the choices of narrational form, often in the "hyperbole, supernatural detail, and ideological distortion." Plaks is surprised when he finds "nonnarrative elements" in Chinese texts. These elements are characterized as stative or digressive, but most pertinently *unlike* western narration that tends towards the sequential narration of discrete events, a chronology heading towards the present. His account of a "characteristic tendency of traditional Chinese thought to posit complementary categories of interrelation," or "nondialectical duality" is a good description of narration that encourages the hiatuses and tensions of mimetic revelation. The status of Plaks's work in Chinese studies is partly due to the originality of his intervention, in particular his introduction of a non-Western view and practice of narration as an alternative normative mode. There have of course been non-Chinese examples of "nondialectical duality" and this is perhaps especially apparent in the development of film aesthetics. The director Robert Bresson struggles in a different philosophical tradition to describe it:

> To create is not to deform or invent persons and things. It is to tie new relationships between persons and things that are, and as they are.
> Your imagination will aim less at events than feelings, while wanting these latter to be as documentary as possible.[16]

Bresson's "documentary" feeling is an evocative description of affective filmic disruption. It suggests the negotiation between ritual and necessity that is the stuff of mimetics and the raw material of social norms. The relationship between the storyteller and the story is intense and symbiotic. The narrative is a document but the narration must take into account the origin and the reception of the document, the possibilities of feeling that it carries through the arcade, or arcades, of translation. There is more in the text than meets the eye, but the elements that *are* seen, that are in Chow's words available for "naive handling" are the moments of successful translation that have historical, political, and contemporary significance.

Guanxi is emotionally, socially, and politically translatable via arcades of virtue that are defined by the interests of a particular set of human networks. As a preliminary concept it helps the spectator focus on relationships within the story and plotline and to reflect on character as defined by a narrative of association. In *Black Snow*, *guanxi* thus defines the organization of narrative space within the frame. Quanzi's relationships with society—whether friendly or ambiguous—are in medium shot and spatial dominance is given to his interlocutors rather than to

Quanzi himself, who hovers at the edge of the frame. Shots of Quanzi alone switch the focus to *place*. He is often in semidarkness, in his home, clubs, or in the park. These spaces may be understood as the film's alternative protagonists. Their common element is the presence of Quanzi, who becomes a plot device linking up different parts of urban life in the late 1980s. Normative virtues do not take precedence here, and this anarchy, or democracy, of experience is such that no particular time or place is established. Each new location deserves its own establishing shot, defined by Quanzi walking through the space. Modes of time, modernity, postmodernity, revolution, and tradition are marked as coterminous but incommensurate.

Quanzi does not understand this. He maintains too many emotional connections with an inappropriate past. His initial romantic interest is removed from him by the workings of class and professional prestige. This childhood sweetheart, the memory of whom plays in his mind with the brightness of a children's movie, marries a doctor. His other most poignant relationship is also his most miserable—that with his fellow criminal and childhood companion Chazi. He displays the virtues of friendship in a situation that undermines his return to civility and normative virtue. He finds work, as a (licensed) market trader, but that brings him into contact with Cui Yongli, a very shady wholesaler, theatrical pimp, and dealer in see-through underwear and pirated blue movies (*huangse*). In a local nightclub Cui introduces him to a young female singer who needs someone to walk her home at night and protect her from street hooligans. Walking through the city backstreets, wheeling his bicycle and listening to her optimistic chattering, he begins to fall in love. But love is not the point. His passion for the young nightclub singer is unrequited. He watches her move into a semiprostituted relationship with her manager in a world of hotel bars. This is her success.

In the final scene of the film the protagonist dies from a stab wound. He is in a strange city, heartbroken, and utterly friendless. He staggers through a public park where comic opera is playing to a crowd, and where lovers and young muggers are working the avenues. The audience is judgmental when Quanzi laughs at the wrong joke. The entertainment's pastiche of the shift from operatic moves to disco dancing has already shown us that the real joke is on postmodernity and those who, like Quanzi, do not know to keep follies of different modes discrete and discreet. When the crowd disperses, the hero dies a victim of random urban violence. His death is an ordinary tragedy of modernity but he is himself caught on a cusp of postmodern rage. Quanzi's premodern romantic sensibility, refined in a childhood of revolutionary prudery, is frustrated by the rhetoric of modern market pragmatism.

Quanzi's dreams of romance originate in his private secret, a vision of three young pioneers playing on a railway line, his memories. As he travels back into society, he cannot find this childish goodness, or the romantic hopes that it signifies. What he remembered as a cohesive society is predicated on a public secret, a common disavowal of the vacuum of contemporary time. The immediate past has been unravelled in the debunking of the Cultural Revolution. The integrity of the mythic revolutionary period is shaken by the processes of reform, and the uneasy relationship it creates with the memory of Maoism and revolutionary heritage. With no historical certainty, and a marketized future that has lost the promise of perfectibility, the present is a moment of impossible fluidity. The contemporary must be survived rather than articulated. In his attempt to make sense of life and bring his past and present together to establish a basis for future happiness Quanzi stumbles disastrously on this nexus of incoherence.

Reality and fantasy are mutually sustaining in human societies, and public secrets are the strategies by which human societies move across spectrums of necessity and experience. Sudden breaks are dangerous, literally *wounding*, to society. If the contingencies of everyday life are confusing or contradictory, then most people pretend that they are not. They have no collective option. Change is perhaps the most inescapable feature of modernity, and one that must be constantly appropriated within existing discourses and structures of power and social organization. If, as in Communist China in the 1980s, political models of behavior are undermined by current economic priorities, the population has to 'think' in more than one time. They must be modern, as socialists *and* as capitalists. The first entails belief in a future paradise; the second will only allow the pleasures of consumption, and unlimited progress. There is no capitalist heaven: it's all in the journey. It is an unspoken achievement, for to speak it is to admit the paradox and to pathologize the process. Quanzi is the symptom of this pathology in *Black Snow*.

The relationship between the criminal and the singer is narrated through the topography of the text—the back streets, the empty hotel, and the thoroughfare of southern development—and it is plotted through the social relations of both parties. The girl seems to like him, she thinks he is a good person, and is surprised and disbelieving when he tells her that he is actually "no good." When success begins to shape her as a performer into an older, more overtly sexual creature, red décolleté evening satins replacing the pink bobby socks, she laughs off his criticism as being "exactly something her father would say." She understands Quanzi better than he realizes. He is indeed an old-fashioned romantic version of *guanxi*, mindful of the *lun* (correct relationships) of a Confucian gentleman, complete with a touch of prudery, and corrupted by a dash of the young scholar: sacrificing his official prospects for love of the prostitute, or the fox maiden, the latter a common metaphor for the fickleness of female beauty. Fox maidens are demons in ravishing disguise.

As Roger Ames and David Hall make clear in their treatise on Confucianism, in the older traditions of thought the individual was responsible for his particular network. It was not simply a case of complying with the dominant virtue system in order to fit in to the comfortable security of social civility.

"There is a symbolic relationship between personal and communal realization: authoritative humanity and authoritative community are coextensive."[17] The highest virtue (*ren*—which could be translated as 'having become a person') is in the hands of the self (*zi*). It is impossible to achieve *ren* without interaction with others, but this does not mean that every individual does not stand at the center of a complete network that is peculiar to her/him, and through which s/he attains agency.[18] Conversely, the pursuit of ego-grounded interests is the unworthy concern of the retarded individual (*xiaoren*). Philosophically then the development of human relationships may ideally not be the repetitive restatement of a fixed social and political civility. It might just entail a journey towards a virtue that will be differently configured in every case. This offers a hopeful and even radical concept of personal and communal politics. Despite the weary story of urban lives that is narrated in contemporary film, this radical hope of the *xiaoren* is embedded in the texts as a public challenge to the hegemony of a state-led social normalcy.[19]

And where is love?

> The first moment in love is that I not wish to be a self-subsistent and independent person and that, if I were, then I would feel defective and incomplete.[20]

This quote is taken from Hegel's description of love, used by Partha Chatterjee to unravel the anomalies of the discourse of state and society that are fundamental to much political philosophy. Chatterjee argues that Hegel's rather beautiful formulation sits uncomfortably with the hierarchy of family power structures that provide the location for private, as opposed to public or political, life in Hegelian terms. Public order stems from a working relationship between state, civil society, and domestic privacy. In its ideal form, public order allows for the autonomy of the second, the modernity of the first, and the inviolability of the third. In fact, all three domains are compromised by the relationship, as it necessitates a shared virtue system. The power to determine the nature of the system will vary with circumstance. The myth of autonomy and personal freedom will be preserved as a legitimating element in a democratic discourse, whereas a rhetoric of social benefit and national honor is a likely component of the binding discourse of an authoritarian regime. Either way the disruptive factor of this otherwise orderly equation will be scrupulously ignored. For Chatterjee that disruption lies in the discourse and the experience of community. He suggests that in Hegel's words of love a "narrative of community is seeping through the interstices of the objectively constructed, contractually regulated structure of civil society."[21] Chatterjee claims that the narrative of community has long been suppressed in European social theory. The virtues of civil society bypass community values and structures of communicable behavior that could qualify as action. He traces this omission to the narratives of capitalism and colonialism. Community cannot be fitted into narratives that demand its destruction nor can it be satisfactorily converted into a recognizable format—nationalism—for that too is potentially injurious to global capital development. "It is not so much the state-civil society opposition but rather the capital-community opposition that seems to be the great unsurpassed contradiction in Western social philosophy."[22] Chatterjee notes that demands of communal difference will either subvert the ethical organization of the modern state, or will disappear into the recesses of invisibility. To return to Rey Chow's metaphor, there is an arcade that is lit by the logic of capital. The translations that occur to those who are hurrying, or who are hurried, through, are not necessarily commensurate with the unyielding optimism of those lights, and as they emerge into the full neon glare of the1990s, people will find their own ways and means—or communities—through which to survive the trauma.

> What, then, are the true categories of universal history? State and civil society? Public and private? Social regulation and individual rights?—all made significant within the grand narrative of capital as the history of freedom, modernity, and progress? Or the narrative of community—untheorized, relegated to the primordial zone of the natural, denied any subjectivity that is not domesticated to the require-ments of the modern state, and yet persistent in its invocation of the love and kin-ship against the homogenizing sway of the normalized individual?[23]

There are various reasons for turning to Chatterjee in this argument. First, his intervention in an argument over the supposed universality of the concept of civil society adds another dimension to the Chinese/European and American perspec-tives. Even where these perspectives note the difficulty of translating political concepts into the particularly inflexible context of the authoritarian state there is little sense that the aspects of virtue and civility may be detachable from the nodes of power.[24] Chatterjee's flexibility is a welcome echo of the breaks in political certainty that Claude Lefort puts forward. Lefort conceives of a psychoanalytic structure to the formation of political society. He writes of the empty space of power and authority that must never be actually filled nor actually seen to be empty if democratic equilibrium is to be maintained.

> But if we must talk of the discorporation of the individual, we must also analyze the disengagement of civil society from a state, itself consubstantial with the body of the king. [. . .] more specifically, we must examine the disentangling of the spheres of power, law, and knowledge that takes place when the identity of the body poli-tic disappears. The modern democratic revolution is best recognized in this muta-tion: there is no power linked to a body. Power appears as an empty place and those who exercise it as mere mortals occupy it only temporarily or could install them-selves in it only by force or cunning.[25]

In the "logic of totalitarianism" this place is filled by the person of the leader and the presence of the Party. Lefort argues that the logic is nonetheless related to the logic of democracy, or incipient democracy. Both result from the disin-corporation of power. In democracy the representative signals but cannot fully occupy the place of power that must also signify the space of freedom. In totali-tarianism incorporation is mimicked by the personality cult of the leader and the space of freedom is filled by the Party and its ideology of a perfected future visible through the organization of the present.[26] Andrew Nathan's account of the Gengshen reforms in the early 1980s, when 'democratic' elections were introduced within an 'administered society', indicates that the space for freedom was not an option. The number of candidates had to match the number of elective positions. More fundamentally perhaps the discourse of the election was decided by the prevailing wisdom of Party policy:

> The people could make constructive suggestions and expose particular corrupt officials, but they had no legitimate need to rise up against or oppose the leadership itself. As Shanghai Radio put it, democracy was like playing basketball: 'the contest should be held in a space confined by four lines'. These lines were Deng's 'four upholds': socialism, dictatorship of the proletariat, Marxism-Leninism/Mao Zedong Thought, and Party leadership. The last, Deng had said, was most important.[27]

This structure precludes the possibility of a divided present, as the socialist vision is of a future perfect that is inevitably unified but which is nonetheless enforceable in the throes of disunity. Thus civil society, which acknowledges interest groups that are not representable through the invisible center of the collective or Party project, is an impossible denial of the promised future-as-present. The danger of this is for the occupier of power. If the place of power is occupied and the space for freedom is closed, s/he experiences the panic of having no god, no past, and no uncertain future, nowhere in fact to place the image of his/her own ideal being. To compensate for this claustrophobia the leader and the figures of ideology become omnipresent in their attempt to verify and escape from their own unbearable presence.

Mao Zedong's definition of the locus of power was through a vision of the concentric circles of an onion. The layers of the onion were made up of the social classes of society but the center around which they were wrapped would be impossible to locate. Mao's four classes corresponded to the Soviet model—working class, peasants, petty bourgeoisie, and national 'exploitative' bourgeoisie in that order from the outside in. There was always a slight anomaly in the Chinese case however as the leadership of the proletariat was in an ambiguously symbiotic relationship with the peasant class. In his report on the 1927 peasant uprisings in Hunan, which was reprinted and widely circulated in the 1950s, Mao makes it very clear that the violent and exclusionary methods of the peasant committees were the correct way to destroy the power of the bourgeoisie. He is insistent that all political action must be subordinate to the committee that should have absolute and strong leadership. Elsewhere he declines to describe exactly how government will be structured other than that it must answer to the will of the people: "As for the question of the 'system of government' this is a matter of how political power is organized, the form in which one social class or another chooses to arrange its apparatus of political power to oppose its enemies and protect itself."[28]

Given that this is premised on his version of democracy as contained in a dictatorship, it seems that the will of the people is synonymous with the will and presence of the dictator. According to his own formulation of democratic dictatorship, he embodies the will of the people and yet has no space in a configuration of power that he has pressed into the public imaginary of itself. It is this claustrophobic mixture of absolute power and utter invisibility that leads to the evermore insistent projection of the dictator as a physical icon.[29] The image of the leader offers the dictator an escape from interiority. It is an ideal projection through which the people, but most importantly the dictator himself, can visualize memories of the past, belief in the present, and faith in a perfect future. "Egocrat coincides with himself, as society is supposed to coincide with itself . . . once the old organic constitution disappears, the death instinct is unleashed into the closed, uniform, and imaginary space of totalitarianism."[30]

Lefort's hermeneutics encourages a psychoanalytic visualization of politics that inspires confidence in Chatterjee's own argument of the communities of the interstices. Lefort escapes from the binary difference between democracy and totalitarianism through a psychoanalysis of the human condition that experiences and manufactures both systems. Chatterjee denies the polarity of the state and civil society by locating the point of denial that shores up this model. He refuses a Habermasian model of life-world and political-economic worlds. Based on a reading of modernity as the separation out of political, economic, and civil functions through institutionalization and the fragmentation of power, definitions such as these deny the experienced residuals of premodernity that still affect the meaning of the modern state and that are themselves affected by the material and economic conditions of modernity. [31] Chatterjee's politics of the interval enables us to see worlds within worlds, and spaces in cultural products that may be realist, spectacular, historical, *and* public. He allows a visualization of the structure of politics in the symbolic world of film.

Second, writers on the problems of locating civil society in the Chinese context have already quoted the exchange between Taylor and Chatterjee to good effect.[32] Wasserstrom and Liu, historians of the public sphere and of mass movements in modern China, emphasize Chatterjee's observation that civil society entails a hegemony of value that undermines many claims to its inherent beneficial relationship to the development of democracy. They show how the Tiananmen Square demonstrations of 1989, and the protest movement, can be better analyzed on more flexible terms. One interesting result of their approach is the revelation that student organization in April to June 1989 closely resembled the structure and dynamics of state organizations, and that even relationships between groups of students could be predicated on preexisting official relationships between their institutions or home provinces.[33] Third, Chatterjee's understanding of the modern state allows insights into the problems of any shift of organizing principles on a state level that entail changes to everyday life, but which can neither accommodate the traces of past behavior nor accept the survival techniques of newly emerging groups.

In *Beijing Bastards* male friendships dominate the narrative, echoing the unfortunate Quanzi's commitment to Chazi. In both films, the protagonists communicate their politics, their ideals, and their anger through the discourses of separated communities. They are singers, artists, roadies, and undecided bohemians, and they tend to waver around the fringes of the law. In Chatterjee's terms, the interstices of community, those that do not sit well with the demands of public order, are driven outside the discourse of morality and decency. The discourses that carry their voice (in *Beijing Bastards* it is Cui Jian's music) are criminalized. The response from the criminals and their sympathizers is to see virtuous society as artificial and to encourage a rhetoric of authenticity for the outsider.

The importance of rock music as an articulation of the political and social imagination of the protagonists is very apparent in *Beijing Bastards*. In one sequence two friends get very drunk and one picks a fight with another of their wider circle. The man he picks on is large, strong, lawless, and closer to a hooligan (*liumang*) than anyone else in either of the films. The less drunk of the two friends manages to break it up. As the night before becomes the morning after, they sit sore-headed in an empty street. Without Cui Jian's sound track their dissolute alienation reports itself as farce. Left to themselves they produce this conversation on the tram tracks, roughly translated as:

"Dickhead."
"You pissed on my head last night."
"Wimp."
"Not."
"Are."
"Race you then."

They then set off to race down the tram tracks to an unspecified finishing post. The camera remains stationary as they stumble away, one dropping his sweater as he goes. The race is going nowhere but it does have a curiously moving effect of reminding us—and them—of their friendship. The effect works from a sense that the sequence is absolutely 'authentic,' which here means unnarrated, or untranslated. The men in *Beijing Bastards* are sharing a contemporary narrative and they need Cui's songs to pull the humor into focus. The viewers, including those who are sharing that contemporaneity, need a translation.

The topography of the scenes maps out the complications of male friendships. There are many intimate scenes in private homes and in the passing public/privacy of the 'party' space. Yet there is also significant emphasis on public spaces where any form of publicity or presence may be a political utterance. In one long sequence, matched on the sound track to Cui's performance, the camera tracks around Tiananmen. The square itself is comparatively empty but the roadway is packed full of bicyclists, taxi drivers, and pedestrians.[34] At this moment, most of the population of Beijing seems to be an outsider. The scene creates a community of outsiders against the symbolic unity of the space of the square. It is a cinematic incorporation of the public secret, but it is neither indivisible nor fixed. The cathartic authenticity of rock music is only one way of touching the nerves of the public secret. The state can itself stumble on a communal interstice and cause an utterance of defiance where nothing was conscious before. Or a public event can become an occasion for a communal response that has not been anticipated. Wu Hung has described the earlier Tiananmen demonstrations that followed the death of Zhou Enlai in 1976. Those demonstrations were eventually broken up by violence. He quotes a mourner saying:

> When Premier Zhou died . . . many people were weeping—in the streets, on the buses . . . it was uplifting, really uplifting. There was a sense of relief. In the past, for so long in China, there had been no occasion when you could feel your feelings uplifted. . . . But with Zhou's death, you came to realize that your grief was their grief too. We were isolated before, but then people became close.[35]

Wu Hung's argument is that the articulating point was not the death itself but the People's Monument in the center of the square, where the demonstrators had been trapped and shot. As a monument to Liberation it had a previously unblemished relationship with the officially sanctioned past and present of the People's Republic. Now it had become an erection of Party hegemony. It was both a desecrated monument and a popular monument to the desecration wreaked by the authorities. The mourner still remembers that she was "uplifted," perhaps that she recognized herself as an insider outside the morality and decency that is to be seen but not spoken. In *Beijing Bastards* she may be riding inside one of those taxis, or getting soaking wet on a bicycle, outside the square. But her presence inside the square is a part of its continuing potency. It is a powerful symbol of the Party's grip on the morality of state and society. It is also the place where that virtual relationship may be shaken by the unforeseeable matching of contemporary community and the realignment of its own processes of organization in an assault on its virtue.

In *Beijing Bastards* the narrative strands are plotted in a "nondialectical" plurality. We are not sure if we are heading anywhere except perhaps for halfway down a tram track. Everyone is looking for something, a place to rehearse, a mislaid girlfriend, a place to be heard and not just seen. Yet despite this seeming aimlessness in the narrative there is a cohesion. Characters do not disappear. The girl who has been thrown out after a one-night stand reemerges in other scenes to discuss herself with other acquaintances. The concert takes place. The girlfriend is found, but not recovered. That consistency is achieved despite the roving episodic plotlines is indicative of a local loyalty to a specific group. This loyalty is such that the values and interests of the group are symbolically legitimated within the text. The film succeeds in making fragments of the contemporary stand out as history.

The civility of certain contemporary Chinese films allows an oppositional reading of publicity and public virtue that breaks open many of our conceptions of democratic governance and communal action. The ownership of history, or simply of narrative, is debated in unfamiliar and unlikely configurations of social networks. Criminality, liminality, and aimlessness accrue meanings that are indicative of a contemporary mode of living that is unlike the virtuous ideals of either the Chinese Communist Party or the governing norms of Western democracies. These visions of *un*civil society are glimpsed in public space created in filmic narrative and text. These visions are not translatable via essays in political or sociological analysis. They do suggest that the relationship between public space and civil society can be developed if the analyst is willing to redefine the virtue of civility. To return once more to Rey Chow's metaphor of the arcade, the virtue of civil society is that which is transmissible through public space, and "what is transmissible is that which, in addition to having meaning or 'sense', is accessible."[36]

Afterword

Whoever Has Money Is Number One

Shei you qian shei jiu shi laoda.

One of the most successful books and television series in recent years was Cao Guilin's (Glen Cao) *Beijinger in New York* (1991). The book was the Chinese bestseller of 1991 and has sold approximately twenty million copies. The television spin-off attracted an audience of nine hundred million.[1] *Beijinger* is a fast-moving potboiler. It is a partly autobiographical story of a journey from poverty to wealth through hard work and all-American/all-Chinese enterprise. Qiming starts out as an immigrant who finds that his previous career as a musician will be useless in America. Together with his wife, Yan, he starts a small-scale enterprise as a knitting manufacturer. Another woman, Ah Chun, who has already made money through restaurants, invests in the business. The business prospers, but the price of success is the corruption of Qiming's family life. He has an affair with Ah Chun, and witnesses the death of his daughter at the hands of drug-crazed kidnappers. His wife goes mad under the strain of accumulated grief.

The book warns against the perils of capitalist adventuring. Yet New York emerges not as a place, but as an experience of capitalism and estrangement. New York is Heaven and Hell; it is where money talks. Glen Cao quotes a popular song as a kind of refrain of Qiming's rise and fall:

> If you love him
> Send him to New York,
> 'Cause that's where Heaven is.
> If you hate him
> Send him to New York,
> 'Cause that's where Hell is . . .[2]

Maybe then the book's appeal lies in its narrative proximity to the experience of Beijingers in Beijing, Wuhaners in Wuhan, and so on. The space of New York is an imaginary arena in which Chinese audiences can play out the trauma and excitement of living in the era of reform. The space of New York in Cao's moral melodrama is another version of the screen space in *Wild Mountains* detailing Hehe's noisy and public nervous breakdown. The wide medium shot frames just too much room for Hehe to flail around, unsupported by those (on screen and off) who stare at his distress. In *Beijinger* the supposed distance from home allows the tragedy to unfold in a vacuum of social disinterest. What makes the narratives so compelling is in fact their proximity to the imaginary spaces of the spectator. Our knowledge of modernity is advanced to the point where we can be both looker and looked-upon. The flexibility of suffering in market-oriented societies teaches us that much humility.

The figure of the entrepreneur who makes a quiet fortune using his family as labor-capital is as familiar to China in the era of Dengist reform as it is to the back streets of New York. Chinese government statistics show that in 1978 the number of people employed in township and village enterprises (TVE) was twenty-eight million. By 1994 that figure had grown to one hundred and twenty million.[3] The answer to the question—what *is* capitalism with (Chinese) (socialist) characteristics?—has at least three possible answers. Jiang Zemin himself was probably thinking of the retention of strong central controls over social, economic, and political policy. The anthropologist Hill Gates has argued that it is a system of petty business ventures working within an overall system of tributary hierarchy. In her argument, petty business is characterized by the use of family labor in place of start-up capital. Tributary hierarchies are the breaks on self-confident business expansion that are experienced by Chinese emigrés through the bureaucracies of citizenship, and by Chinese in China through the power of the cadres. For both groups there is the conundrum of finding themselves acting outside the virtuous norms of either citizenship or State/Party led enterprise—and yet doing so by following the logic of Western capitalism or the ethos of the Four (Dengist) modernizations. Third, there is a parallel between economic emigrés and the internal migrants who have become a floating population within China itself (*mangliu*—a slang word referring to internal migrants). Both groups are responding to economic realities created by state policies or—in the case of America—ideological expectations of self-help, but both groups are characterized as outsiders.[4] Migrants produce an alternative virtue system that is dependent on global capitalisms in and out of China, but which is not legitimated by state governments and legal systems. Capitalism with Chinese, or American, characteristics is experienced, by migrants, as alienation from the system that creates the conditions of its development.

The audience's response to Glen Cao's story suggests that the outsider mentality was both fearsome and familiar to them. This may help to account for the bonding and overlapping between different outsider 'types' in contemporary cultural production. Characters are outside mainstream society, or perceive themselves to be outside it at certain moments and in certain situations. In crime fictions, there is an obvious disjuncture between the mainstream and the world of the fiction. In 'hooligan fictions' this is complicated as illegal and marginal activities are sometimes hard to distinguish. The law is no longer the ultimate arbiter of affective relationships and appropriate behavior. In 'apartment block' or 'alley' drama, the importance of habitation overrides wider social arrangements. These narratives are primarily interested in the correspondences of the everyday, and the networks of proximity and mutual interest. Thus, in many different ways, all these narratives are organized through human associations running parallel to social organizations approved and maintained by Party and State. The mainstream is nonetheless an important player in these dramas. It is the moments of overlap between the mainstream and alternative associative systems that cause meaningful tensions in the narrative. These tensions shift the function of the text from an articulation of alternative networking to a public negotiation between civil codes and standards of virtue. These moments in the films are functional but uncivil public spaces.

Returning to Taussig's term, it is the public secret, or secrets, which lies exposed in the fractures between network and another or one virtue system and another. In *Black Snow* Quanzi's death is a dramatic exposition of the vulnerability of a supposedly 'unvirtuous' man in modern China. Quanzi's emotional and moral connections with patterns of virtuous society are sufficient to cast doubt on simple divisions of good and bad, outsider and insider, in the era of market reform. In *Beijing Bastards* the rock and roll band is shown to be friendly with hooligan elements but it is also aligned to the average Beijing citizen. The point is made by the sound track. Cui Jian's music links scenes of illegal partying with the sight of bicyclists riding around Tiananmen in the rain. In this sequence all Beijingers are shown as outsiders to the central space of symbolic power, Tiananmen. The link between these films and others like them is the relationship between events and the creation of publics. The event is explicit (the death of Quanzi) or implicit. Tiananmen Square is a spatial memory encompassing the demonstrations of 1976, 1978, and 1989, which were themselves embedded in memories of Liberation in 1949, and the rallies of the1960s. The event is never a casual thing in visual culture and public memory. It is a spectacular political and public marker of change in the contemporary moment. In the late-twentieth century, a hundred years into the cinematic age, where visual literacy is common and sophisticated, the event in film summons the contemporary and is part of the ensuing debate. If a sphere of nonviolent dialogue and negotiation between competing interests and ideas exists in any society, it may do so in the symbolic spaces conjured between film and spectator.

THE POLITICAL FILM

The argument of this book is that film has the capacity to produce virtual public space. This is to claim that the activity of spectatorship can move beyond the cognitive to the political. There are conditions through which such a horizontal shift might occur. The constituency of the public must share experiences or interests that make a mutual and synchronous recognition of the contemporary nature of the film text possible. The recognition might roll throughout the film or may be sparked by a single shot or sequence. It should be at least conceivable that such recognition might also at times produce a culturally disparate public. Insofar as this approach acknowledges the polysemic identity of any text, I follow Lola Young's claim that a film is more than the sum of the constraints of its production: "A cinematic text cannot be attributed exclusively to those directly involved in its production but should be analyzed as part of a complex web of interrelated experiences, ideas, fantasies and unconscious expressions of desire, anxiety, and fear that need to be located in their historical, political and social contexts."[5]

Young's analysis of the representation of race in British film is an interrogation of analytic patterns as well as of the political nature of the filmic text and the world in which it is produced. Her study is an example of detailed and insightful textual analysis that benefits from the hindsights of postcolonial theory and from recent challenges to hegemonic white feminism. Young describes films as conscious interventions into the discourses of 'race' in Britain and British cinema. She shows how such interventions, whatever their intention, are themselves so embedded in the thinking about race contemporary to their production that the interventions have generally served as representational bolsters to the status quo. She argues that in particular the social status of black women is apparent in the films, both in terms of their narrative status and also in that their roles pander to the desires and fears of black and white male filmmakers and audiences.

Our analyses differ in that I take films to offer symbolic forms of a social and political imaginary, rather than accurate reflections of social and political realities. In the conclusion to her work Young calls for "a continual public and social questioning of imagery and representations to which people have become habitualized."[6] I am arguing that public questioning may be articulated within the texts, and that such articulation is not necessarily a reflection or reiteration of other forms of public discourse. It may in fact be one of very few articulations of a contemporary public imaginary that differs from the representations and images of an ideal of reality favored by the State. In this official scenario, lived experience and the public imaginary are exactly and identically described by the policies of the State and the ideology of the Party. Research into social disorder, whether ostensibly political, criminal, or economic, offers powerful critiques of the notion that State ideology has the same control over the public imaginary of contemporary China as it has maintained over the institutional formations of public life. Cultural and symbolic forms of 'disorder' provide a symptomatic reading of contemporary Chinese consciousness.

The recognition of the contemporary in these texts does not necessarily provoke radical interventions in the spheres of *real politik* or in indications of social unrest. Yet the arguments around the effects of visual texts on the spectator is a question that constantly returns in any debate that links the cultural and the political.[7] For the German filmmakers and theorists, Oskar Negt and Alexander Kluge, the classical public sphere is "an illusory synthesis of the totality of society."[8] It may be challenged by cultural and political intrusions onto its synthetic territory. Their argument stems in part from the intense frustration with the problems of getting a film 'out' at all. Without spectators, there is a film but no event, and nothing can come of it. Negt and Kluge identify the event as a sphere of action, made visible in film. Their alternative public sphere lies in the punctures to the form and content of the "illusory synthesis." In films that deal with criminality and alternative urban lifestyles, the intrusion is effected through surrogacy. Spectatorial processes of identification, cognition, and attraction are subverted into an attention to subjects, and subjectivities, outside the normal rules of engagement.

A text may also be political on its own terms and within its own aesthetic texture. If the political moment in a filmic text becomes public when it becomes an event, it is because it has been recognized as contemporary from a certain spectatorial position. Intrusions onto synthetic territory may also be seen as irruptions, points of failure within the heretofore dominant mode of address. The Lacanian psychoanalytic model allows for symptoms of the Real, the missing dimension of the psyche, to escape into the symbolic and thus into visibility. This model is a key to understanding the way in which reality, the missing dimension of experience, can be glimpsed in representations of imagined experience. Thomas Elsaesser's warning that: "One . . . has to respect both the autonomy of the historical dimension and the autonomy of the textual level" complements the Lacanian perspective.[9] Keeping that respect in mind, we can claim that textual symbolic public space is symptomatic of the contemporary political imaginary. The kind of films championed by Negt and Kluge are radical interventions into the suture of the capitalist European culture industries. Radicalism in the Chinese context shares only the generality that sensitive areas of contemporary experience are made visible. Radical moments are characteristically disruptive, stylistic or generic moves, and ironic or shocking juxtapositions of the political and the private. As Rey Chow has remarked on the topic of Cui Jian's rock music, the discomfort of the radical lies not in his lyrics as such, but in the defiant chaos that characterizes his appeal to the contemporary listener.

Instead of words with sonorous historical meanings, Cui Jian's lyrics read more like grammatically incoherent utterances. Even though they conjure up "historical" images, his words speak against literate and literary culture by their choppiness and superficiality. The Long March, one of the nation's bestselling stories since 1949, is a signifier for something vague and distant, and Chairman Mao is a mere name to complete a rhyme.[10]

VERTOV'S TRAIN: READING THE CONTEMPORARY

Little attention had been paid to the notion of the symbolic in the study of contemporary Chinese society and politics. Interesting work on civil society has been done in terms of historical or contemporary case studies, such as David Strand's work on rickshaw boys at the turn of the century and Dorothy Sollinger's hypothesis—which in the end she discards—that economic internal migrants form an alternative civil society in modern China.[11] These scholars are working within, and against, an idealized concept of civil society. It is extremely unlikely to emerge in the current political landscape. They therefore couch their conclusions in negative comparisons with the implicit Western example. I suggest that we are asking the wrong question, or rather, that the question needs to be reworked before being applied to China. Film studies are often divided between general theories and area focus. My emphasis here has been on acknowledging the need for local contextualization, but also for cultural translation in the formation of an analytic framework. I have translated my interest with civil society into a concern with symbolic public space and the idea of a political imaginary. These have become the basic ideas with which I have inflected theories developed in film analysis. I have attempted to offer politicized interpretations, without forcing the entire text or body of texts into an ideological paradigm, which does not respect the integrity and difference of each film.

A model example of this approach to film analysis is Annette Michelson's work on Dziga Vertov and *The Man with a Movie Camera*. In "The Wings of Hypothesis," written to accompany an exhibition of modernism and montage, Michelson draws together the discourses of modern science, political fantasy, and cinematic metaphysics of the 1920s.[12] Her work explains why and how the cinematic imaginations of early Soviet filmmakers were fired by the genius of Einstein and the theory of relativity. The logic of her argument, that metatheory is a determining factor in the development of an aesthetic mode, also suggests that no one element of the contemporary imaginary has determinancy. The theory of relativity, the scientism of Marxism-Leninism, and the theory of the interval that emerges in the films and writings of Vertov and Sergei Eisenstein are discrete, but mutually implicated. In her hermeneutic emphasis on film, Michelson elaborates the different directions in which Vertov and Eisenstein travelled in their interpretation of the consequences of Einstein's work. Eisenstein used political and musical metaphor to describe his instinct for what he called the fourth dimension. The construction of film through montage, if done within a framework of equivalence for all stimulants, would lead the filmmaker towards a sense of unpredictable autonomy in the filmic text. "Here we observed one further curious parallel between the visual and musical overtone; it cannot be traced in the static frame, just as it cannot be traced in the musical score. Both emerge as genuine values only in the dynamics of the musical or cinematographic process."[13]

Vertov's notion of the interval was characterized by the control of the director's cinematic eye, not the potential anarchy of Eisenstein's vision. He tended to prioritize the reliable rhythms of the machine in his montage of modernity. Even so he too conceptualized a fourth dimension of meaning that was available in film. The "'truth value' of cinema [would convert] the invisible into the visible, [render] the hidden manifest, [convert] falsehood into truth."[14] His key to the truth was to release time deliberately and to make visible the causal space between action and intention. In a documentary account of the delivery of grain between collective farms and consumer, a train is edited to run backwards, and the point is made. Vertov's scientistic, revolutionary agenda was, ironically perhaps, to work in a way echoed by films that debate the collapse of the science of everyday life in a marketized Marxist-Leninist scenario.[15] The revelatory qualities of the interval fall between the technologism of Vertov and the spiritual awe of Eisenstein. Through the medium of montage, both men played with time, chronology, speed, and direction to reveal their own, and for Eisenstein, unexpected ideas of reality. A contemporary mood is similarly revealed, or made visible, in Chinese filmmaking, through the exposure of moments in film that are suggestive of the interval.

The prime revelation of the cinematic public secret in China must be that there *is no one coherent historical, social, or moral narrative* at work in these films. This is obvious to some, but often blurred by international renditions of China as a closed and totalitarian space on the global stage. What cinema reveals is that there are many constituents and constituencies in film culture in the People's Republic. These spaces are public and sometimes unexpectedly so. Politically, the dominant force for social and political cohesion is the will of the State and the Party, neither of which has an interest in the construction or maintenance of a "space of uncoerced human association."[16] Culturally, there is a nuanced symbolic debate taking place, which acknowledges both the mimetic core of cultural practice and the fluctuations of contemporary experience. The radicalism of this publicness indicates that the contemporary political imaginary is alive and at work in the symbolic life of contemporary China.

Notes

PREFACE

1. Michael Walzer, "The Civil Society Argument," in *Dimensions of Radical Democracy*, ed. Chantal Mouffe (London: Verso, 1992), 89.

2. Perhaps primary reading would be Zhang Yingjin's overview of studies of Chinese cinema in English: "Screening China: Recent studies of Chinese Cinema in English," *Bulletin of Concerned Asian Scholars* 29, no.3 (1997): 59–66.

3. Sheldon Hsiao-peng Lu, ed., *Transnational Chinese Cinemas: Identity, Nationhood, Gender* (Honolulu: University of Hawaii Press, 1997).

4. See also Arjun Appadurai's account of the imagination in modernity. Arjun Appadurai, *Modernity at Large: Cultural Dimensions of Globalization* (Minneapolis: University of Minnesota Press, 1996), 144–45.

5.Walter Benjamin, "The Work of Art in the Epoch of its Technical Reproducibility" [Final version] (1939), quoted in *Walter Benjamin: The Colour of Experience*, Howard Caygill (London: Routledge, 1998), 112. For a full translation of the piece (but an earlier draft—1935), see Gerald Mast, Marshall Cohen, and Leo Braudy, eds., *Film Theory and Criticism: Introductory Readings*, fourth edition (Oxford: Oxford University Press, 1992), 665–81.

6. Caygill, *Walter Benjamin*, 112.

7. Andrew Light and Johnathan M. Smith, eds., *The Production of Public Space*, Philosophy and Geography II (Lanham: Rowman & Littlefield, 1998).

8. Neil Smith, "Antimonies of Space and Nature in Henri Lefèbvre's *The Production of Space*," *The Production of Space*, eds. Light and Smith, 49–70; Hugh Mason, "The Rights of Rights of Way," *The Production of Space*, eds. Light and Smith, 179–88. Henri Lefèbvre, *The Production of Space*, trans. Donald Nicholson-Smith (Oxford: Blackwell, 1991).

9. Victor Burgin, "Brecchiated Time," in *In Different Spaces: Place and Memory in Visual Culture* (Berkeley: University of California, 1996), 213.

10. Burgin, *Different Spaces*, 239–45.

11. Caygill, *The Colour of Experience*, 10–12, 82–83.

CHAPTER ONE

1. "He told me that the content of the film *Red Detachment of Women* was very good." Extract from Chinese language primer, *Elementary Chinese I* (Beijing: Foreign Languages Press, 1976), 28.

2. Socialist realism with Chinese characteristics.

3. Chen Xiaomei, "Growing up with posters in Maoist China: Memory, Multiplicity and Masquerade in Visual Culture," in *Picturing Power in the People's Republic of China: Posters of the Cultural Revolution*, eds. Harriet Evans and Stephanie Donald, (Lanham: Rowman & Littlefield, forthcoming).

4. David Bordwell and Kristin Thompson, *Film Art: An Introduction* (New York: McGraw Hill, 1997).

5. See Ackbar Abbas, *Hong Kong: Culture and the Politics of Disappearance* (Minneapolis: University of Minnesota Press, 1997), 22–47, passim. Also Jo Law, *Memory and Disappearance: Representing Space and Time in Four Contemporary Hong Kong Films*, (unpublished masters' thesis, University of Western Australia, 1998); June Yip, "Constructing a Nation: Taiwanese History and the Films of Hou Hsiao-hsien"; and Jon Kowallis, "The Diaspora in Postmodern Taiwan and Hong Kong Film: Framing Stan Lai's *The Peach Blossom Land* with Allen Fong's *Ah Ying*," both in *Transnational Cinemas*, ed. Lu (1997), 139–86.

6. This point has also been made by Ann Anagnost, "Socialist Ethics and the Legal System," in *Popular Protest and Political Culture in Modern China: Learning from 1989*, eds. Jeffrey N. Wasserstrom and Elizabeth J. Perry, (Boulder: Westview, 1992), 179. She makes an argument for community rather than formal civil society as an organizing structure of liberalization on China. On contingency and political correspondence in the Marxian analysis of civil society and beyond: see John Keane, *Democracy and Civil Society: Predicaments of European Socialism, the Prospects for Democracy and the Problem of Controlling Social and Political Power* (London: Verso, 1988), xiii, 57–59.

7. For detailed chronologies of early Chinese filmmaking and exhibition see *Griffithiana*, issues 54; 60-61 (October 1995 and 1997), 7–78, 127–33.

8. Derek Elley, "Chinese Cinema Remembered," *Griffithiana*, 60-61 (October 1997): 135.

9. Yun, 'Zhongguo dianying qiantude zhanwang—zhi Ruan Lingyu yu Jin Yan' [Chinese Cinema's Future Prospects—For Ruan Lingyu and Jin Yan], *Yingxi shenghuo* [Movie life], 1: 48: 1931. Quoted in "Chinese Cinema Remembered," Elley, 137.

10. Kristine Harris has analyzed Ruan's last film *The New (Modern) Woman*, suggesting that Ruan's performance, and subsequent death exemplify the ambiguous access to public speech of women in 1930s 'modern' China. Kristine Harris, "The New Woman Incident: Cinema, Spectacle and Scandal in 1935 Shanghai," in *Transnational Cinemas*, ed. Lu (1997), 227–302.

11. Ruan Lingyu (1910–1935) began her career with the Mingxing Studios in 1926 with *Man and Wife in Name Only* (Gua ming de fu qin). Her last films were in 1935: *The Modern Woman* (Xin nü xing), and *Wind of the Nation* (Guo feng). She made thirty films in total. *Zhongguo dianying da cidian* (Shanghai Publishing House, 1993), 806.

12. Régis Bergeron, *Le cinéma chinois 1949-1983* (Paris: L'Harmatton, 1984), 8–9. Lee, Ou-fang Leo, eds. John K. and Albert Feuerwerker, (1991), *The Cambridge History*

of China, Vol. 13, Republican China 1912-1949 (Cambridge: Cambridge University Press), 487–91.

13. Paul G. Pickowicz, "Melodramatic Representation and the 'May Fourth' Tradition of Chinese Cinema," in *From May Fourth to June Fourth: Fiction and Film in Twentieth Century Literature*, eds. Ellen Widmer and David der-dei Wang, (Cambridge: Harvard University Press, 1993), 295–326.

14. He has won 'Best Picture' three times: 1962—*Red Detachment of Women*, 1983—*Herdsman*, 1987—*Hibiscus Town*.

15. Ni Zhen, "After *Yellow Earth*," in *Film in Contemporary China: Critical Debates 1979-1989*, eds. George S. Semsel, Chen Xihe, and Xia Hong, trans. Fu Binbin. (New York, London: Praeger, 1989), 31–37, quotation 33. For further collection of Chinese film criticism in translation see: George S. Semsel, ed., *Chinese Film: The State of the Art in the People's Republic*, (New York, London: Praeger, 1987); and George S. Semsel, Xia Hong, and Hou Jianping, eds., *Chinese Film Theory: A Guide to the New Era* (New York, London: Praeger, 1990).

16. Chen Xihe, *The Major Developments and their Ideological Implications of Chinese Film and Film Education since the Cultural Revolution*, (Ph.D. dissertation, Ohio State University, 1994). Chen Kaige, interview in *Playboy*, Chinese edition, no. 22 (May 1988), 48. Chen Kaige and Tony Rayns, *King of the Children and the New Chinese Cinema* (London: Faber and Faber, 1989), 19–22.

17. Chris Berry has also picked up on the work of Peng Xiaolian in his article on the viewing subject in Chinese cinema. Chris Berry, "Neither One Thing Nor Another: Toward a Study of the Viewing Subject and Chinese Cinema in the 1980s," in *New Chinese Cinemas: Forms, Identities, Politics*, eds. Nick Browne et al. (Cambridge: Cambridge University Press, 1993), 88–113, especially 104–6. *Me and My Classmates* won a junior film award, 'The Ox', which according to the Director of the Children's Film Studio, Yu Lan, was the level to which Peng was aiming, knowing that "she was not good enough for senior prizes." Given Yu Lan's acknowledgment that children's film is not accorded equivalent status to adult movies in the industry, it is interesting to see the conflation of a fifth generation woman's first film with a 'low' self-expectation. Personal conversation with the author, Beijing, 1998.

18. Mary Ann Farquhar, *Chinese Children's Literature* (Ph.D. dissertation, Griffith University, 1983), 40, 173, 181, and passim.

19. Li Shaohong (1992), " 'Director's Statement', *Notes to 'Bloody Morning*," Beijing Film Studio (Distributed by Era International, Hong Kong, Los Angeles, Taipei, 1990) (London International Film Festival Leaflet, 1992).

20. Paul Clark, *Chinese Cinema: Culture and Politics since 1949* (Cambridge: Cambridge University Press, 1987), 58–61, 139; John Lent, "China," in *The Asian Film Industry*, ed. John Lent (1990), 11–34 (studio system 12–16). Raw data taken from the *China Statistical Yearbooks*, 1995, 1996, 1997. (China State Statistical Bureau: Beijing).

21. Tony Rayns, "Between Ideologues and Bankers," *Britain-China* (London: Great Britain China Centre, Spring 1992): 10–11.

22. Paul Clark, *Chinese Cinema*, 136–46.

23. Useful summaries of the events of that period can be found in June Teufel Dreyer, *China's Political System: Modernization and Tradition* (London: Macmillan, 1996), 264–66; and in "Creativity and Politics," Douwe Fokkema, in *The Cambridge History of China*,

Revolutions within the Chinese Revolution 1966-1982, Vol. 15, Part 2, eds. Denis Twitchett and John K. Fairbank, (Cambridge: Cambridge University Press, 1991), 595–610.

24. William Kessen, ed., *Childhood in China* (London: Yale University Press, 1975), 26–28.

25. "So I would say that these seven months [the start of the Cultural Revolution] were the most terrible in my life. Yet they were also the most wonderful. I had never felt so good about myself, nor have I ever since," Rae Yang, *Spider Eaters*, (Berkeley: University of California Press, 1997), 115. "I retrieve my own experience of growing up with posters—returning to the early 1960s before the Cultural Revolution, when I was touched, intrigued, and indeed constructed by the posters that offered me space to play in what seemed like a simple world of bright colors and thrilling events," Chen, "Growing Up with Posters," in *Picturing Power*, eds. Evans and Donald, (Lanham: Rowman & Littlefield, 1999).

26. See the anecdote of a fancy red jacket made and worn only once, as its redness did not disguise the daringly retrotraditional design of the cut. Claire Roberts, ed., *Evolution and Revolution: Chinese Dress 1700s-1900s* (Sydney: Powerhouse Publishing, 1997): 50–51.

27. "China cancels domestic flight of award-winning *The Blue Kite*," *Japan Times*, (19.10.93.), 8. Tony Rayns, "Chaos and Anger: Blacklisted Directors in China," *Sight and Sound* 4, no. 10 (Sept./Oct. 1994): 12. Also Dru Gladney, "Tian Zhuangzhuang, the Fifth Generation, and Minorities Film in China," *Public Culture* 8 (1995), 161–75, especially 173.

28. This was the reason given to me at the NFT box office when my ticket fee was returned with apologies. I later saw the film on an illegal video copy, but have since found it easy to purchase from a 'respectable' distributor (China Film Import and Export, Los Angeles).

29. *Beijing Bastards* was co-opted as a generic title for a short season of new Chinese film at the Institute of Contemporary Arts in London in February 1995. The film has also been screened on Channel Four. His latest piece, *East Palace, West Palace*, has done well at festivals in 1998, also touring as part of the Gay and Lesbian film festival in Western Australia in 1999.

30. Miriam Hansen, *Babel and Babylon: Spectatorship in American Silent Film* (Cambridge, Mass.: Harvard University Press, 1991), 36.

31. For an interesting take on the politics of the live event see Joseph W. Esherick, and Jeffrey N. Wasserstrom, "Acting Out Democracy: Political Theatre in Modern China," *Journal of Asian Studies*, no. 49 (Nov. 1990): 835–65.

32. Thomas Elsaesser, "Social Mobility and the Fantastic: German Silent Cinema," in *Fantasy and the Cinema*, ed. James Donald (London: British Film Institute, 1989), 22–38, quotation 29. Also see Siegfried Kracauer, *Theory of Film: The Redemption of Physical Reality* (Oxford: Oxford University Press, 1976), 160–61.

33. Siegfried Kracauer, *From Caligari to Hitler: A Psychological History of the German Film* (Princeton: Princeton University Press, 1947). The problem is encapsulated in the title. A film is not a subject of analysis or psychological investigation. It may be approached as bearing the traces of psychoanalytic formations of fantasy, but Kracauer's mix of psychology and history inevitably makes claims on both which are not sustainable.

34. Many examples that take the color red (*hong*) into the title include revolutionary classics: *Red Banners on Mount Cuigang* (Cui gang hong qi) (1951); *Red Children* (Hong hai zi) (1958); *Red Seeds* (Hong se de zhong zi) (1958); *Red Sun Over Ke Mountains* (Ke shan hong ri) (1960); *Song of the Red Flag* (Hong qi pu) (1960); *The Red Basket* (Hong se bei lou) (1965). There are also animated films mainly designed for children: *Red Army Bridge* (Hong jun qiao) (1964). Nor should we forget a continuing tradition of film adaptations of the Ming classic, *Dream of Red Mansions* (Hong lou meng), where redness accrues a very different 'hue' with its attachment to a rich family epic, but one which nevertheless still occupies an important spot in Chinese cultural consumption. (Adaptations were made in 1927, 1928, 1948, 1962) and television serials have also been screened regularly on Chinese television (Beijing TV, 1988-89). *Dianying cidian* 359–63, Donald J. Marion, *The Chinese Filmography: The 2444 Feature Films Produced by Studios in the People's Republic of China from 1949 through 1995* (Jefferson: McFarland and Co., 1997), 469–81.

CHAPTER TWO

1. Thanks to Harriet Evans, Wendy Parkins, Cao Li, Stephan Feuchtwang, John Frow, John Cayley, Chen Hong, and Kate Lacey for constructive suggestions. Thanks, too, to my niece Kate Fowler who helped me get started on a walk around Fremantle, and to participants and audience in events arranged around the 'In and Out' exhibition at the John Curtin Art Gallery in April-May 1998 (including my co-panellists, Binghui Huangfu, Brenda Crofts, and Lisa Reihana).

2. Jürgen Habermas, *The Structural Transformation of the Public Sphere* (Cambridge: Polity Press, 1989); and *Moral Consciousness and Communicative Action* (Cambridge: Polity Press, 1990).

3. Antonio Gramsci (edited collection, 1977), *Selected Political Writings 1910-1920*, ed. Quentin Hoare, trans. John Mathews (London: Lawrence and Wishart, 1977), 11–13.

4. The available scholarship is extensive. For representative examples see: Paul Bowles and Gordon White, "Contradictions in China's Financial Reforms: The relationship between banks and enterprises," *Cambridge Journal of Economics* 13, no. 4 (Dec.1989): 481–95; Heath B. Chamberlain, "Party-Management Relations in Chinese Industries: Some Political Dimensions of Economic Reform," *The China Quarterly*, no.112 (Dec.1987): 631–61; He Baogang and David Kelly, "Emergent Civil Society and the Intellectuals in China," in *The Development of Civil Society in Communist Systems*, ed. Robert Miller (Sydney: Allen and Unwin, 1992); W. J. F. Jenner, *The Tyranny of History: The Roots of China's Crisis* (London: Allen Lane, 1992); Elizabeth Perry, "China in 1992: An Experiment in Neo-Authoritarianism," *Asian Survey*, Vol. XXXIII, no.1 (January 1993): 12–21; William Rowe, "The Public Sphere in Modern China," *Modern China* 16, part 3 (1990): 309–29; Tony Saich, "Party and State Reforms in the People's Republic of China," *Third World Quarterly* 5, no.3 (1983): 627–39; Saich, "Much Ado About Nothing: Party Reform in the 1980s," in *Discos and Dictatorship: Party-State and Society Relations in the People's Republic of China*, ed. Gordon White (Leiden: RUL, 1993); Dorothy Sollinger, "China's Transients and the State: A Form of Civil Society?"; *Politics and Society* 21, no.1 (Mar. 1993): 91–122; Frederick Wakeman, "Civil Society

and Public Sphere Debate : Western Reflections on Chinese Political Culture," in *Modern China* 19, no. 2, (1993): 108–38 for a skeptical account of Rowe's Habermasian standpoint; and Gordon White, "Prospects for Civil Society in China," *Australian Journal of Chinese Affairs*, no. 29 (Jan. 1993): 63–87.

5. Richard Madsen, "The Public Sphere, Civil Society, and Moral Community; A Research Agenda for Contemporary China Studies," *Modern China* 19, no. 2 (Apr. 1993): 183–98, quotation 189.

6. Madsen, "The Public Sphere," 190.

7. Which is not the same as Habermas' later concept of *communicative action* but which may describe his understanding of seventeenth-century coffee shop politicking.

8. Edward Shils, "The Virtue of Civil Society" in *Government and Opposition* 26, no. 1 (winter 1991): 3–20; Alasdair MacIntyre, *After Virtue: A Study in Moral Theory* (London: Duckworth, 1985), 181–200.

9. John F. Starr, "On Participation and Representation," in *Continuing the Revolution: The Political Thought of Mao* (Princeton: Princeton University Press 1979), 188–222.

10. Phrase borrowed from Christina Buci-Glucksmann, "Hegemony and Consent: A Political Strategy," in *Approaches to Gramsci*, ed. Anne Showstack Sassoon (London: Writers and Readers Co-operative Society, 1982), 116–26.

11. Norberto Bobbio, "Gramsci and the Concept of Civil Society," in *Democracy and Civil Society: Despotism and Democracy: The Origins and Development of the Distinction between Civil Society and the State 1750-1850*, ed. John Keane (London: Verso, 1988), 73–99, especially 86.

12. For a discussion of unified collective action see Walter L. Adamson, "Gramsci and the Politics of Civil Society," *Praxis International* 7, nos. 3-4 (Winter 1987-88): 318–39. Adamson's hope for a new-world order is taken further by Richard Falk, "The World Order between Inter-state Law and the Law of Humanity: The Role of Civil Society Institutions," in *Cosmopolitan Democracy—An Agenda for a New World Order*, eds. Daniele Archibugi and David Held, (Cambridge: Polity Press 1995), 163–79. For a discussion of the meaning of human rights in *Chinese* political thought see Merle Goldman, "Human Rights in the People's Republic of China," *Daedalus* 112, no. 4 (1983): 111–38.

13. He Baogang, *The Dual Roles of Semi-Civil Society* (written in 1993) (Institute of Development Studies Discussion Paper no. 327, 1993), 12–13. For a reading of Gramsci in the 'post' political see Sue Golding, *Gramsci's Democratic Theory—Contributions to a Post-Liberal Democracy* (Toronto: University of Toronto Press, 1992).

14. Professor Su Shaozhi's *avoidance* of the topic while discussing political and ideological reform—and while obviously keen to promote the role of mass organizations and government as separate from the main policy function of the Party—is telling: Tony Saich, "Political and Ideological Reform in the People's Republic of China: An Interview with Professor Su Shaozhi," *China Information* 1, no. 2 (1986): 19–25.

15. Shu-Yun Ma lists the many western sinologists who were influenced by the availability of Habermas' work in translation and by the 1989 demonstrations to seize on the concept of civil society as a way of evaluating China's democratic progress. Ma Shu-yun, "The Chinese Discourse on Civil Society," *The China Quarterly* (1994): 180–93. Influential pieces include: Elizabeth J. Perry and Ellen V. Fuller, "China's Long March to Democracy," *World Policy Journal* 53, no. 4 (Fall 1991): 663–85; Elizabeth J. Perry, "State and Society in Contemporary China," *World Politics* 41, no. 4 (July 1989): 579–

91; Tony Saich, ed., *The Chinese People's Movement: Perspectives on Spring 1989* (London: ME Sharpe, 1990); Andrew G. Walder, "The Political Sociology of the Beijing Upheaval of 1989," *Problems of Communism* (Sept.-Oct. 1989): 39–40; Dorothy Sollinger, "Democracy with Chinese Characteristics," *World Policy Journal* (Fall 1989): 621–32. For a more general overview and bibliography of the question see Gordon White (1994-95), "The Dynamics of Civil Society in Post-Mao China" in *The Individual and the State in China*, ed. Brian Hook (Oxford: Clarendon Press, 1996), seen in draft October 1994. Also Gordon White, Jude Howell, and Shang Xiaoyuan, *In Search of Civil Society: Market Reform and Social Change in Contemporary China* (Oxford: Clarendon Press, 1996).

16. This connection is made by François Jullien, *The Propensity of Things: Toward a History of Efficacy in China*, trans. Janet Lloyd (New York: Zone Books, 1995), 55–56.

17. Michel Foucault quoted in "Truth and Power," in *The Foucault Reader: An Introduction to Foucault's Thought*, ed. Paul Rabinow (London: Penguin, 1984), 51–75.

18. Hannah Arendt, *On the Human Condition* (Chicago: Anchor Books/University of Chicago Press, 1959), 195. For Hannah Arendt's theory of action as a successor to Kant see Kimberley Hutchings, *Kant, Critique, and Politics* (London, New York: Routledge, 1996), 83–89. For a wider discussion of Arendt see Mauricio Passerin D'Entreves, *The Political Philosophy of Hannah Arendt* (London: Routledge, 1994), 64–100, 149–63.

19. Discussion held in the Beijing Language and Culture University, August 1998.

20. There is an explicit agenda in these debates to determine who is complicit with State versions of history and narrative, and who can formulate opposition. The argument ranges from accusations of antipolitics from Ben Xu—to claims for alternative politics from Xudong Zhang. Ben Xu, " 'From Modernity to Chineseness': The Rise of Nativist Cultural Theory in Post-1989 China," *Positions: East Asia Cultures Critique* 6, no. 1 (Spring 1998): 203–37. Xudong Zhang, "Nationalism, Mass Culture, and Intellectual Strategies in Post-Tiananmen China," *Social Text* 55, vol. 16, no. 2 (Summer 1998): 109–40.

21. *Far Eastern Economic Review*, Feb. 17, 1994. It is also well known that the PLA controls much of the Arms Industry in China. China is the sixth largest supplier of conventional weapons world-wide: *SIPRI Yearbook*, (1995), 493. Although in this respect note John Frankenstein and Bates Gill: "Is the true nature of the PLA the modernizing aggressive force seen in its 'pockets of excellence'? and recently imported weapons—the atomic weapons, missiles, fighters, submarines, and rapid reaction units—or is it the bureaucratic, technology-inhibited organization that devotes at least as much time growing vegetables to make ends meet as it does to training?" Frankenstein and Gill, "Current and Future Challenges facing Chinese Defence Industries," *The China Quarterly*, no.6 (1996): 426.

22. Wu Hung has made an extended argument of this kind in respect to the people's monument in the center of the square. Wu Hung, "Tiananmen Square: A Political History of Monuments," *Representations*, no. 35 (Summer 1991): 84–117.

23. The kitsching of Mao is discussed in great detail in Geremie Barmé's *Shades of Mao: The Posthumous Cult of the Great Leader* (Armonk: ME Sharpe, 1996); also Robert Benewick and Stephanie Donald, "Badgering the People: Mao Badges—a Retrospective," in *Belief in China: Art and Politics, Deities and Mortality*, eds. Benewick and Donald, (Brighton: Green Foundation, Brighton Royal Pavilion, 1996), 29–39.

24. As note 4.

25. Rey Chow, "Can One Say No to China?," *New Literary History* 28 (Winter 1997): 147–51. See also articles in *Postmodernism and China*, special issue *Boundary 2*, 24:3, eds. Zhang Xudong and Arif Dirlik, (Fall 1997). Also Jing Wang, *High Culture Fever: Politics, Aesthetics, and Ideology in Deng's China* (Berkeley: University of California Press, 1996).

26. Ien Ang, "Comment on Felski's 'The Doxa of Difference': The Uses of Incommensurability," *Signs: Journal of Women in Culture and Society* 23, no. 1 (1997): 56–57, 59.

27. This phrase is borrowed from Laura Mulvey's article on reinventing film practice, "Visual Pleasure and Narrative Cinema" (1975), reprinted in Laura Mulvey, *Visual and Other Pleasures* (London: Macmillan, 1989), 14–26, quotation 25.

28. William Outhwaite, *Habermas: A Critical Introduction* (Cambridge: Polity Press, 1984), especially Chapter 8: 'Modernity and Philosophy', 121–36.

29. Sheldon Hsiao-peng Lu looks at the 'post-new' in "Global POSTmodernIZATION: The Intellectual, the Artist, and China's Condition," *Boundary 2*, 24:3 (Fall 1997): 65–98.

30. Liu Kang, "Popular Culture and the Culture of the Masses in Contemporary China," *Boundary 2*, 24, no. 3 (1997): 99–122.

31. Benewick and Donald, *Belief in China*, 29–30.

32. Current debate between pro and anti-*houxue* scholars in China and America as to the political purchase of postmodern theoretical approaches is reminiscent of Habermas' argument with French philosophers. Habermas makes the accusation against Foucault of the destruction of historiography through a conflation of different kinds of power, the power of "transcendental generativity, *and* of empirical self-assertion simultaneously." Similarly (although not identically) *houxue* scholars are accused of avoiding the choice of self-assertion in the face of Party generated power. Jürgen Habermas, "The Critique of Reason as an Unmasking of the Human Sciences: Michel Foucault," in *The Philosophical Discourse of Modernity* (Cambridge: MIT Press, 1987), 256.

33. In a recent conference on globalization Wang Ning, a major player in debates on postmodernism in China, referred to Habermas as one of his primary sources. *The International Conference on Globalization and the Future of the Humanities*, Beijing Language and Culture University, August 1998. There was also an interesting discussion of communicative action in the context of cultural defence in a paper offered by Mai Yongxiong, "Misreading of Civilisation and Cultural Communication" at the same conference. See also Jonathan Arac, "Postmodernism and Postmodernity in China: an Agenda for Inquiry," *New Literary History* 28 (Winter 1997): 134–38.

34. John Frow, 1997, "What is Postmodernism?," in *Time, Commodity, Culture: Essays in Cultural Theory and Postmodernity* (Oxford: Oxford University Press, 1997), 30.

35. Frow, *Postmodernism*, 32.

36. Trinh Minh-ha, "Which Way to Political Cinema?," *Framer Framed* (London/New York: Routledge, 1992), 248.

37. For other work on strategic gender placement see Chris Berry, "Sexual Difference and the Viewing Subject in *Li Shuangshuang* and *The In-laws*," ed. Chris Berry, *Perspectives on Chinese Cinema* (London: BFI, 1991), 30–39.

38. Tian Hua's other films include: *Blooming Flowers in the Moonlight* (Hua hao yue yuan) (1958), *Daughter of the Party* (Dang de nü er) (1958), *So Lovely a Landscape* (Jiang

shan duo jiao) (1959), *Storm* (Feng bao) (1959), *Loyal Hearts on a Green Sea* (Bi hai dan xin) (1962), *The Fight for Power* (Duo yin) (1963), *Secret Drawing* (Mimi tu zhi) (1965), *Eventful Years* (Zheng rong sui yue) (1978), *Liezi No. 99* (Liezi jiu shi jiu hao) (1978), *The Slave's Daughter* (Nü li de nüer) (1978), *In and Out of Court* (Fating nei wai) (1980), *Xumao and his Daughters* (Xumao he tade nüren) (1981), *Highrise Pagoda* (Tong tian ta) (1986), *Liu Fei's Will* (Liu fei de yi shu) (1988). Her latter films see her cast as an official with a nose for justice.

39. Much thinking about class and sexuality which informs critiques of this film (including the present analysis) has been inspired by Meng Yue's piece—first published in *Ershi yi shijie* 4 (April 1991): 103–12, republished as Meng Yue, "Female Images and National Myth," in *Gender Politics in Modern China: Writing and Feminism*, ed. Tani E. Barlow (Durham: Duke University Press, 1993), 118–36. See particularly pages 120–23.

40. An excellent account of the association between death rites and the feminine is in Emily Martin's "Gender and Ideological Differences in Representations of Life and Death," in *Death Ritual in Late Imperial and Modern China*, eds. James Watson and Evelyn Rawski, (Berkeley: University of California Press, 1988), 164–179. The story of the lady Linshui, who is both goddess and demon in her incarnations as girl, Guanyin, and snake, is told by Brigitte Baptandier, "'The Lady Linshui: How a Woman became a Goddess," in *Unruly Gods: Divinity and Society in China*, eds. Meir Shahar and Robert P. Weller, (Honolulu: University of Hawaii Press, 1996), 105–49.

41. Meng Yue, "Female Images and National Myth," 118–36.

42. Julian Petley, "The Lost Continent," in *All Our Yesterdays: 90 Years of British Cinema*, ed. Charles Barr (London: BFI, 1986), 106.

43. Peter Wollen, "Art into Film—The Western and the Bather," *Sight and Sound* Supplement (October 1994).

44. "One should never wear anything white in one's hair, as this is very unlucky. It is often said that white is the color of mourning in China. This is not quite correct: the word in question is *su* which means a kind of unbleached sackcloth, and the mourning apparel made from it is a brownish yellow rather than white." Wolfram Eberhard, *A Dictionary of Chinese Symbols: Hidden Symbols in Chinese Life and Thought* (London: Routledge, Kegan Paul, 1988), 313. Nevertheless, filmic accounts of mourning use very white material to get the point across (the funeral scene in Zhang Yimu's *Ju Dou,* 1990). Anecdotal discussions with Chinese colleagues also suggest that the idea of whiteness as *bai* in mourning is quite common, *su* is understood to be on the yellow end of the spectrum—and in these days of industrial bleach is not always associated with funerals.

45. Ruth Frankenberg, "Local Whitenesses, Localizing Whiteness," *Displacing Whiteness: Essays in Social and Cultural Criticism* (Durham: Duke University Press, 1997), 4.

46. Chéla Sandoval, "Theorizing White Consciousness for a post-Empire World: Barthes, Fanon, and the Rhetoric of Love," in Displacing Whiteness, ed. Ruth Frankenberg, (1997), 96.

47. *Serf* (Nong nü) (1963), and the much more recent *Temple Mountain* (1998). Meanwhile the film *Kundun* (1998) was screened in Australia with a preparatory reading from the declaration of Human Rights by Buddhist Americans, including Goldie Hawn and Harrison Ford. One began to wonder who was saving whose soul, and on what grounds?

48. See for example posters of the 1960s and 1970s where minority peoples are generally feminine and dressed in 'traditional' costume. Examples in Stefan Landsberger,

Chinese Propoganda Posters: From Revolution to Modernization (Amsterdam: Pepin Press, 1995), 163–64. A large poster on the road around Tiananmen Square is of a similar genre, and models (dolls) of minority women are on sale in Beijing Capital Airport.

49. This was perhaps why the huge painting of a wizened, sun-blackened peasant man, Luo Zhongli's *Father*, made such a stir as a piece of wound art in 1980.

50. Hunter (1984): 216, quoted in Janet Lee (1996), "Between Subordination and the She-Tiger: Social Constructions of White Femininity in the Lives of Single, Protestant Missionaries in China, 1905-1930," *Women's Studies International Forum* 19, no.6 (1996): 621–32.

51. Although 'redness' is the color of political correctness, pure white (*qingbai*) is used as a more general term to describe oneself as good, 'on the level', 'beyond criticism', in all sociopolitical senses.

52. Edward H. Schafer, "The Great Water Goddesses in T'ang Poetry," in *The Divine Woman: Dragon Ladies and Rain Maidens in T'ang Literature* (Berkeley: University of California Press, 1973), 89. Poets quoted: Li Po: "kan hsing, pa shou," Li chiao "Su"; Liu Ts'ang, Lo shen yuan; Wen T'ing-yun "Lien Hua."

53. bell hooks, "Whiteness in the Black Imagination," in *Killing Rage, Ending Racism* (London: Penguin Books, 1996), 31-32.

54. Filmed in London studios.

55. Binghui Huangfu, "Inside and Outside. A Forum on Contemporary Chinese Art and the Complexities of Cultural Exchange," a paper given at a symposium "Cultural Difference" at the John Curtin Gallery, Perth, 29 April 1998.

56. The artists: Ah Xian, Guan Wei, Jiangjie, Li Tianyuan, Liu Xiaoxian, Wang Guangyi, Wang Jianwei, Wang Luyan, Wang Youshen, and Wang Zhiyuan.

57. Binghui Huangfu, *Catalogue: In and Out: Contemporary Art from China and Australia* (LaSalle-SIA College of Arts, 1997), 36–38.

CHAPTER THREE

1. The age of children is not easily defined. Many respondents to a recent survey in Beijing thought that under twelve was the age of childhood (*ertong*) (reasons included: that children in primary school are different from teenagers; that children may not ride bicycles on the street by themselves until they are twelve) others opted for under sixteen, because the entry to Senior High School at sixteen entails a shift in focus towards adult responsibilities and the job market, or because Chinese law defines childhood as under sixteen. (Interviews in Beijing with Yu Lan and other film professionals, with the author and Yingchi Chu, November, 1998)

2. *Adventure on a Small Island* (Xiao dao xing shen) (1994); *The Beginning of Life* (Ren zhi chu) (1992); *Frustrated Childhood* (Feng yu gu yuan) (1992); *I Only Cried Three Times* (Wo zhi liu san ci lei) (1987); *The Drummer from Flame Mountain* (Huo yan shan lai de gu shou) (1991), *Child's Song in War* (Zhan zheng tong yao) (1994); *The Magic Watch* (Mo Biao) (1990); *Boys and Girls* (Shao nan shao nu men) (1987); and *Ma Jia and Ling Fei* (Ma Jia he Ling Fei) (1982).

3. Li Suyuan, in conversation with the author, Beijing, 1998. See also Li Suyuan, "ertong xin li yu ertong dianying" (Child Psychology and Children's Film), *Dangdai*

dianying (Contemporary Film) (June 1990): 70–79. Comments below with Yu Lan and Tian Zhuangzhuang also recorded in Beijing, 1998.

4. Interview recorded at The Children's Film Studio, 1998.

5. Interview recorded at The Children's Film Studio, 1998.

6. Li Suyuan, 1998.

7. Gertrud Koch, "Exchanging the Gaze: Revisioning Feminist Film Theory," *New German Critique*, no. 34 (1985): 139–53.

8. Theodor Adorno, "Transparencies on Film," (1966), *New German Critique*, no. 24–25 (Fall/Winter 1981-1982): 199–205, quotation 203.

9. Theodor Adorno and Max Horkheimer, *The Dialectic of Enlightenment*, trans. John Cumming (London: Verso, 1979), 120–67 and passim. Theodor Adorno, *The Culture Industry* (London: Routledge, 1991). Miriam Hansen, "Introduction to Adorno's 'Transparencies'," *New German Critique*, no. 24-25 (Fall/Winter 1981–1982): 186–98.

10. For a discussion of identification and recognition in mass spectatorship see Vicky Lebeau's article "Daddy's Cinema: Femininity and Mass Spectatorship," *Screen* 33, no. 3 (Autumn 1992): 244–58.

11. Tian Zhuangzhuang, recorded Beijing Film Studio, 1998.

12. D.W. Winnicott, *Playing and Reality*, (London: Tavistock Books, 1971), quote taken from "Playing: A Theoretical Statement" in the Penguin Books edition (London: Penguin, 1980), 55. This study reworks the earlier statement of the child psychologist, Margaret Loewenfeld, ". . . play in children is the expression of the child's relation to the whole of life. . . . Play . . . is taken as applying to all activities in children that are spontaneous and self-generated;" in Loewenfeld, *Play in Childhood* (London: Victor Gollancz, 1935), 36–37.

13. See chapter one, note 27.

14. *Ying-hs'i Hua*, (Paintings of Children at Play), (Taipei: China Printing Company, 1996), 96–97, and passim.

15. Beijing, 1998.

16. The clinical implications of childhood dependence on external stimuli for the development of workable patterns of representation are discussed in D. W. Winnicott (1965),"The Psychology of Madness: A Contribution from Psychoanalysis," reprinted in *New Formations*, no. 26 (Autumn 1995): 45–53.

17. Mladen Dolar, "Hitchcock's Objects," in *Everything You Always Wanted to Know about Lacan but Were Afraid to Ask Hitchcock*, ed. Slavoj Zizek (London: Verso, 1992), 45.

18. Dolar, "Hitchcock's Objects," 31–46

19. Loewenfeld, *Play in Childhood*, 35–38. Thanks to Lesley Caldwell for her advice on sources for this chapter.

20. See Dominique Scarfone, "In Praise of Conflictuality," *New Formations*—Issue on Psychoanalysis and Culture 26 (autumn 1995): 36; For discussions around the concept of passionate, agonistic democracy see Bernard-Henri Lévi, *La Pûreté dangereuse* (Paris: Grasset, 1994); Chantal Mouffe, "Pluralism and Modern Democracy: Around Carl Schmitt," *New Formations* 14 (Summer 1991): 1–16; Chantal Mouffe, ed., *Dimensions of Radical Democracy*, (London: Verso, 1992); Chantal Mouffe, "For a Politics of Agonistic Pluralism," in *Identity, Authority and Democracy*, Research Papers in Media and Cultural Studies, eds. James Donald and Stephanie Donald, (Falmer: University of Sussex, 1995), 111–22.

21. Scarfone, *Conflictuality*, 44.

22. Michael Taussig, *Mimesis and Alterity: A Particular History of the Senses* (London: Routledge, 1993), 86.

23. Winnicott, *Psychology of Madness*, 49.

24. Caygill, *Colour of Experience*, 10–11.

CHAPTER FOUR

1. Sheldon Hsiao-peng Lu, "National Cinema, Cultural Critique, Transnational Capital: The Films of Zhang Yimou," in Lu, *Transnational Cinemas: Identity, Nationhood, Gender* (Honolulu: University of Hawaii Press, 1997), 111–12.

2. The section on landscape and agency in *Yellow Earth* was first published as Stephanie Donald, "Landscape and Agency: *Yellow Earth* and the Demon Lover" in *Theory, Culture and Society* 14, no. 1 (Spring 1997): 97–112.

3. *Wild Mountains* won six Golden Rooster awards in 1986, including Best Picture, Best Director, Best Actress, Best Supporting Actor, Best Costume, and Best Sound. It also won the Grand Prix at the Eighth Nantes Tri-Continental Festival. *Yellow Earth* won Zhang Yimou the cinematography Golden Rooster in 1985.

4. Li Tuo, *"Yellow Earth*—An Unwelcome Guest" quoted in *Seeds of Fire*, Geremie Barmé, (Far Eastern Economic Review Publications, 1986), 252–69, quotation, 253.

5. Laura Mulvey, "Visual Pleasure," and "Afterthoughts on 'Visual Pleasure and Narrative Cinema' inspired by *Duel in the Sun*," in *Visual and Other Pleasures*, ed. Mulvey, 14–28, 29–38.

6. Chris Berry, "Neither One Thing Nor Another—Towards a Study of the Viewing Subject and the Chinese Cinema in the 1980s" in Browne: *New Chinese Cinemas*, 89–90.

7. See for example the report of his speech "Speed Up the Pace of Reform, the Open Door and Modernisation Construction in Order to Strive for Even Greater Victories in the Cause of Socialism with Chinese Characteristics," *People's Daily*, 21 October 1992.

8. Chen Kaige and Tony Rayns, *King of the Children and the New Chinese Cinema* (London, Boston: Faber and Faber, 1989), 26–29.

9. Synopsis of *Yellow Earth* and translation of Hanhan's song by Bonnie McDougall, in *Seeds of Fire: Chinese Voices of Conscience*, eds. Geremie Barmé and John Minford, (Newcastle upon Tyne: Bloodaxe Books, 1988), 254–59.

10. Mao Tse-tung (Zedong), *Report of an Investigation into the Peasant Movement in Hunan* (1926/7), (Beijing: Foreign Languages Press, 1953), 4–6.

11. Bonnie McDougall, *Mao Zedong's "Talks at the Yan'an Conference on Literature and Art": A Translation of the 1943 Text with Commentary* (Ann Arbor: The University of Michigan Center for Chinese Studies no. 39, 1980), 57–86.

12. This early cut of the film has been reduced in later cuts for distribution. An original version—with full and accurate subtitles—can be obtained for loan from the British Film Institute, London. Full versions of the script may be found (in Chinese), *Tansuo dianying ji* (1987), Shanghai: Shanghai Wenyi Chubanche and (in English) Bonnie MacDougall, *The Yellow Earth: A Film by Chen Kaige with a Complete Translation of the Film Script* (Hong Kong: The Chinese University Press, 1991).

13. "Gelovani, the actor who . . . 'incarnates' (Stalin) in *The Vow* is a specialist whom the Russians had, since 1938, already seen play Stalin many times." André Bazin, "The

Stalin Myth in Soviet Cinema," (written in 1950), in *Movies and Methods Part II*, ed. Bill Nichols (Berkeley: University of California Press, 1984), 29–39.

14. Gina Marchetti, *"Two Stage Sisters*: The Blossoming of a Revolutionary Aesthetic," reprinted in Sheldon Lu, *Transnational Cinemas,* 59–80. Marchetti's article has a useful bibliographic note on other writings on Xie Jin in English, 59–80.

15. Having reread Rey Chow's article "Silent is the Ancient Plain," *Discourse* 12, no.2 (spring-summer 1990), I think that her remarks on 90–91 regarding the emptying out of silence probably led me into this discussion. I quote briefly so readers also have the benefit of her very fruitful suggestions: "There is . . . something incompatible between the notion of emptiness and the notion of representation—especially graphic representation . . . in film criticism, 'space' and 'emptiness', though visually nonsignifying, are bound to become occasions for a narrative filling. Why belabour the paradox? Because in it lie the reasons why an alternative . . . agency, in order to be politically effective, cannot simply be argued by way of imagistic nonpresence alone. The argument of 'blanks' must be supplemented by a different kind of perception—one that understands space . . . as an emptying of representation. . . ."

16. Bazin, "Stalin," 33 and 35. Bazin is one of the Western film theorists cited as a possible influence on modern Chinese film in Li Tuo and Zhang Nuanxin's article—influential with Fourth Generation filmmakers especially—"The Modernization of Film Language," *Beijing Film Art* 3 (1979): 40–52. I would like to quote Claire Huot's comment (by fax August 1995) that Zhang's espousal of a western aesthetic was not always evident in her filmmaking, which always retained a strong sense of Chinese modes and tradition.

17. Sergei Eisenstein, "The Cinematographic Principle and the Ideogram," in *Film Theory and Criticism*, eds. Cohen and Braudy, (1992), 127–37. (First published 1930 as 'The Cinematographic Principle and Japanese Culture; with a digression on Montage and the Shot', *Transition* [Paris], no.19 [spring-summer], 1930)

18. Julia F. Andrews, *Painters and Politics in the People's Republic of China* (Berkeley: University of California Press, 1994), 254, 282, 287.

19. Paul Clark, *Chinese Cinema*, 105–37.

20. Paul Clark, *Chinese Cinema*, 135–37.

21. Roger T. Ames and David L. Hall, *Thinking Through Confucius* (New York: SUNY Press, 1987), 63.

22. Denis Cosgrove and Stephen Daniels, *The Iconography of Landscape: Essays on the Symbolic Representation, Design and Use of Past Environments* (Cambridge: Cambridge University Press, 1988), 1.

23. Ann Anagnost, "Who is Speaking Here? Discursive Boundaries and Representation in Post-Mao China," in *Boundaries in China*, ed. John Hay (London: Reaktion Books, 1994), 265.

24. David E. Apter and Tony Saich, *Revolutionary Discourse in Mao's Republic* (Cambridge: Harvard University Press, 1994).

25. Apter and Saich, *Revolutionary Discourse*, 114–15.

26. Joseph Needham, "Time and Eastern Man," *The Henry Myers Lecture 1964* (London: Royal Anthropological Institute of Great Britain and Ireland, 1964), 3–6, 31.

27. Johnathan Hay, "The Suspension of Dynastic Time" in *Boundaries*, ed. John Hay, 171–97, (on dates) 172, (on the symbolic) 194.

28. Slavoj Zizek, *The Sublime Object of Ideology* (London: Verso, 1989), 160–73.

29. Andrews, *Painters and Politics*, 294–97; Joan Lebold Cohen, *The New Chinese Painting 1949-1986* (New York: Harry Abrams, 1987), 120–21.

30. Stuart Schram, *Mao Tse-tung* (London: Penguin, 1966), 293.

31. Simon Schama, *Landscape and Memory* (London: Harper Collins, 1995), 407.

32. John Hay, "The Body Invisible in Chinese Art," in *Body, Subject and Power in China*, eds. Angela Zito and Tani E. Barlow, (Chicago: Chicago University Press, 1994), 75; and Judith Farquhar, "Multiplicity, Point of View, and Responsibility in Traditional Chinese Healing," in *Body, Subject*, eds. Zito and Barlow, 84–87. See also my review article, "The Winds of Change," *Women: A Cultural Review* 6, no.1 (1995): 119–22.

33. D. C. Lau, "Introduction" to *Mencius* (Harmondsworth: Penguin, 1970), 24–25.

34. Ames and Hall, *Thinking Through Confucius*, 17–25, 85.

35. Needham, *Time*, 6.

36. Rey Chow, "Silent is the Ancient Plain: Music, Film-making, and the Concept of Change in the New Chinese Cinema" in Rey Chow, *Primitive Passions: Visuality, Sexuality, Ethnography, and Contemporary Chinese Cinema* (New York: Columbia University Press, 1995), 81.

37. Peter Hitchcock's article on alienation and aesthetic form in Fifth Generation film was suggestive in the formulation of this argument, especially in his use of a Lacanian model of analysis. Peter Hitchcock, "The Aestetics of Alienation, or China's 'Fifth Generation'," *Cultural Studies* 6, no.1 (January 1992): 116–41, esp. 121–25.

38. Ching-mei Esther Yau, *Filmic Discourses on Women in Chinese Cinema (1949-1965): Art, Ideology, and Social Relations* (Ph.D. thesis, University of California, 1990), 267.

39. Translation: MacDougall, *Yellow Earth*, 192–93.

40. Raymond Williams, "Base and Superstructure in Marxist Cultural Theory," in *Problems in Materialism and Culture* (London: Verso, 1980), 41.

41. Information from an interview by Klaus Eder with the director recorded in *New Chinese Cinema*, eds. Klaus Eder and Deac Rossell, (Dossier 1, National Film Theatre of Great Britain, 1993), 120–21.

42. "Rules are normative in the sense of external ordering principles with respect to historical cultures, while in traditional cultures rules are constitutive and immanent in the sense that, as ritualistic forms, they constitute the being or agent in the performance of the ritual." Ames and Hall, *Confucius*, 22.

43. Elisabeth Croll, *From Heaven to Earth: Images and Experiences of Development in China*, (London: Routledge, 1994), 25.

44. Ames and Hall, *Confucius*, 325.

45. Andrew Kipnis, "(Re)inventing *Li: Koutou* and Subjectification in Rural Shandong" in *Body, Subject*, eds. Zito and Barlow, (Chicago: Chicago University Press, 1994), 216.

CHAPTER FIVE

Part of this chapter published as Stephanie Donald, "Women Reading Chinese Films: Between Orientalism and Silence," *Screen* 36, no. 4 (winter 1995): 325–40.

1. Trinh T. Minh-ha, "Difference—A Special Third World Women's Issue," *Discourse* 8 (fall/winter 1986-87): 27.

2. Julia Kristeva, *About Chinese Women*, trans. Anita Barrows (New York: Marion Boyars, 1977), 68. First published: Paris: Editions de femmes, 1974.

3. Kristeva, *Women*, 199–200.

4. Meng Yue, "Female Images and National Myth" in *Gender Politics in Modern China: Writing and Feminism*, ed. Tani E Barlow (Durham: Duke University Press, 1993), 118–36; quotations, 121, 134.

5. Anchee Min, "Extract from *Red Fire Farm*," in *Granta* 39 (Spring 1992): 200.

6. Chen Xiaomei, "Growing Up with Posters," forthcoming.

7. Mary Ann Doane, "Film and the Masquerade: Theorising the Female Spectator," in *Film Theory*, eds. Mast, Cohen, and Braudy, (Oxford: Oxford University Press, 1992), 758–72; Gaylyn Studlar, "Masochism, Masquerade, and the Erotic Metamorphoses of Marlene Dietrich," in *Fabrications and the Female Body*, eds. Jane Gaines and Charlotte Herzog, (AFU Readers, New York: Routledge, 1990), 229–49.

8. *Quanguo funü lianhuanhui*, (National Association of Women) abbreviated to *Fulian*.

9. Tani E. Barlow, "Politics and Protocols of *Fünü*" in *Engendering China: Women, Culture and the State*, eds. Christina K. Gilmartin et al. (Cambridge: Harvard University Press, 1994), 339–59, 349–50.

10. Trinh T. Minh-ha, "Difference," 15–16.

11. Trinh, "Difference," 23–24.

12. Su Tong, *Raise the Red Lantern* (Da hong denglong gaogao gua) (Yuan-Liou Publishing Co. 1990), trans. Michael Duke (London: Touchstone, 1994).

13. Esther Ching-mei Yau, "Is China the End of Hermeneutics? Or, Political and Cultural Usage of Non-Han Women in Mainland Chinese Films," *Discourse* 11, no. 2 (1989): 99.

14. Frank Dikötter, *The Discourse of Race in Modern China* (London: Hurst and Co., 1992), 193–94, quotation 182.

15. For a discussion of this and other debates around the visual arts see: Marie Claire Huot, *La Petite Révolution Culturelle* (Arles: Editions Philippe Picquier, 1994). See also Joan Lebold Cohen's account of the mural incident, in Cohen, *New Chinese*, 39–40. She describes how the reaction to Yuan Yunsheng's *Water Festival: Song of Life*, painted in 1979 as one of a series of commissioned murals at the airport, was orchestrated more by official prudery than genuine Dai disquiet. The offending scene of bathing nudes was covered up in 1981 as part of the brief Socialist Morality campaign.

16. Dru C. Gladney, "Representing Nationality in China: Refiguring Majority/Minority Identities," *Journal of Asian Studies* 53, no.1 (February 1994): 92–123, quotation 103.

17. Yau, "Hermeneutics," 129.

18. Yau, "Hermeneutics," 129.

19. Its reinvention in May Fourth literature was a reworking of a long history of nature as a mark of cultural authenticity. See for example the discussion of evocation *xing* as an antidote to the prosaic tendencies of early *baihua* writings in Zhang Zao, "Development and Continuity of Modernity in Chinese Poetry Since 1917," in *Inside Out: Modernism and Postmodernism in Chinese Literary Culture*, eds. Wendy Larson and Anne Wedell Wedellsborg, (Aarhus: Aarhus University Press, 1993), 38–59. For a discussion of the traditions and tropes of Chinese poetry see James J. Y. Liu, *The Art of Chinese Poetry*

(University of Chicago, 1962), esp. Part II. See also Chow's remarks on Buddhist texts, where Daoist *wuwei* (doing nothing) seems to have been incorporated. The acolyte must achieve the transmission of truth/natural content through a renunciation of overdetermined form. Rey Chow, "Ethics after Idealism," *Diacritics* 23, no. 1 (1993): 19.

20. Yingchi Chu, "Introduction," in *Coloniser, Motherland and Self in Hong Kong Cinema*, (unpublished Ph.D. dissertation, Murdoch University, 1999), 2–5.

21. The autonomous regions: Tibet; Xinjiang-Uygur; Inner Mongolia; Ningxia Hui; Guangxi-Zhuang. These do not enjoy self-government but they exercise more social control than the provinces in some matters—family planning, education, legal jurisdiction, and religious expression. In Xinjiang there has been recent publicity for attempts to rebuild ethnic identity and create Islamic ties with central Asian republics of the former USSR. Dominic Ziegler, "Survey: China," *The Economist*, (pullout) (8.3.97): 6. There are fifty-five national minorities in China (currently others, including the Hakka, are applying for legal visibility). In 1995 the largest group was the Zhuang (18.7 million), follwed by the Manchu (11.5 million) and the Miao (10.6 million). There were 1.4 million Dai in 1995—The total population breaks down into Han 90.1 percent (1.125 billion) and national minorities 9.9 percent (111.2 million). However national minorities occupy 64 percent of total land area in China, mostly to the west and south. Source: *China State Statistical Yearbook*, 1997. Urban and rural Chinese are projected at 34.49 percent urban to 65.51 percent in the year 2000. In 1975 only 17.25 percent of the population were 'urban'. At current rates (1995) China's urban population is on a par with India's (30.3 percent China; 26.8 percent India) and less than that of Indonesia (35.4 percent). Sources: UN Center for Human Settlements, *An Urbanizing World: Global Report on Human Settlements, 1996*; Asian Development Bank: UN *World Urbanization Prospects*, 1997.

22. Zhang Nuanxin's films include: *Sha Ou* (1981, Youth Film Studio) This is a morality and nation story of woman volleyball player who loses her own career, and then her husband, but trains China's team to beat Japan to a gold medal. *A Woman Pianist's Story* (Gui ge qing yuan, 1990, Shanghai, France Aifeier, Beiersite Film) is another story of a woman's career—this time told through her relationship with her father, rather than her country. *Yunnan Story* (Yun nan gu shi, 1993, Taiwan Zhingsheng, Taiwan Golden Tripod, Beijing)—the story of a Japanese woman living her life in China after WWII. After a visit to her family in Japan forty years later she realizes that she is now happier in China. South China 1994 (Nan zhong guo1994, Tianjin, Shenzhen)—A story of progressive management in an Special Economic Zone (her last completed film). Yu Le ed., *Cao zong yin mu de nü xing: zhongguo nü lin gdao*, (Women operators in film: Chinese female directors), (Beijing: Women and Children's Press, 1989), 118–45.

23. Li Tuo and Zhang Nuanxin, "The Modernization of Film Language," *Beijing Film Art* 3 (1979): 40–52.

24. Nancy Fraser, "What's Critical about Critical Theory?" in *Feminism as Critique*, eds. Seyla Benhabib, and Drucilla Cornell, (Oxford: Polity Press, 1987), 31–55; Seyla Benhabib, "Models of Public Space: Hannah Arendt, the Liberal Tradition, and Jürgen Habermas" in *Habermas and the Publc Sphere,* ed. Craig Calhoun (Cambridge, Mass.: MIT Press, 1992), 73–98.

25. Fraser, "What's Critical," 39–40.

26. Chris Berry and Mary Ann Farquhar, "Post Socialist Strategies: An Analysis of *Yellow Earth* and *The Black Cannon Incident*" in *Cinematic Landscapes: Observations*

on the Visual Arts of China and Japan, eds. Linda.C. Ehrlich and David Desser, (Austin: University of Texas Press, 1994), 91–116, 102.

27. There are three terms, *dangdai, niandai, xiandai*, which can all be translated as 'now'. They also however suggest a spectrum of time within the contemporary mode. *Dangdai* is the contemporary moment that includes the age in which it is experienced. Thus in 1977 a mainland dictionary could say: 'Comrade Mao was the greatest Marxist-Leninist of our time'. *Niandai* is the disengaged, ahistorical moment; it has currency but no fixed chronological place. *Xiandai* is perhaps the most chronologically loaded term. It is the contemporary but also bears a connotation of the modern age, of the years of conflict with the encroaching world since the mid-nineteenth century. For the rest of this argument then I assume that the new contemporary is *dangdai*, which is susceptible to experience as well as history.

28. Arif Dirlik, *Revolution and History: The Origins of Marxist Historiography in China 1919–1937* (Los Angeles, Berkeley, London: University of California Press, 1978), 229.

29. For further discussion of the relationship between narcissism and the idealizing mutual gaze, see: Esther Yau, "International Fantasy and the New Chinese Cinema," *Quarterly Review of Film and Video* 14, no. 3 (1993): 95–107, and Chow, "Ethics," 3–22.

30. It seemed a pity then that at the screening at the National Film Theatre in London in 1993 a translation was given by one male voice through headphones that rather destroyed the schematic.

31. National Film Theater (London, now Royal National Film Theater) (NFT) program notes to the screening in July 1993. Also reiterated by Peng at the NFT Guardian debate 4 July 1993.

32. Rey Chow, "Seeing Modern China," in *Women and Chinese Modernity—The Politics of Reading between East and West* (Minneapolis: University of Minnesota Press, 1991), 7.

33. Homi Bhabha, "The Other Question" in *The Location of Culture* (London: Routledge, 1994), 70.

34. Chow's argument is traced throughout her collection of essays: Rey Chow, *Writing Diaspora, Tactics of Intervention in Contemporary Cultural Studies* (Bloomington: Indiana University Press, 1993), esp. 51–54, 56–57.

35. Much of Chow's perspective is argued through her reading of Gayatri Chavrakorty Spivak, "Can the Subaltern Speak?" in *Marxism and the Interpretation of Culture*, eds. Lawrence Grossberg and Cary Nelson, (Urbana: University of Illinois Press, 1988), 271–313.

36. Rey Chow, "Violence in the Other Country," in *Third World Women and the Politics of Feminism*, eds. Chandra Talpede Mohanty, Ann Russo, and Lourdes Torres, (Bloomington: Indiana University Press, 1992), 81–100, quotation 91.

37. Bhabha, *Location*, 86–86.

CHAPTER SIX

A substantial proportion of this chapter has previously appeared as Stephanie Donald, "Symptoms of Alienation: The Female Body in Recent Chinese Film," *Continuum: Journal of Media and Cultural Studies* 12, no.1 (1998): 91–113.

1. Kristeva, *Chinese Women*, 68.

2. Hill Gates, "Owner, Worker, Mother, Wife," in *Putting Class in its Place: Worker Identities in East Asia*, ed. Elizabeth Perry (Berkeley: University of California Press, 1996), 136.

3. Katherine Carlitz, "Desire, Danger and the Body: Stories of Women's Virtue in Late Ming China," in *Engendering China: Women, Culture and the State*, eds. Christina K. Gilmartin et al. (Cambridge: Harvard University Press, 1994), 124.

4. Jiang Zemin's China?

5. Cornelius Castoriades, *L'Institution imaginaire de la societe*, (Paris: Seuil, 1975), 293.

6. Arif Dirlik, "Postsocialism? Reflections on 'Socialism with Chinese Characteristics'," in *Marxism and the Chinese Experience: Issues in Contemporary Chinese Socialism*, eds. Arif Dirlik and Maurice Meisner, (London: ME Sharpe, 1989).

7. 'The Hundred Singers' Concert' celebrating the International Year of Peace, Beijing Workers' Stadium, May 1986.

8. Linda Jaivin, "Blowing His Own Trumpet," *Far Eastern Economic Review* 139, no. 12 (24 March 1988): 84–87. Cui Jian has been almost permanently banned in Beijing, although he does play occasional approved gigs and 'parties', as well as shows outside Beijing and internationally. Thanks to David Matthew Stoke of Melbourne University for his advice and information on Cui Jian's career to date.

9. Liang Heping and Ulrike Stobbe, *China Avant-garde, 1993* (Berlin: Haus der Kulturen der Welt, 1993), 90–93.

10. Liang and Stobbe, *Avant-garde*, 93.

11. The Criminal Justice and Public Order Act 1994 criminalizes gatherings in the open air of two or more people preparing for a rave, and ten or more people waiting for a rave to start. The clauses stipulate land 'in the open air' but this includes 'a place partly open to the air'. The CJPO Act, clause 63: 1; 2; 10 c.

12. Jeremy Gilbert, "Soundtrack to an Uncivil Society: Rave Culture, the Criminal Justice Act, and the Politics of Modernity," *New Formations* 31 (1997): 5–22. Tara Brabazon, "Disco(urse) dancing: reading the body politic," *Australian Journal of Communication* 24, no. 1 (1997): 104–08.

13. Gilbert, "Soundtrack," 15.

14. John Minford, quoted in Geremie Barmé, "Wang Shuo and *Liumang* (hooligan) culture," *The Australian Journal of Chinese Affairs* 28 (July 1992): 28.

15. Screening at midnight, 26 June 1995.

16. Elizabeth Grosz, *Volatile Bodies: Towards a Corporeal Feminism* (Bloomington: Indiana University Press, 1995), 86.

17. Judith Farquhar, "Multiplicity, Point of View, and Responsibility in Traditional Chinese Healing," *Body Subject and Power in China*, eds. Angela Zito and Tani Barlow, (Chicago: University of Chicago Press, 1994), 94.

18. Harriet Evans, *Women and Sexuality in China: Dominant Discourses of Female Sexuality and Gender Since 1949* (Cambridge: Polity Press, 1997), 220.

19. Charlotte Furth, "Rethinking Van Gulik: Sexuality and Reproduction in Traditional Chinese Medicine," *Engendering China*, ed. Gilmartin (Cambridge: Harvard University Press, 1994), 145.

20. Huot, *La Petite Révolution*, 57.

21. Thanks to Harriet Evans whose work on *jiefang* and gender suggested this line of argument. Harriet Evans, "Jiefang," *Intersections: Gender, History and Culture in the Asian Context* 1, no. 1. <http://wwwsshe.murdoch.edu.au/hum/as/intersections/> (accessed November 10 1998).

22. Gates, "Owner, Worker," 127–30.

23. Evans, *Gender and Sexuality*, 187–88.

24. Esther Ching-mei Yau, *Filmic Discourses,* 270.

25. T'ien Ju-k'ang, *Male Anxiety and Female Chastity: A Comparative Study of Chinese Ethical Values in Ming-Ch'ing Times* (Leiden: Brill; Monographes du T'oung-Pao, 1988): viii.

26. T'ien Ju-k'ang, *Male Anxiety,* 66.

CHAPTER SEVEN

1. Rey Chow, "Film as Ethnography; or, Translation between Cultures in the Post-colonial World," in *Primitive Passions* (New York: Columbia University Press, 1995), 173–202, quotation 199.

2. Geremie Barmé, "Wang Shuo and *Liumang* (hooligan) Culture," *The Australian Journal of Chinese Affairs* (July 1992): 23–64, 45.

3. Barmé, "Wang Shuo," Quoting the *Beijing Economic Weekly*, 27 November 1988, 30.

4. Victor C. Falkenheim, "Citizen and Group Politics in China: An Introduction," in *Citizens and Groups in Contemporary China*, ed. Falkenheim (Ann Arbor: Michigan University Press, 1987), 1–19, quotation 4. For an account of the extent of state involvement in daily life after marketization see Vivienne Shue, "State Sprawl," in *Urban Spaces in Contemporary China: The Potential for Autonomy and Community in Post-Mao China,* eds. Deborah S. Davis et al. (Cambridge: Cambridge University Press, 1995), 93–99.

5. See Merle Goldman's account, "Dissident Intellectuals in the PRC," in *Citizens and Groups in Contemporary China*, ed. Victor Falkenheim, 159–87. She stresses that in order to dissent effectively intellectuals need to engage in informal politics so that their case is heard ". . . they were held together less by their professional interests than by similar positions on such issues as the Great Leap Forward, and *by their personal connections*" (my emphasis), 165.

6. Ambrose Yeo-chi King, "Kuan-hsi and Network Building—a Sociological Interpretation," *Daedalus* 120, no. 2 (spring 1991): 63–84.

7. Andrew J Nathan, "Is Chinese Culture Distinctive?," *The Journal of Asian Studies* 52, no.4 (Nov. 1993): 923–36.

8. S. Duan, *Village Leadership in Contemporary China*, (unpublished Ph.D. dissertation, University of Sussex, 1994), quotations taken from draft (with author's permission).

9. Nancy N. Chen, "Urban Spaces and *Qigong*," in *Urban Spaces*, ed. Deborah S. Davis (Cambridge: Cambridge University Press, 1995), 354.

10. Andrew Kipnis, "(Re)inventing *Li: Koutou* and Subjectification in Rural Shandong," in *Body, Subject*, eds. Zito and Barlow, (Chicago: Chicago University Press, 1994), 211.

11. Duan, *Village Leadership*, quote from draft.

12. *Yin wen sheng shi,* quoted from Jin Shengtan's introduction to *Shui Hu Zhuan,* quoted by Andrew Plaks, *Chinese Narrative: Critical and Theoretical Essays* (Princeton: Princeton University Press, 1977), 316–17.

13. Plaks, *Narrative,* 312. See also Sheldon Hsiao-peng Lu, "From History to Verisimilitude," in *From Historicity to Fictionality: The Chinese Poetics of Narrative* (Stanford: Stanford University Press, 1994), 129–31.

14. Michael Taussig, *Mimesis and Alterity: A Particular History of the Senses* (London, New York: Routledge, 1992), 77–86.

15. Plaks, *Narrative,* 312–13.

16. Robert Bresson, *Notes on the Cinematographer,* trans. Jonathan Griffin. (London: Quartet, 1975), 14–15.

17. Roger T. Ames and David Hall, *Thinking Through Confucius* (New York: SUNY, 1987), 124.

18. Gender neutral language is not appropriate in Confucian texts, and should be understood as a deliberate intrusion.

19. Ames and Hall, *Confucius,* 114–24. For an account of the influence of Neo-Confucian philosophy on contemporary Chinese thought see Lin Tongqi, Henry Rosemont Jr., and Roger T. Ames, "Chinese Philosophy: a Philosophical Essay on the 'State of the Art'," *The Journal for Asian Studies* 54, no. 3 (August 1995): 727–58.

20. Partha Chatterjee, "A Response to Taylor's 'Modes of Civil Society'," in *Public Culture* 3, no.1 (Fall 1990): 119–32, quotation 124. See also Partha Chatterjee, *The Nation and its Fragments* (Princeton: Princeton University Press, 1993), 230–34.

21. Chatterjee, "Response," 130.

22. Chatterjee, "Response," 131.

23. Chatterjee, "Response," 130–32.

24. See He Baogang, *The Dual Roles of Semi-Civil Society* (Sussex: Institute of Development Studies Discussion Paper, 1993); "Special Issue on Public Sphere and Civil Society in China," *Modern China* 19, no. 2 (April 1993). Lowell Dittmer's work on informal politics and the public sphere argues that virtue and civility are entirely questions of policy, Lowell Dittmer, *China Under Reform* (Boulder: Westview Press, 1994). Andrew Nathan, argues that civil rights as enshrined in the *six* Chinese Constitutions since 1949, were entirely at the disposal of state interests: ". . . the writers of Chinese constitutions included rights prominently . . . their purpose was not to protect the individual against the state, but to enable the individual to function more effectively within the state." *Chinese Democracy* (London: Tauris, 1986), 125.

25. Claude Lefort, *The Political Forms of Modern Society—Bureaucracy, Democracy, Totalitarianism* (Cambridge: Polity Press, 1986), 297–303. See also Renata Salecl, "Nationalism, Anti-Semitism and Anti-Feminism in Eastern Europe," *New German Critique: An Interdisciplinary Journal of German Studies,* no. 57 (1992): 51–67; Slavoj Zizek, "Eastern European Liberalism and its Discontents," *New German Critique: An Interdisciplinary Journal of German Studies,* no. 57 (1992): 25–49.

26. Note François Jullien's perceptive work on authoritarianism in early Chinese political thought. He notes that the manipulation carried out from the central presence of the ruler worked (at least in theory) only when the ruler was invisible: Michel Foucault, *Surveiller et Punir,* (Paris: Gallimard, 1975), described in François Jullien, (New York, Zone Books, 1995), 52–56. His argument allows one to speculate on a break between Legalist authoritarian procedure and the modern psychosis of totalitarian rule.

27. Nathan, *Chinese Democracy*, 83.

28. Mao Zedong, *Report of an Investigation into the Peasant Movement in Hunan* (Beijing: Beijing Foreign Languages Press, 1953), 4ff.

29. Introductions to Maoist thought taken from Roderick McFarquhar, and John K. Fairbank, eds., *The Cambridge History of China, Vol. 15, Part 2: Revolutions within the Chinese Revolution 1966-1982* (Cambridge: Cambridge University Press, 1991), 1–96; Stuart R. Schram, ed., *Mao Tsetung* (London: Penguin Books, 1966); Mao Tse-tung, *On Art and Literature* (Beijing: Foreign Languages Press, 1960).

30. Lefort, *Political Forms*, 306.

31. J. L. Cohen and A. Arato, *Civil Society and Political Theory* (Cambridge: MIT Press, 1992), 427–28.

32. Charles Taylor, "Modes of Civil Society," *Public Culture* 3, no. 1 (1990): 95–118.

33. Jeffrey N. Wasserstrom and Liu Xinyong, "Student Associations and Mass Movements," in *Urban Spaces*, ed. Deborah S. Davis, 362–393. See also Elizabeth Perry, "Labor's Battle for Political Space: The Role of Worker Associations in Contemporary China," in *Urban Spaces*, ed. Deborah S. Davis, 302–25.

34. Following the Film Bureau's procedures against him in March 1994, Zhang Yuan made a documentary called *The Square*, as a 'riposte'. Tony Rayns, *Index on Censorship* 24, no. 6 (1995): 79.

35. Wu Hung, "Tiananmen Square: A Political History of Monuments," *Representations*, no. 35 (summer 1991): 84–117, quotation, 102–3.

36. Chapter seven, note 1.

AFTERWORD

1. Cao Guilin, *Beijinger in New York* (*Beijing ren zai Niu Yue*, 1991), English translation, (San Francisco: Cypress Book Company, 1994). See Huot, *La Petite Revolution*, 165–66, for a further account.

2. Cao, *Beijinger*, 211.

3. Tables 3–12; 11–29; 11–28; *China Statistical Yearbook 1995*, Beijing: China Statistical Publishing House, 72, 363, 364.

4. Gates, "Owner, Worker, Mother, Wife," and Emily Honig, "Regional Identity, Labor, and Ethnicity in Contemporary China," both in *Putting Class*, (Berkeley: University of California, 1996), 225–43, 127–65.

5. Lola Young, *Fear of the Dark: 'Race', Gender and Sexuality in the Cinema* (London: Routledge, 1996), 175.

6. Lola Young, *Fear*, 190.

7. David Gauntlett, "Ten things wrong with the effects model," <http:www.theory.org.uk> (accessed 9 September 1999).

8. Oskar Negt and Alexander Kluge, *Public Sphere and Experience: Towards and Analysis of the Bourgeois and Proletarian Public Sphere* (Minneapolis: Minnesota University Press, 1993), 56.

9. Elsaesser, "Social Mobility," 29.

10. Rey Chow, "Listening Otherwise, Music Miniaturized: A Different Type of Question about Revolution," in *Writing Diaspora: Tactics of Intervention in Contemporary Cultural Studies* (Bloomington: Indiana University Press, 1993), 151.

11. David Strand, *Rickshaw Beijing: City People and Politics in 1920s China* (Berkeley: University of California Press, 1993); Dorothy Sollinger, "China's Transients and the State? A Form of Civil Society?," *Politics and Society* 21, no. 1 (March 1993): 91–122.

12. Annette Michelson, "The Wings of Hypothesis: On Montage and the Theory of the Interval," in *Montage and Modern Life 1919-1942*, ed. M. Teitelbaum (Cambridge: MIT Press, 1992), 61–81.

13. Sergei Eisenstein, "The Filmic Fourth Dimension," in *Film Form: Essays in Film Theory*, ed. Jay Leyda (New York: Harcourt, Brace and World, 1949) quoted in Michelson, "Wings," 69 passim. For an account of the autonomy of the filmic text see: Vlada Petric, *Constructivism in Film: 'The Man with the Movie Camera', A Cinematic Analysis* (Cambridge: Cambridge University Press, 1987), 70–128. For a discussion of the effects of science and on science in an authoritarian regime see Perry Link and Fang Lizhi's review article of H. Lyman Miller's *Science and Dissent in Post-Mao China: The Politics of Knowledge* (1996), "The Hope for China," *The New York Review of Books* (17 October 1996): 43–47.

14. Michelson, "Wings," 79.

15. Michelson, "Wings," 80–81.

16. Walzer, "The Civil Society Argument," 89.

Bibliography

Abbas, Ackbar. *Hong Kong: Culture and the Politics of Disappearance.* Minneapolis: University of Minnesota Press, 1997.

Adamson, Walter. L. "Gramsci and the Politics of Civil Society." *Praxis International* 7, nos. 3-4 (winter 1987-88): 318–339.

Adorno, Theodor. "Transparencies on Film" (written in 1966). *New German Critique*, no. 24-25 (fall/winter 1981-82): 199–205.

———. *The Culture Industry.* London: Routledge, 1991.

Adorno, Theodor, and Max Horkheimer. *The Dialectic of Enlightenment.* Trans. John Cumming. London: Verso, 1979.

Ah Cheng. "The Chess Master." *Chinese Literature* (summer 1985): 84–132.

Ames, Roger T., and David L. Hall. *Thinking through Confucius.* New York: State University of New York, 1987.

Anagnost, Ann. "Socialist Ethics and the Legal System." In *Popular Protest and Political Culture in Modern China: Learning from 1989.* Eds. Jeffery N. Wasserstrom and Elizabeth Perry. Boulder: Westview, 1992.

———. "Who Is Speaking Here? Discursive Boundaries and Representation in Post-Mao China." In *Boundaries in China.* Ed. John Hay. London: Reaktion Books, 1994.

Anderson, Perry. "The Antimonies of Antonio Gramsci." *New Left Review* (November 1976-January 1977): 5–78.

Andrews, Julia F. *Painters and Politics in the People's Republic of China 1949-1979.* Berkeley: University of California Press, 1994.

Ang, Ien. "Comment on Felski's 'The Doxa of Difference': The Uses of Incommensurability." *Signs: Journal of Women in Culture and Society* 23, no. 1 (1997): 57–64.

Appadurai, Arjun. *Modernity at Large: Cultural Dimensions of Globalization.* Minneapolis: University of Minnesota Press, 1996.

Apter, David E., and Tony Saich. *Revolutionary Discourse in Mao's Republic.* Cambridge, Mass.: Harvard University Press, 1994.

169

Archibugi, Daniele, and David Held. *Cosmopolitan Democracy: An Agenda for a New World Order*. Cambridge: Polity Press, 1995.

Arendt, Hannah. *The Human Condition: A Study of the Central Dilemmas Facing Modern Man*. Chicago: University of Chicago Press, 1958.

Baptandier, Brigitte. "The Lady Linshui: How a Woman Became a Goddess." In *Unruly Gods: Divinity and Society in China*. Eds. Meir Shahar and Robert P. Weller. Honolulu: University of Hawaii Press, 1996.

Barlow, Tani E., ed. *Gender Politics in Modern China: Writing and Feminism*. Durham: Duke University Press, 1993.

_____. "Politics and Protocols of *Fünü*." In *Engendering China: Women, Culture, and the State*. Eds. Christine Gilmartin et al. Cambridge, Mass.: Harvard University Press, 1994.

Barmé, Geremie. "Wang Shuo and *Liumang* (Hooligan) Culture." *The Australian Journal of Chinese Affairs* (July 1992): 23–64.

_____. *Shades of Mao: The Posthumous Cult of the Great Leader*. Armonk, N.Y.: ME Sharpe, 1996.

Barmé, Geremie, and John Minford. *Seed of Fire: Chinese Voices of Conscience*. Newcastle upon Tyne: Bloodaxe Books, 1988.

Bazin, Andre. "The Stalin Myth in Soviet Cinema." In *Movies and Methods Part II*. Ed. Bill Nicholls, 29–40. Berkeley: University of California Press, 1984.

Ben Xu. "From Modernity to Chineseness: The Rise of Nativist Cultural Theory in Post-1989 China." *Positions-East Asia Cultures Critique* 6, no. 1 (spring 1998): 203–37.

Benewick, Robert, and Paul Wingrove, eds. *Reforming the Revolution*. London: Macmillan, 1988.

_____. *China in the 1990s*. London: Macmillan, 1995.

Benewick, Robert, and Stephanie Donald. "Badgering the People: Mao Badges, A Retrospective." In *Belief in China: Art and Politics, Deities and Mortality*. Eds. Benewick and Donald. Brighton: Green Centre for Non-Western Art, 1996.

Benhabib, Seyla. "Models of Public Space: Hannah Arendt, the Liberal Tradition, and Jürgen Habermas." In *Habermas and the Public Sphere*. Ed. Craig Calhoun. Cambridge, Mass.: MIT, 1992.

Benhabib, Seyla, and Drucilla Cornell, eds. *Feminism As Critique*. Oxford: Polity Press, 1987.

Benjamin, Walter. "The Work of Art in the Age of Technical Reproduction." In *Film Theory and Criticism: Introductory Readings*. Eds. Gerald Mast, Marshall Cohen, and Leo Braudy. Fourth Edition. Oxford: Oxford University Press, 1992.

Bergeron, R. *Le Cinéma Chinois 1949-1983*. Paris: L'Harmatton, 1984.

Berry, Chris, ed. *Perspectives on Chinese Cinema*. London: British Film Institute, 1991.

_____. "Neither One Thing Nor Another-Towards a Study of the Viewing Subject and the Chinese Cinema in the 1980s." In *New Chinese Cinema: Forms, Identities, Politics*. Eds. Nick Browne et al. Cambridge: Cambridge University Press, 1993.

Berry, Chris, and Mary Ann Farquhar. "Post-Socialist Strategies: An Analysis of *Yellow Earth* and *Black Cannon Incident*." In *Cinematic Landscapes: Observations on the Visual Arts of China and Japan*. Eds. Linda C. Ehrlich and David Desser. Austin: University of Texas Press, 1994.

Bhabha, Homi K. *The Location of Culture*. London: Routledge, 1994.

Bobbio, Norberto. "Gramsci and the Concept of Civil Society." In *Civil Society and the State: New European Perspective: On the Predicaments of European Socialism, the Prospects for Democracy, and the Problem of Controlling Social and Political Power*. Ed. John Keane. London: Verso, 1988.

Bordwell, David, and Kristin Thompson. *Narration in the Fiction Film*. London: Methuen, 1985.

———. *Film Art: An Introduction*. Fifth Edition. New York: McGraw Hill, 1997.

Bowles, Paul, and Gordon White. "Contradictions in China's Financial Reforms: The Relationship between Banks and Enterprises." *Cambridge Journal of Economics* 13, no. 4 (December 1989): 481–95.

Brabazon, Tara. "Disco(urse) Dancing: Reading the Body Politic." *Australian Journal of Communication* 24, no. 1 (1997): 104–14.

Bresson, Robert. *Notes on the Cinematographer*. Trans. Jonathan Griffin. London: Quartet, 1975.

Browne, Nick, Paul Pickowicz, Vivienne Sobchack, and Esther Ching-mei Yau, eds. *New Chinese Cinema: Forms, Identities, Politics*. Cambridge: Cambridge University Press, 1993.

Buci-Glucksmann, Christina. "Hegemony and Consent: A Political Strategy." In *Approaches to Gramsci*. Ed. Anne Showstack Sassoon. London: Writers and Readers Cooperative Society, 1982.

Burgin, Victor. *In Different Spaces: Place and Memory in Visual Culture*. Berkeley: University of California Press, 1996.

Calhoun, Craig, ed. *Habermas and the Public Sphere*. Cambridge, Mass.: MIT, 1992.

Cao Guilin (Glen). *Beijinger in New York (Beijing ren zai Niu Yue)*. San Francisco: Cypress Book Co., 1993.

Carlitz, Katherine. "Desire, Danger, and the Body: Stories of Women's Virtue in Late Ming China." In *Engendering China: Women, Culture, and the State*. Eds. Christina K. Gilmartin et al. Cambridge, Mass.: Harvard University Press, 1994.

Castoriadis, Cornelius. *L'Institution imaginaire de la société*. Paris: Seuil, 1975.

Caygill, Howard. *Walter Benjamin: The Colour of Experience*. London: Routledge, 1998.

Chamberlain, Heath B. "Party-Management Relations in Chinese Industries: Some Political Dimensions of Economic Reform." *The China Quarterly*, no. 112 (December 1987): 631–61.

Chang, David Wen-wei. *China under Deng Xiaoping: Political and Economic Reform*. London: Macmillan, 1988.

Chatterjee, Partha. "A Response to Taylor's 'Modes of Civil Society'." *Public Culture* 3, no. 1 (fall 1990): 119–32.

———. *The Nation and Its Fragments: Colonial and Postcolonial Histories*. Princeton: Princeton University Press, 1993.

Chen Kaige, and Tony Rayns. *King of the Children and the New Chinese Cinema*. London: Faber and Faber, 1989.

Chen Xiaomei. "Growing Up with Posters in Maoist China: Memory, Multiplicity and Masquerade in Visual Culture." In *Picturing Power in the People's Republic of China: Posters of the Cultural Revolution*. Eds. Harriet Evans and Stephanie Donald. Lanham: Rowman & Littlefield, 1999.

Chen Xihe. *The Major Developments and Their Ideological Implications of Chinese Film and Film Education since the Cultural Revolution*. Ph.D. dissertation, Ohio State University, 1994.

China Statistical Yearbook(s). Beijing: China Statistical Publishing House, 1995, 1996, 1997.

Chong Woei Lien. "Rock Star Cui Jian." *CHIME Journal*, no. 4 (autumn 1991): 90–91.

Chow, Rey. "It's You and Not Me: Domination and Othering in Theorizing the Third World." In *Coming to Terms*. Ed. Elizabeth Weed. New York: Routledge, 1989.

———. "Silent Is the Ancient Plain: Music, Film-making, and the Conception of Reform in China's New Cinema." *Discourse* 12, no. 2. (spring/summer 1990): 82–109.

———. *Women and Chinese Modernity-The Politics of Reading between East and West*. Minnesota: University of Minnesota Press, 1991.

———. "Violence in the Other Country." In *Third World Women and the Politics of Feminism*. Eds. Chandra Talpade Mohanty, Ann Russo, and Lourdes Torres. Bloomington: Indiana University Press, 1992.

———. "Ethics after Idealism." *Diacritics* 23, no. 1 (1993): 3–22.

———. *Writing Diaspora: Tactics of Intervention in Contemporary Cultural Studies*. Bloomington: Indiana University Press, 1993.

———. *Primitive Passions: Visuality, Sexuality, Ethnography and Contemporary Chinese Cinema*. New York: Columbia University Press, 1995.

———. "Can One Say No to China?" *New Literary History* 28 (winter 1997): 147–51.

Chu Yingchi. *Coloniser, Motherland, and Self in Hong Kong Cinema*. Ph.D. dissertation, Murdoch University, 1999.

Clark, Paul. *Chinese Cinema: Culture and Politics since 1949*. Cambridge: Cambridge University Press, 1987.

Cohen, Jean, and Andrew Arato. *Civil Society and Political Theory*. Cambridge, Mass.: MIT Press, 1992.

Cohen, Joan Lebold. *The New Chinese Painting 1949-1986*. New York: Harry Abrams, 1987.

Cosgrove, Denis, and Stephen Daniels. *The Iconography of Landscape: Essays on the Symbolic Representation, Design and Use of Past Environments*. Cambridge: Cambridge University Press, 1988.

Croll, Elisabeth. *From Heaven to Earth: Images and Experiences of Development in China*. London: Routledge, 1994.

Dai Jinhua. "Invisible Women: Contemporary Chinese Cinema and Women's Film." *Positions* 3, no. 1 (spring 1995).

Davis, Deborah S., Richard Kraus, Barry Naughton, and Elizabeth Perry, eds. *Urban Spaces in Contemporary China: The Potential for Autonomy and Community in Post-Mao China*. Cambridge: Cambridge University Press/Wilson Woodrow Center, 1995.

D'Entrèves, Mauricio Passerin. *The Political Philosophy of Hannah Arendt*. London: Routledge, 1994.

Dikötter, Frank. *The Discourse of Race in Modern China*. London: Hurst and Co., 1992.

Dirlik, Arif. *Revolution and History: The Origins of Marxist Historiography in China 1919-1937*. Los Angeles: University of California Press, 1978.

———. "Postsocialism? Reflections on 'Socialism with Chinese Characteristics'." In

Marxism and the Chinese Experience: Issues in Contemporary Chinese Socialism. Eds. Arif Dirlik and Maurice Meisner. London: ME Sharpe, 1989.

Dirlik, Arif, and Xudong Zhang, eds. *Postmodernism in China.* Special Issue: *Boundary 2* 24, no. 3 (fall 1997).

Dittmer, Lowell. "Public and Private Interests and the Participatory Ethic in China." In *Citizens and Groups in Contemporary China.* Ed. Victor Falkenheim. Michigan Monographs in Chinese Studies, no. 56. Ann Arbor: Michigan University Press, 1987.

_____. *China under Reform.* Series: "Politics in Asia and the Pacific-Interdisciplinary Perspectives." Boulder: Westview Press, 1994.

Doane, Mary-Ann. "Film and Masquerade: Theorising the Female Spectator." In *Film Theory and Criticism.* Eds. Gerald Mast, Marshall Cohen, and Leo Braudy. Fourth Edition. Oxford: Oxford University Press, 1992.

Dolar, Mladen. "Hitchcock's Objects." In *Everything You Always Wanted to Know about Lacan but Were Afraid to Ask Hitchcock.* Ed. Slavoj Zizek. London: Verso, 1992.

Donald, James, ed. *Fantasy and the Cinema.* London: British Film Institute, 1991.

Donald, James, and Stephanie Donald. "The Publicness of Cinema." In *Re-inventing Film Studies.* Eds. Christine Gledhill and Linda Williams. London: Edward Arnold, 2000.

Donald, Stephanie. "Chinese Women and Chinese Film: Problems with History and Feminism." In *Women in Market Societies East and West: Crisis and Opportunity.* Eds. Barbara Einhorn and Eileen Janes Yeo. Aldershot: Edward Elgar, 1995.

_____. "Winds of Change." *Women: A Cultural Review: Gender, Islam, and Orientalism* 6, no. 1 (1995): 9–122.

_____. "Women Reading Chinese Films: Between Orientalism and Silence." *Screen* 36, no. 4 (1995): 325–46.

_____. "Landscape and Agency: *Yellow Earth* and the Demon Lover." *Theory, Culture and Society* 14, no. 1 (February 1997): 91–112.

_____. "Symptoms of Alienation: The Female Body in Recent Chinese film." *Continuum: Journal of Media and Cultural Studies* 12, no. 1 (1998): 91–113.

Dreyer, June Teufel. *China's Political System: Modernization and Tradition.* London: Macmillan, 1996.

Duan Shu-yun. *Village Leadership in Contemporary China.* Unpublished Ph.D. dissertation, University of Sussex (file no. 3893), 1994.

Eberhard, Wolfram. *A Dictionary of Chinese Symbols: Hidden Symbols in Chinese Life and Thought.* London: Routledge, Kegan Paul, 1988.

Eder, Klaus, and Deac Rossell, eds. *New Chinese Cinema.* Dossier 1. London: National Film Theatre of Great Britain, 1993.

Ehrlich, Linda C., and David Desser, eds. *Cinematic Landscapes: Observations on the Visual Arts of China and Japan.* Austin: University of Texas Press, 1994.

Eisenstein, Sergei. "The Filmic Fourth Dimension" (written in 1929). In *Film Form: Essays in Film Theory.* Ed. and trans. Jay Leyda. New York: Harcourt, Brace and World, 1949.

_____. "The Cinematographic Principle and the Ideogram" (written in 1930). In *Film Theory and Criticism,* 2nd edition. Eds. Gerald Mast and Marshall Cohen. Oxford: Oxford University Press, 1979.

Elley, Derek. "Chinese Cinema Remembered." *Griffithiana* 60-61 (October 1997): 127–81.

Elsaesser, Thomas. "Social Mobility and the Fantastic: German Silent Cinema." In *Fantasy and the Cinema*. Ed. James Donald. London: British Film Institute, 1991.

Esherick, Joseph W., and Jeffrey N. Wasserstrom. "Acting Out Democracy: Political Theatre in Modern China." *Journal of Asian Studies*, no. 49 (November 1990): 835–65.

Evans, Harriet. *Women and Sexuality in China: Dominant Discourses of Female Sexuality and Gender since 1949*. Cambridge: Polity Press, 1997.

_____. "The Language of Liberation: Gender and Jiefang in Early CCP Discourse." Intersections 1, no. 1 < http://wwwsshe.murdoch.edu.au/hum/as/intersections/current_issue.htm>, October, 1998. (accessed 10 November 1998).

Fairbank, John K., and Albert Feuerwerker, eds. *The Cambridge History of China: Vol. 13, Republican China 1912-1949*. Cambridge: Cambridge University Press, 1991.

Falk, Richard. "The World Order between Inter-state Law and the Law of Humanity: The Role of Civil Society Institutions." In *Cosmopolitan Democracy-An Agenda for a New World Order*. Eds. Daniele Archibugi and David Held. Cambridge: Polity Press, 1995.

Falkenheim, Victor, ed. *Citizens and Groups in Contemporary China*. Michigan Monographs in Chinese Studies, no. 56. Ann Arbor: University of Michigan Press, 1987.

Farquhar, Judith. "Multiplicity, Point of View, and Responsibility in Traditional Chinese Healing." In *Body, Subject, and Power in China*. Eds. Angela Zito and Tani E. Barlow. Chicago: University of Chicago Press, 1994.

Farquhar, Mary. *Chinese Children's Literature*. Ph.D. dissertation, Griffith University, 1983.

_____. "The 'Hidden' Gender in *Yellow Earth*." *Screen* 33, no. 2 (1992): 4–164.

Foucault, Michel. *Madness and Civilisation: A History of Insanity in the Age of Reason*. London: Tavistock Publications, 1967 (first published Paris: Librairie Plon, 1961).

_____. *Surveiller et Pûnir*. Paris: Gallimard, 1975.

Frankenberg, Ruth, ed. *Displacing Whiteness: Essays in Social and Cultural Criticism*. Durham: Duke University Press, 1997.

Fraser, Nancy. "What's Critical about Critical Theory?" In *Feminism As Critique*. Eds. Seyla Benhabib and Drucilla Cornell. Cambridge: Polity Press, 1987.

Frow, John. *Time, Commodity, Culture: Essays in Cultural Theory and Postmodernity*. Oxford: Oxford University Press, 1997.

Furth, Charlotte. "Rethinking Van Gulik: Sexuality and Reproduction in Traditional Chinese Medicine." In *Engendering China: Women, Culture, and the State*. Eds. Christina K Gilmartin et al. Cambridge, Mass.: Harvard University Press, 1994.

Gates, Hill. "Owner, Worker, Mother, Wife." In *Putting Class in Its Place: Worker Identities in East Asia*. Ed. Elizabeth Perry. Berkeley: University of California Press, 1996.

Gauntlett, David. "Ten Things Wrong with the Effects Model." <www.theory.org.uk> 26 August 1999. [accessed 03 September 1999].

Gilbert, Jeremy. "Soundtrack to an Uncivil Society: Rave Culture, the Criminal Justice Act and the Politics of Modernity." *New Formations* 31 (spring/summer 1997): 5–22.

Gilmartin, Christina K., Gail Hershatter, Lisa Rofel, and Tyrene White, eds. *Engendering China: Women, Culture, and the State*. Cambridge, Mass.: Harvard University Press, 1994.

Gladney, Dru C. "Representing Nationality in China: Refiguring Majority/Minority Identities." *Journal of Asian Studies* 53, no. 1 (February 1994): 92–123.

_____. "Tian Zhuangzhuang, the Fifth Generation, and Minorities Film in China." *Public Culture* 8 (1995): 161–75.

Golding, Sue. *Gramsci's Democratic Theory-Contributions to a Post-Liberal Democracy.* Toronto: University of Toronto Press, 1992.

Goldman, Merle. "Human Rights in the People's Republic of China." *Daedalus* 112, no. 4 (1983): 111–38.

_____. "Dissident Intellectuals in the PRC." In *Citizens and Groups in Contemporary China.* Ed. Victor Falkenheim. Ann Arbor: University of Michigan Press, 1987.

Gramsci, Antonio. *Selections from Political Writings 1910-1920.* Ed. Quintin Hoare. Trans. John Mathews. London: Lawrence and Wishart, 1977.

Grosz, Elizabeth. *Volatile Bodies: Towards a Corporeal Feminism.* Bloomington: Indiana University Press, 1994.

Habermas, Jürgen. *The Past As Future.* Trans. Mark Pensky. Cambridge: Polity Press, 1994.

_____. *Moral Consciousness and Communicative Action.* Cambridge: Polity Press, 1990.

_____. *The Structural Transformation of the Public Sphere- An Inquiry into a Category of Bourgeois Society* (written in 1962). Trans. Thomas Burger. London: Polity Press, 1989.

_____. *The Philosophical Discourse of Modernity.* Cambridge, Mass.: MIT Press, 1987.

_____. "The Public Sphere: An Encyclopaedia Article." *New German Critique* 1, no. 3 (fall 1974): 49–55.

Hansen, Chad. "Chinese Ideography and Western Ideas." *The Journal of Asian Studies* 52, no. 2 (May 1993): 373–99.

Hansen, Miriam. "Introduction to Adorno's 'Transparencies'." *New German Critique*, no. 24-25 (fall/winter 1981-1982): 186–98.

_____. *Babel and Babylon: Spectatorship in American Silent Film.* Cambridge, Mass.: Harvard University Press, 1991.

Harris, Kristine. "The New Woman Incident: Cinema, Spectacle, and Scandal in 1935 Shanghai." In *Transnational Chinese Cinemas: Identity, Nationhood, Gender.* Ed. Sheldon Hsiao-peng Lu. Honolulu: University of Hawaii Press, 1997.

Hay, Johnathan. "The Suspension of Dynastic Time." In *Boundaries in China.* Ed. John Hay. London: Reaktion Books, 1994.

_____. "The Body Invisible in Chinese Art." In *Body, Subject, and Power in China.* Eds. Angela Zito and Tani E. Barlow. Chicago: University of Chicago Press, 1994.

_____, ed. *Boundaries in China.* London: Reaktion Books, 1994.

He Baogang. *The Dual Roles of Semi-Civil Society.* Institute of Development Studies Discussion Paper no. 327, 1993.

He Baogang, and David Kelly. "Emergent Civil Society and the Intellectuals in China." In *The Development of Civil Society in Communist Systems.* Ed. Robert Miller. Sydney: Allen and Unwin, 1992.

Held, David. "Democracy and the New International Order." In *Cosmopolitan Democracy-An Agenda for a New World Order.* Eds. Daniele Archibugi and David Held. Cambridge: Polity Press, 1995.

Hemelryk [Donald], Stephanie. "The Chinese Horizon and the Socialist-Realist Gaze." *Diatribe*, University of Southampton: Centre for the Study of Language and Cultural Theory (winter 1994/95): 31–41.

Hitchcock, Peter. "The Aesthetics of Alienation, or, China's Fifth Generation." *Cultural Studies* 6, no. 1 (January 1992): 116–41.

Honig, Emily. "Regional Identity, Labor, and Ethnicity in Contemporary China." In *Putting Class in Its Place: Worker Identities in East Asia.* Ed. Elizabeth Perry. Berkeley: University of California Press, 1996.

hooks, bell. *Killing Rage: Ending Racism.* London: Penguin Books, 1996.

Huangfu, Binghui. *Catalogue: In and Out: Contemporary Art from China and Australia.* LaSalle: College of Arts, 1997.

Huot, Marie Claire. *La Petite Révolution Culturelle.* Arles: Editions Philippe Picquier, 1994.

Hutchings, Kimberley. *Kant, Critique, and Politics.* London: Routledge, 1996.

Jenner, W. J. F. *The Tyranny of History: The Roots of China's Crisis.* London: Allen Lane and Penguin, 1992.

Jullien, Francois. *The Propensity of Things: Toward a History of Efficacy in China.* Trans. Janet Lloyd. New York: Zone Books, 1995.

Keane, John. *Democracy and Civil Society: Despotism and Democracy: The Origins and Development of the Distinction between Civil Society and the State 1750-1850.* London: Verso, 1988.

———, ed. *Civil Society and the State: New European Perspectives: On the Predicaments of European Socialism, the Prospects for Democracy, and the Problem of Controlling Social and Political Power.* London: Verso, 1988.

———. *The Media and Democracy.* Cambridge: Polity Press, 1991.

———. "Structural Transformations of the Public Sphere." *The Communication Review* 1, no. 1 (1995): 1–22.

Kessen, William, ed. *Childhood in China.* London: Yale University Press, 1975.

King, Ambrose Yeo-chi. "Kuan-hsi and Network Building: A Sociological Interpretation." *Daedalus* 120, no. 2 (spring 1991): 63–84.

Kipnis, Andrew. "(Re)inventing *Li: Koutou* and Subjectification in Rural Shandong." In *Body, Subject, and Power in China.* Eds. Angela Zito and Tani E. Barlow. London: University of Chicago Press, 1994.

Klein, Melanie. "The Psycho-analytic Play Technique: Its History and Significance" (written in 1955). In *The Selected Melanie Klein.* Ed. Juliet Mitchell. London: Penguin, 1986.

Koch, Gertrud. "Exchanging the Gaze: Revisioning Feminist Film Theory." *New German Critique*, no. 34 (1985): 139–53.

Kowallis, Jon. "The Diaspora in Postmodern Taiwan and Hong Kong Film: Framing Stan Lai's *The Peach-blossom Land* with Allen Fong's *Ah Ying.*" In *Transnational Chinese Cinemas: Identity, Nationhood, Gender.* Ed. Sheldon Hsiao-peng Lu. Honolulu: University of Hawaii Press, 1997.

———. *From Caligari to Hitler: A Psychological History of the German Film.* Princeton: Princeton University Press, 1947.

Kracauer, Siegfried. *Theory of Film: The Redemption of Physical Reality.* Oxford: Oxford University Press, 1976. Also published as: *Nature of Film: The Redemption of Physical Reality.* London: Dennis Dobson, 1961.

Kristeva, Julia. *About Chinese Women.* Trans. Anita Barrows. New York: Marion Boyars, 1977. (First published Paris: Editions de femmes, 1974.)

Landsberger, Stefan. *Chinese Propaganda Posters: From Revolution to Modernization.* Amsterdam: Pepin Press, 1995.

Larson, Wendy, and Anne Wedell-Wedellsborg, eds. *Inside Out, Modernism and Postmodernism in Chinese Literary Culture.* Aarhus: Aarhus University Press, 1993.

Lau, D. C. *Mencius.* London: Penguin, 1970.

Law, Jo. *Memory and Disappearance: Representing Space and Time in Four Contemporary Hong Kong Films.* Master's thesis (MFA), University of Western Australia, 1998.

Lebeau, Vicky. "Daddy's Cinema: Femininity and Mass Spectatorship." *Screen* 33, no. 3 (1992): 244–58.

Lee, Janet. "Between Subordination and the She-Tiger: Social Constructions of White Femininity in the Lives of Single, Protestant Missionaries in China, 1905-1930." *Women's Studies International Forum* 19, no. 6 (1996): 621–32.

Lefèbvre, Henri. *The Production of Space.* Trans. Donald Nicholson-Smith. Oxford: Blackwell, 1991.

Lefort, Claude. *The Political Forms of Modern Society-Bureaucracy, Democracy, Totalitarianism.* Cambridge: Polity Press, 1986.

Lent, John. *The Asian Film Industry.* London: Christopher Helm, 1990.

Lévi, Bernard-Henri. *La Pûreté dangereuse.* Paris: Grasset, 1994.

Leyda, Jay, ed. *Film Form: Essays in Film Theory.* New York: Harcourt, Brace and World, 1949.

Li Suyuan. "Ertong xin li yu ertong dianying." *Dangdai dianying* (June 1990): 70–79.

Li Tuo, and Zhang Nuanxin. "*Lun dianying yuyande xiandaihua*" ("The Modernization of Film Language") *Beijing Film Art* 3 (1979): 40–52.

———. "*Yellow Earth*-An Unwelcome Guest." In *Seeds of Fire: Chinese Voices of Conscience.* Eds. Geremie Barmé and John Minford. Newcastle upon Tyne: Bloodaxe Books, 1988.

Liang Heping, and Ulrike Stobbe. "Cui Jian and the Birth of Chinese Rock Music." *China Avant Garde* (catalogue). Berlin: Haus der Kulturen der Welt, 1993.

Light, Andrew, and Johnathan M. Smith, eds. *The Production of Public Space.* Lanham: Rowman & Littlefield, 1998.

Lin Tongqi, Henry Rosemont, Jr., and Roger T. Ames. "Chinese Philosophy: A Philosophical Essay on the 'State-of-the-Art'." *The Journal for Asian Studies* 54, no. 3 (August 1995): 727–58.

Liu, James J.Y. *The Art of Chinese Poetry.* Chicago: University of Chicago Press, 1962.

Liu Kang. "Popular Culture and the Culture of the Masses in Contemporary China." *Boundary 2* 24, no. 3 (fall 1997): 99–122.

Liu Kang, and Xiaobang Tang, eds. *Politics, Ideology, and Literary Discourse in Modern China.* Durham: Duke University Press, 1993.

Loewenfeld, Margaret. *Play in Childhood.* London: Victor Gollancz, 1935.

Lu, Sheldon Hsiao-peng. *From Historicity to Fictionality: The Chinese Poetics of Narrative.* Stanford: Stanford University Press, 1994.

———, ed. *Transnational Chinese Cinemas: Identity, Nationhood, Gender.* Honolulu: University of Hawaii Press, 1997.

———. "Global POSTmodernIZATION: the Intellectual, the Artists, and China's Condition." *Boundary 2* 24, no. 3 (fall 1997): 65–98.

Ma Ning. "The Textual and Critical Difference of Being Radical: Reconstructing Chinese Leftist Films of the 1930s." *Wide Angle* 11, no. 2 (1989): 22–31.

Ma Shu-yun. "The Chinese Discourse on Civil Society." *The China Quarterly* (spring 1994): 180–193.

Madsen, Richard. "The Public Sphere, Civil Society, and Moral Community; A Research Agenda for Contemporary China Studies." *Modern China* 19, no.2 (April 1993): 183–98.

McDougall, Bonnie. *Mao Zedong's "Talks at the Yan'an Conference on Literature and Art": A Translation of the 1943 Text with Commentary.* Ann Arbor: The University of Michigan Center for Chinese Studies, 1980.

———. *The Yellow Earth: A Film by Chen Kaige with a Complete Translation of the Filmscript.* Hong Kong: The Chinese University Press, 1991.

MacIntyre, Alasdair. *After Virtue: A Study in Moral Theory.* London: Duckworth, 1985.

Mao Zedong (Tse-tung). *Report of an Investigation into the Peasant Movement in Hunan,* (written in 1927). Beijing: Foreign Languages Press, 1953.

———. *On Art and Literature.* Beijing: Foreign Languages Press, 1960.

Marchetti, Gina. *"Two Stage Sisters*: The Blossoming of a Revolutionary Aesthetic." In *Transnational Chinese Cinemas: Identity, Nationhood, Gender.* Ed. Sheldon Hsiao-peng Lu. Honolulu: University of Hawaii Press, 1997.

Marion, Donald J. *The Chinese Filmography: The 2444 Feature Films Produced by Studios in the People's Republic of China from 1949 through 1995.* Jefferson: McFarland and Co., 1997.

Martin, Emily. "Gender and Ideological Differences in Representations of Life and Death." In *Death Ritual in Late Imperial and Modern China.* Eds. James Watson and Evelyn Rawski. Berkeley: University of California Press, 1988.

Mason, Hugh. "The Rights of Rights of Way." In *The Production of Space.* Eds. Light and Smith. Lanham: Rowman & Littlefield, 1998.

Mast, Gerald, and Marshall Cohen, eds. *Film Theory and Criticism.* Second Edition, Oxford: Oxford University Press, 1979.

Meng Yue. "Female Images and National Myth." In *Gender Politics in Modern China: Writing and Feminism.* Ed. Tani E. Barlow. Durham: Duke University Press, 1993.

Michelson, Annette. "The Wings of Hypothesis: On Montage and the Theory of the Interval." In *Montage and Modern Life, 1919-1942: Catalogue of a Travelling Exhibition 7 April 1992-3 Jan 1993.* Ed. M. Teitelbaum. Cambridge, Mass.: MIT Press, 1992.

Miller, H. Lyman. *Science and Dissent in Post-Mao China: The Politics of Knowledge.* Seattle: University of Washington Press, 1996.

Miller, Robert, ed. *The Development of Civil Society in Communist Systems.* Sydney: Allen and Unwin, 1992.

Min, Anchee. "Extract from *Red Fire Farm.*" *Granta,* no. 39 (1992).

Mouffe, Chantal. "Pluralism and Modern Democracy: Around Carl Schmitt." *New Formations,* no. 14 (summer 1991): 1–16.

———, ed. *Dimensions of Radical Democracy: Pluralism, Citizenship, Community.* London: Verso, 1992.

———. "For a Politics of Agonistic Pluralism." In *Identity, Authority, and Democracy.* Eds. James Donald and Stephanie Donald. Brighton: University of Sussex, 1995.

Mulvey, Laura. *Visual and Other Pleasures.* London: Macmillan, 1989.

Nathan, Andrew. *Chinese Democracy.* London: Tauris, 1986.

_____. "Is Chinese Culture Distinctive? A Review Article." *The Journal of Asian Studies* 52, no. 4 (November 1993): 923–36.

Needham, Joseph. "Time and Eastern Man." *The Henry Myers Lecture 1964.* London: Royal Anthropological Institute of Great Britain and Ireland, 1964.

Negt, Oskar, and Alexander Kluge. *The Public Sphere and Experience: Towards an Analysis of the Bourgeois and Proletarian Public Sphere.* Trans. Peter Labanyi, Jamie Owen Daniel, and Assenka Oksiloff. Minneapolis: University of Minnesota Press, 1992.

Ni Zhen. "After *Yellow Earth.*" In *Films in Contemporary China: Critical Debates 1979-1989.* Eds. George Semsel, Chen Xihe, and Xia Hong. Trans. Fu Binbin. London: Praeger, 1989.

Nicholls, Bill, ed. *Movies and Methods Part II.* Berkeley, Los Angeles, London: University of California Press, 1984.

Outhwaite, William. *Habermas: A Critical Introduction.* Cambridge: Polity Press, 1994.

Perry, Elizabeth. "State and Society in Contemporary China." *World Politics* 41, no. 4 (July 1989): 579–91.

_____. "China in 1992: An Experiment in Neo-Authoritarianism." *Asian Survey* 33, no. 1 (January 1993): 12–21.

_____, ed. *Putting Class in Its Place: Worker Identities in East Asia.* Berkeley: University of California Press, 1996.

Perry, Elizabeth, and Ellen V. Fuller. "China's Long March to Democracy." *World Policy Journal* 53, no. 4 (fall 1991): 663–85.

Perry, Elizabeth J., and Christine Wong, eds. *The Political Economy of Reform in Post-Mao China.* Cambridge, Mass.: Harvard University Press, 1985.

Petley, Julian. "The Lost Continent." In *All Our Yesterdays: 90 Years of British Cinema.* Ed. Charles Barr. London: British Film Institute, 1986.

Petric, Vlada. *Constructivism in Film: "The Man with a Movie Camera": A Cinematic Analysis.* Cambridge: Cambridge University Press, 1987.

Pickowicz, Paul. "Melodramatic Representation and the 'May 4th' Tradition of Chinese Cinema." In *From May Fourth to June Fourth: Fiction and Film in Twentieth Century Literature.* Eds. David Der-wei Wang and Ellen Widmer. Cambridge, Mass.: Harvard University Press, 1993.

_____. "Huang Jianxin and the Notion of Postsocialism." In *New Chinese Cinema.* Eds. Nick Browne et al. Cambridge: Cambridge University Press, 1993.

Plaks, Andrew H. *Chinese Narrative: Critical and Theoretical Essays.* Princeton: Princeton University Press, 1977.

Rabinow, Paul, ed. *The Foucault Reader: An Introduction to Foucault's Thought.* London: Penguin, 1984.

Rayns, Tony. "Dream On." *Sight and Sound* (July 1993): 16–17.

_____. "Chaos and Anger: Black-listed Directors in China." *Sight and Sound* 4, no. 10 (September/October 1994): 12–14.

_____. "China: Censors, Scapegoats, and Bargaining Chips." *Index on Censorship* 24, no. 6 (1995): 69–79.

Red Detachment of Women (Hong se niang zi jun). *"Revolutionary Operas of Today" (Geming xiandai jingju).* Beijing: August First Printing, 1972.

Roberts, Claire, ed. *Evolution and Revolution: Chinese Dress 1700s-1900s.* Sydney: Powerhouse Publishing, 1997.

Rowe, William. "The Public Sphere in Modern China." *Modern China* 16, Part 3 (1990): 309–29.

Saich, Tony. "Party and State Reforms in the People's Republic of China." *Third World Quarterly* 5, no. 3 (July 1983): 627–39.

_____. "Political and Ideological Reform in the People's Republic of China: An Interview with Professor Su Shaozhi." *China Information* 1, no. 2 (1986): 19–25.

_____. "Much Ado about Nothing: Party Reform in the 1980s." In *The Chinese State in the Era of Reform: The Road to Crisis*. Ed. Gordon White. London: Macmillan, 1991.

_____. *Discos and Dictatorship: Party-State and Society Relations in the People's Republic of China*. Leiden: RUL, 1993.

Salecl, Renata. "Nationalism, Anti-Semitism and Anti-Feminism in Eastern Europe." *New German Critique: An Interdisciplinary Journal of German Studies*, no. 57 (1992): 51–67.

Sandoval, Chéla. "Theorizing White Consciousness for a Post-Empire World: Barthes, Fanon, and the Rhetoric of Love." In *Displacing Whiteness: Essays in Social and Cultural Criticism*. Ed. Ruth Frankenberg. Durham: Duke University Press, 1997.

Scarfone, Dominique. "In Praise of Conflictuality." *New Formations*, Issue on Psychoanalysis and Culture, no. 26 (autumn 1995): 36–44.

Schafer, Edward H. *The Divine Woman: Dragon Ladies and Rain Maidens in T'ang Literature*. Berkeley: University of California Press, 1973.

Schama, Simon. *Landscape and Memory*. London: Harper Collins, 1995.

Schram, Stuart R., ed. *Mao Tsetung*. London: Penguin, 1966.

Semsel, George, ed. *Chinese Film: The State of the Art in the People's Republic*. London: Praeger, 1987.

_____. "China." In *The Asian Film Industry*. Ed. John Lent. London: Christopher Helm, 1990.

Semsel, George, Chen Xihe, and Xia Hong, eds. *Film in Contemporary China: Critical Debates 1979-1989*. New York: Praeger, 1989.

Semsel, George, Xia Hong, and Hou Jianping, eds. *Chinese Film Theory: A Guide to the New Era*. New York: Praeger, 1990.

Shils, Edward. "The Virtue of Civil Society." *Government and Opposition* 26, no. 1 (winter 1991): 3–20.

Shue, Vivienne. "State Sprawl." In *Urban Spaces in Contemporary China: The Potential for Autonomy and Community in Post-Mao China*. Eds. Deborah S. Davis et al. Cambridge: Cambridge University Press/Woodrow Wilson Center, 1995.

Sollinger, Dorothy. "Democracy with Chinese Characteristics." *World Policy Journal* (fall 1989): 621–32.

_____. "China's Transients and the State: A Form of Civil Society?" *Politics and Society* 21, no.1 (March 1993): 91–122.

Spivak, Gayatri Chavrakorty. "Can the Subaltern Speak?" In *Marxism and the Interpretation of Culture*. Eds. Lawrence Grossberg and Cary Nelson. Urbana: University of Illinois Press, 1988.

Starr, John F. *Continuing the Revolution: The Political Thought of Mao*. Princeton: Princeton University Press, 1979.

Strand, David. *Rickshaw Beijing: City People and Politics in 1920s China*. Berkeley: University of California Press, 1989.

_____. "Protest in Beijing: Civil Society and Public Sphere in China." *Problems of Communism* 39, no. 3 (1990): 1–19.

Studlar, Gaylyn. "Masochism, Masquerade, and the Erotic Metamorphoses of Marlene Dietrich." In *Fabrications and the Female Body*. Eds. Jane Gaines and Charlotte Herzog. New York: Routledge, 1990.

Su Tong. *Raise the Red Lantern*. Trans. Michael Duke. London: Touchstone, 1994.

Tansuo Dianying Ji. Shanghai: Shanghai Wenyi Chubanche, 1987 (*Experimental Films' Scripts*, Shanghai Literary Publishing).

Taussig, Michael. *Mimesis and Alterity: A Particular History of the Senses*. London: Routledge, 1993.

Taylor, Charles. "Modes of Civil Society." *Public Culture* 3, no. 1 (1990): 95–118.

Thompson, John D. *The Media and Modernity: A Social Theory of the Media*. Cambridge: Polity Press, 1995.

T'ien Ju-k'ang. *Male Anxiety and Female Chastity: A Comparative Study of Chinese Ethical Values in Ming-Ch'ing Times*. Monographes du T'oung Pao, Vol. 14, Leiden: Brill, 1988.

Trinh T. Minh-Ha. "Difference-A Special Third World Women's Issue." *Discourse* 8 (fall/winter 1986-1987): 11–37.

_____. *Framer Framed*. London: Routledge, 1992.

Twitchett, Denis, and John K. Fairbank, eds. *The Cambridge History of China*, Vol. 15, Part 2: *Revolutions within the Chinese Revolution 1966-1982*. Cambridge: Cambridge University Press, 1991.

UN Center for Human Settlements, *An Urbanizing World: Global Report on Human Settlements*. New York, 1996.

Wakeman, Frederick. "Civil Society and Public Sphere Debate: Western Reflections on Chinese Political Culture." *Modern China* 19, no. 2 (1993): 108–38.

Walder, Andrew G. "The Political Sociology of the Beijing Upheaval of 1989." *Problems of Communism* (September-October 1989): 39–40.

Walzer, Michael. "The Civil Society Argument." In *Dimensions of Radical Democracy: Pluralism, Citizenship, Democracy*. Ed. Chantal Mouffe. London: Verso, 1992.

Wang, David Der-wei, and Ellen Widmer, eds. *From May Fourth to June Fourth: Fiction and Film in Twentieth-Century Literature*. Cambridge, Mass.: Harvard University Press, 1993.

Wang Jing. *High Culture Fever: Politics, Aesthetics, and Ideology in Deng's China*. Berkeley: University of California Press, 1996.

Wang, Yuejin. "The Cinematic Other and the Cultural Self?: De-centering the Cultural Identity on Cinema." *Public Culture* 2, no. 1 (1989): 31–53.

Wasserstrom, Jeffrey N., and Liu Xinyong. "Student Associations and Mass Movements." In *Urban Spaces in Contemporary China: The Potential for Autonomy and Community in Post-Mao China*. Eds. Deborah S. Davis et al. Cambridge: Cambridge University Press, 1995.

White, Gordon. "The New Economic Paradigm: Towards Market Socialism" In *Reforming the Revolution*. Eds. Robert Benewick and Paul Wingrove. London: Macmillan, 1988.

_____, ed. *The Chinese State in the Era of Economic Reform: The Road to Crisis*. London: Macmillan, 1991.

_____. *Riding The Tiger*. London: Macmillan Books, 1993.

_____. "Prospects for Civil Society in China." *Australian Journal of Chinese Affairs* 29 (January 1993): 63–87.

_____. "The Dynamics of Civil Society in Post-Mao China" In *The Individual and the State in China*. Ed. Brian Hook. Oxford: Clarendon Press, 1996.

Winnicott, D. W. "The Psychology of Madness: A Contribution from Psychoanalysis" (written in 1965), reprinted in *New Formations*, no. 26 (autumn 1995): 45–53.

_____. *Playing and Reality* (written in 1971). London: Penguin Books, 1980.

Wu Hung. "Tiananmen Square: A Political History of Monuments." *Representations*, no. 35 (summer 1991): 84–117.

Yang, Rae. *Spider Eaters*. Berkeley: University of California Press, 1997.

Yau, Esther Ching-mei. "Yellow Earth: Western Analysis and a Non-Western Text." *Film Quarterly* 41, no. 2 (winter 1987-88): 22–33.

_____. "Is China the End of Hermeneutics? Or, Political and Cultural Usage of Non-Han Women in Mainland Chinese Films." *Discourse* 11, no. 2 (1989): 115–36.

_____. *Filmic Discourses on Women in Chinese Cinema (1949-1965): Art, Ideology, and Social Relations*. Ph.D. dissertation, University of California, 1990.

_____. "International Fantasy and the New Chinese Cinema." *Quarterly Review of Film and Video* 14, no. 3 (1993): 95–107.

Ying-hs'i hua. Taipei: China Printing Company, 1996.

Yip, June. " Constructing a Nation: Taiwanese History and the Films of Hou Hsiao-hsien." In *Transnational Chinese Cinemas: Identity, Nationhood, Gender*. Ed. Sheldon Hsiao-peng Lu. Honolulu: University of Hawaii Press, 1997.

Young, Lola. *Fear of the Dark: "Race," Gender, and Sexuality in the Cinema*. London: Routledge, 1996.

Yu Le, ed. *Cao zong yin mu de nüxing: zhongguo nü lingdao*. Beijing: Women and Children's Press, 1989.

Zhang, Xudong. "Nationalism, Mass Culture, and Intellectual Strategies in Post-Tiananmen China." *Social Text 55* 16, no. 2 (summer 1998): 109–40.

Zhang, Yingjin. "Screening China: Recent Studies of Chinese Cinema in English." *Bulletin of Concerned Asian Scholars* 29, no. 3 (1997): 59–66.

Zheng Dongtian. "Starting from the Loess Plateau." *China Screen* 1 (1985): 12–13.

Zhongguo dianying da cidian. Shanghai chubanshe, 1993.

Zito, Angela, and Tani E. Barlow, eds. *Body, Subject, and Power in China*. Chicago: University Press of Chicago, 1994.

Zizek, Slavoj. *The Sublime Object of Ideology*. London: Verso, 1989.

_____. "Eastern European Liberalism and Its Discontents." *New German Critique: An Interdisciplinary Journal of German Studies*, no. 57 (1992): 25–49.

Filmography

BY YEAR

Title	Chinese Translation	Year Released	Director
Birth of a Nation		1919	D. W. Griffiths
Yan ruishen		1921	Ren Pengnian
Battleship Potemkin		1925	Sergei Eisenstein
Sunrise		1927	F. W. Murnau
October		1928	Sergei Eisenstein
Man with a Movie Camera	*Kino Eye*	1929	Dziga Vertov
Wild Flower	*Yecao xianhua*	1930	Sun Yu
The Peach Girl	*Taohua qi xue ji*	1932	Richard Poh (Bu Wancang)
Big Road	*Da lu*	1935	Sun Yu
Children of the Storm	*Fengyun ernü*	1935	Xu Xingzhi
Lost Lamb	*Mitu de gaoyang*	1936	Cai Chusheng
Snow White		1937	Walt Disney
Street Angel	*Malu tianshi*	1937	Yuan Muzhi
The Lady Vanishes		1939	Alfred Hitchcock
Gone with the Wind		1939	David O. Selznick
Black Narcissus		1947	Powell and Pressburger
A Make Believe Couple	*Jiafeng xuhuang*	1947	Sang Hu, Zuo Lin
Joys and Sorrows of Middle Age	*Aile zhongnian*	1949	Sang Hu
Sanmao's Travels	*Sanmao liulang ji*	1949	Zhao Ming

183

Title	Chinese Translation	Year Released	Director
A Peaceful Spring	*Taiping chun*	1950	Sang Hu
The White-haired Girl	*Bai mao nü*	1950	Shui Ha
Corruption	*Fu shi*	1950	Zuo Lin
Strangers on a Train		1951	Alfred Hitchcock
Land	*Tudi*	1954	Shui Ha
New Year Sacrifice	*Zhu fu*	1956	Xia Yan
Mother India		1957	Mehboob Khan
Woman Basketball Player No. 5	*Nü lan wu hao*	1957	Xie Jin
Daughter of the Party	*Dang de nü er*	1958	Lin Nong
The Kite	*Fengzheng*	1958	Wang Jiayi
Young Masters of the Great Leap Forward (Service)	*Da yue jin zhong de xiao zhuren (Fuwu)*	1958	Xie Jin
Lin Family Shop	*Lin jia puzi*	1959	Shui Ha
The Red Sun over the Ke Mountains	*Keshan hong ri*	1960	Dong Zhaoqi
Breathless	*A Bout de Souffle*	1960	Jean-Luc Godard
Red Detachment of Women	*Hongse niangzi jun*	1961	Xie Jin
Little Soldier	*Xiao bing zhangga*	1963	Cui Wei, Ouyang Hongying
Serfs	*Nong nü*	1963	Li Jun
Red Flower of Mount Tan	*Tianshan de hong hua*	1964	Cui Wei, Chen Huaiai, Liu Baode
Two Stage Sisters	*Wutai jiemei*	1964	Xie Jin
Four Loves (Taiwan)	*Wanjun biao mei*	1965	Li Hsing (Li Xing)
Living in Flames	*Liehuo zhong yong sheng*	1965	Shui Ha
On the Docks	*Haigang*	1972	Xie Jin/Xie Tieli
Tout Va Bien (Everything is Fine)		1973	Jean-Luc Godard
Shining Red Star	*Shanshan de hong xing*	1974	Li Jun, Li Ang
Youth in the Heat of Battle	*Feng huo shaonian*	1975	Dong Kena
Hai xia	*Haixia*	1974	Qian Jiang, Chen Huaiai, Wang Haowei
The Second Spring	*Di erge chuntian*	1975	Sang Hu
Twins Come in Pairs	*Talia he talia*	1979	Sang Hu
Three Monks	*Sange heshang*	1980	Ah Da
The Legend of Tianyun Mountain	*Tianyunshan chuanqi*	1980	Xie Jin
Herdsman	*Muma ren*	1982	Xie Jin
Summer at Grandpa's (Taiwan)	*Dongdong de jiaqi*	1983	Hou Hsiao-hsien (Hu Xiaoxian)

Title	Chinese Translation	Year Released	Director
Yellow Earth	*Huang tudi*	1984	Chen Kaige
Wild Mountains	*Ye shan*	1984	Yan Xueshu
The Big Parade	*Da yuebing*	1985	Chen Kaige
The Time to Live, The Time to Die (Taiwan)		1985	Hou Hsiao-hsien (Hu Xiaoxian)
Army Nurse	*Nüer lou*	1985	Hu Mei
A Good Woman	*Liang jia funü*	1985	Huang Jianzhong
Me and My Classmates	*Wo he wode tongxuemen*	1985	Peng Xiaolian
Hailibu	*Hailibu*	1985	Huang Wei
On the Hunting Ground	*Lie chang zhasa*	1985	Tian Zhuang-zhuang
Sacrifice of Youth	*Qingchun ji*	1985	Zhang Nuanxin
The Horse Thief	*Daoma zei*	1986	Tian Zhuang-zhuang
Girl from Hunan	*Xiangnü xiaoxiao*	1986	Xie Fei, Wu Lan
Hibiscus Town	*Furong zhen*	1986	Xie Jin
King of the Children	*Haizi wang*	1987	Chen Kaige
Far Away from War	*Yuan li zhanzheng de niandai*	1987	Hu Mei
Rouge	*Yanzhi kou*	1987	Stanley Kwan (Guan Jinpeng)
Red Sorghum	*Hong gaoliang*	1987	Zhang Yimou
A Marksman without a Gun	*Wu qiang qiangshou*	1988	Hu Mei
A Story of Women	*Nüren de gushi*	1988	Peng Xiaolian
Black Snow	*Ben mingnian*	1989	Xie Fei
Ju Dou	*Ju dou*	1989	Zhang Yimou
Life on a String	*Bian zou bian chang*	1990	Chen Kaige
Bloody Morning	*Xuese qingche*	1990	Li Shaohong
Don't Cry Mummy	*Bie ku mama*	1990	Zhang Yuqiang
Good Morning Beijing	*Beijing, nizao*	1991	Zhang Nuanxin
Raise the Red Lantern	*Da hong deng long gao gao gua*	1991	Zhang Yimou
Urban Gunman	*Dushi qiangshou*	1992	Hu Mei
A Family Portrait	*Sishi buhuo*	1992	Li Shaohong
For Fun	*Zhao le*	1992	Ning Ying
Divorce	*Lihun*	1992	Wang Haowei
1966—My Time in the Red Guards	*1966—Wode hong weibing rizi*	1992	Wu Wenguang
Twilight Star	*Qi mingxing*	1992	Xie Jin
The Story of Qiu Ju	*Qiu Ju da guansi*	1992	Zhang Yimou
Farewell My Concubine	*Bawang bieji*	1993	Chen Kaige
In the Heat of the Sun	*Yang guang can lan de rizi*	1993	Jiang Wen

Title	Chinese Translation	Year Released	Director
The Blue Kite	*Lan fengzheng*	1993	Tian Zhuang-zhuang
The Days	*Dongchun de rizi*	1993	Wang Xiaoshuai
Beijing Bastards	*Beijing zazhong*	1993	Zhang Yuan
Ermo	*Ermo*	1994	Zhou Xiaowen
Red Firecracker, Green Firecracker	*Pao da shuang deng*	1995	He Ping
Blush	*Hongfen*	1995	Li Shaohong
Vive L'amour	*Aiqing wansui*	1995	Tsai ming-liang
Women's Valley	*Nüer gu*	1995	Xie Jin
Shanghai Triad	*Yaoya yao, yao dao waipo qiao*	1995	Zhang Yimou
Happy Angels	*Kuaile de tianshi*	1996	Guang Chunlan
East Palace, West Palace	*Dong gong, xi gong*	1996	Zhang Yuan
Titanic		1997	James Cameron
Red Hot Lover	*Hongse lianren*	1998	Ye Daying

BY DIRECTOR

Director	Title	Chinese Title	Year Released
Ah Da	*Three Monks*	*Sange heshang*	1980
Cai Chusheng	*Lost Lamb*	*Mitu de gaoyang*	1936
Cameron (James)	*Titanic*		1997
Chen Kaige	*Yellow Earth*	*Huang tudi*	1984
Chen Kaige	*The Big Parade*	*Da yuebing*	1985
Chen Kaige	*King of the Children*	*Haizi wang*	1987
Chen Kaige	*Life on a String*	*Bian zou bian chang*	1990
Chen Kaige	*Farewell My Concubine*	*Bawang bieji*	1993
Cui Wei, Chen Huaiai, Liu Baode	*Red Flower of Mount Tan*	*Tianshan de hong hua*	1964
Cui Wei, Ouyang Hongying	*Little Soldier*	*Xiao bing zhangga*	1963
Disney (Walt)	*Snow White*		1937
Dong Kena	*Youth in the Heat of Battle*	*Feng huo shaonian*	1975
Dong Zhaoqi	*The Red Sun over the Ke Mountains*	*Keshan hong ri*	1960
Dziga Vertov	*Man with a Movie Camera*	*Kino Eye*	1929
Eisenstein (Sergei)	*Battleship Potemkin*		1925
Eisenstein (Sergei)	*October*		1928
Godard (Jean-Luc)	*Breathless (A Bout de Souffle)*		1960
Godard (Jean-Luc)	*Tout Va Bien (Everything is Fine)*		1973
Griffiths (D.W.)	*Birth of a Nation*		1919
Guang Chunlan	*Happy Angels*	*Kuaile de tianshi*	1996
He Ping	*Red Firecracker, Green Firecracker*	*Pao da shuang deng*	1995
Hitchcock (Alfred)	*The Lady Vanishes*		1939
Hitchcock (Alfred)	*Strangers on a Train*		1951
Hou Hsiao-hsien (Hu Xiaoxian)	*Summer at Grandpa's (Taiwan)*	*Dongdong de jiaqi*	1983
Hou Hsiao-hsien (Hu Xiaoxian)	*The Time to Live, The Time to Die (Taiwan)*		1985
Hu Mei	*Army Nurse*	*Nüer lou*	1985
Hu Mei	*Far Away from War*	*Yuan li zhanzheng de niandai*	1987
Hu Mei	*A Marksman without a Gun*	*Wu qiang qiangshou*	1988
Hu Mei	*Urban Gunman*	*Dushi qiangshou*	1992
Huang Jianzhong	*A Good Woman*	*Liang jia funü*	1985
Huang Wei	*Hailibu*	*Hailibu*	1985

Director	Title	Chinese Title	Year Released
Jiang Wen	*In the Heat of the Sun*	*Yang guang can lan de rizi*	1993
Kwan (Stanley) (Guan Jinpeng)	*Rouge*	*Yanzhi kou*	1987
Li Hsing (Li Xing)	*Four Loves (Taiwan)*	*Wanjun biao mei*	1965
Li Jun	*Serfs*	*Nong nü*	1963
Li Jun, Li Ang	*Shining Red Star*	*Shanshan de hong xing*	1974
Li Shaohong	*Bloody Morning*	*Xuese qingchen*	1990
Li Shaohong	*A Family Portrait*	*Sishi buhuo*	1992
Li Shaohong	*Blush*	*Hongfen*	1995
Lin Nong	*Daughter of the Party*	*Dang de nüer*	1958
Mehboob Khan	*Mother India*		1957
Murnau (F. W.)	*Sunrise*		1927
Ning Ying	*For Fun*	*Zhao le*	1992
Peng Xiaolian	*Me and My Classmates*	*Wo he wode tongxuemen*	1985
Peng Xiaolian	*A Story of Women*	*Nüren de gushi*	1988
Poh, Richard (Bu Wancang)	*The Peach Girl*	*Taohua qixue ji*	1932
Powell and Pressburger	*Black Narcissus*		1947
Qian Jiang, Chen Huaiai, Wang Haowei	*Hai xia*	*Haixia*	1974
Ren Pengnian	*Yan ruishen*		1921
Sang Hu	*Joys and Sorrows of Middle Age*	*Aile zhongnian*	1949
Sang Hu	*A Peaceful Spring*	*Taiping chun*	1950
Sang Hu	*The Second Spring*	*Di erge chuntian*	1975
Sang Hu	*Twins Come in Pairs*	*Talia he talia*	1979
Sang Hu/Zuo Lin	*A Make-Believe Couple*	*Jiafeng xuhuang*	1947
Selznick (David O.)	*Gone with the Wind*		1939
Shui Ha	*The White-haired Girl*	*Bai mao nü*	1950
Shui Ha	*Land*	*Tudi*	1954
Shui Ha	*Lin Family Shop*	*Lin jia puzi*	1959
Shui Ha	*Living in Flames*	*Liehuo zhong yong sheng*	1965
Sun Yu	*Wild Flower*	*Yecao xianhua*	1930
Sun Yu	*Big Road*	*Da lu*	1935
Tian Zhuangzhuang	*On the Hunting Ground*	*Lie chang zhasa*	1985
Tian Zhuangzhuang	*The Horse Thief*	*Daoma zei*	1986
Tian Zhuangzhuang	*The Blue Kite*	*Lan fengzheng*	1993
Tsai Ming-liang	*Vive L'amour*	*Aiqing wansui*	1995
Wang Haowei	*Divorce*	*Lihun*	1992

Director	Title	Chinese Title	Year Released
Wang Jiayi	*The Kite*	*Fengzheng*	1958
Wang Xiaoshuai	*The Days*	*Dongchun de rizi*	1993
Wu Wenguang	*1966—My Time in the Red Guards*	*1966—Wo de hong-weibing rizi*	1992
Xia Yan	*New Year Sacrifice*	*Zhu fu*	1956
Xie Fei	*Black Snow*	*Ben mingnian*	1989
Xie Fei, Wu Lan	*Girl from Hunan*	*Xiangnü xiaoxiao*	1986
Xie Jin	*Woman Basketball Player No. 5*	*Nü lan wu hao*	1957
Xie Jin	*Young Masters of the Great Leap Forward (Service)*	*Da yue jin zhong de xiao zhuren (Fuwu)*	1958
Xie Jin	*Red Detachment of Women*	*Hongse niangzi jun*	1961
Xie Jin	*Two Stage Sisters*	*Wutai jiemei*	1964
Xie Jin	*The Legend of Tianyun Mountain*	*Tianyunshan chuanqi*	1980
Xie Jin	*Herdsman*	*Muma ren*	1982
Xie Jin	*Hibiscus Town*	*Furong zhen*	1986
Xie Jin	*Twilight Star*	*Qi mingxing*	1992
Xie Jin	*Women's Valley*	*Nüer gu*	1995
Xie Jin/Xie Tieli	*On the Docks*	*Haigang*	1972
Xu Xingzhi	*Children of the Storm*	*Fengyun ernü*	1935
Yan Xueshu	*Wild Mountains*	*Ye shan*	1984
Ye Daying	*Red Hot Lover*	*Hongse lianren*	1998
Yuan Muzhi	*Street Angel*	*Malu tianshi*	1937
Zhang Nuanxin	*Sacrifice of Youth*	*Qingchun ji*	1985
Zhang Nuanxin	*Good Morning Beijing*	*Beijing, nizao*	1991
Zhang Yimou	*Red Sorghum*	*Hong gaoliang*	1987
Zhang Yimou	*Ju Dou*	*Ju dou*	1989
Zhang Yimou	*Raise the Red Lantern*	*Da hong deng long gao gao gua*	1991
Zhang Yimou	*The Story of Qiu Ju*	*Qiu Ju da guansi*	1992
Zhang Yimou	*Shanghai Triad*	*Yaoya yao, yao dao waipo qiao*	1995
Zhang Yuan	*Beijing Bastards*	*Beijing zazhong*	1993
Zhang Yuan	*East Palace, West Palace*	*Dong gong, xi gong*	1997
Zhang Yuqiang	*Don't Cry Mummy*	*Bie ku mama*	1990
Zhao Ming, Yan Gong	*Sanmao's Travels*	*Sanmao liulang ji*	1949
Zhou Xiaowen	*Ermo*	*Ermo*	1994
Zuo Lin	*Corruption*	*Fu shi*	1950

Chinese Glossary 中文术语汇编

Dianying (Films) 电影

Aile zhongnian	哀乐中年
Aiqing wansui	爱情万岁
Bai mao nü	白毛女
Bawang bieji	霸王别姬
Beijing zazhong	北京杂种
Beijing, nizao	北京，你早
Ben mingnian	本命年
Bian zou bian chang	边走边唱
Bieku mama	别哭妈妈
Da lu	大路
Da yuebing	大阅兵
Dahong denglong gaogao gua	大红灯笼高高挂
Dang de nüer	党的女儿
Daoma zei	盗马贼
Dayuejin zhong de xiao zhuren	大跃进中的小主人
Di erge chuntian	第二个春天
Dongchun de rizi	冬春的日子
Dongdong de jiaqi	冬冬的假期
Donggong xigong	东宫西宫
Dushi qiangshou	都市枪手
Ermo	二嫫
Fenghuo shaonian	峰火少年
Fengyun ernü	风云儿女
Fengzheng	风筝
Fu shi	腐蚀
Furong zhen	芙蓉镇
Haigang	海港

Hai li bu	海力布
Haixia	海霞
Haizi wang	孩子王
Hong gaoliang	红高粱
Hong fen	红粉
Hongse lianren	红色恋人
Hongse niangzi jun	红色娘子军
Huang tudi	黄土地
Jiafeng xuhuang	假风虚凰
Ju Dou	菊豆
Keshan hongri	柯山红日
Kuaile de tianshi	快乐的天使
Lan fengzheng	蓝风筝
Liangjia funü	良家妇女
Lie chang zhasa	猎场札撒
Liehuo zhong yongsheng	烈火中永生
Lihun	离婚
Linjia puzi	林家铺子
Malu tianshi	马路天使
Mitu de gaoyang	迷途的羔羊
Muma ren	牧马人
Nong nu	农奴
Nü lan wu hao	女蓝五号
Nüer gu	女儿谷
Nüer lou	女儿楼
Nüren de gushi	女人的故事
Paoda shuangdeng	炮打双灯
Qi mingxing	启明星
Qingchun ji	青春祭
Qiuju da guansi	秋菊打官司
Sange heshang	三个和尚
Sanmao liulang ji	三毛流浪记
Shanshan de hongxing	闪闪的红星
Sishi buhuo	四十不惑
Taiping chun	太平春
Talia he talia	她俩和他俩
Taohua qixue ji	桃花泣血记
Tianshan de honghua	天山的红花
Tianyun shan chuanqi	天云山传奇
Tudi	土地

Wanjun biao mei	婉君表妹
Wo de hongweibing rizi	我的红卫兵日子
Wo he wode tongxue men	我和我的同学们
Wu qiang qiangshou	无枪枪手
Wutai jiemei	舞台姐妹
Xiangnü xiaoxiao	湘女潇潇
Xiaobing zhangga	小兵张嘎
Xuese qingchen	血色清晨
Yan Ruishen	阎瑞生
Yangguang canlan de rizi	阳光灿烂的日子
Yanzhi kou	胭脂扣
Yaoya yao, yaodao waipo qiao	摇呀摇，摇到外婆桥
Ye shan	野山
Yecao xianhua	野草闲花
Yuanli zhanzheng de niandai	远离战争的年代
Zhao le	找乐
Zhu fu	祝福

Dianying daoyan (Directors)	电影导演
Ah Da	阿达
Cai Chusheng	蔡楚生
Chen Huaiai	陈怀皑
Chen Kaige	陈凯歌
Cui Wei	崔嵬
Dong Kena	董克娜
Dong Zhaoqi	董兆琪
Guang Chunlan	广春兰
He Ping	何平
Hou Hsiao-hsien (Hou Xiaoxian)	候孝贤
Hu Mei	胡玫
Huang Wei	黄炜
Huang Jianzhong	黄建中
Huang Zuolin	黄左临
Jiang Wen	姜文
Li Ang	李昂
Li Hsing (Li Xing)	李行
Li Jun	李俊
Li Shaohong	李少红

Lin Nong	林农
Liu Baode	刘保德
Ning Ying	宁瀛
Ouyang Hongying	欧阳红樱
Peng Xiaolian	彭小连
Qian Jiang	钱江
Ren Pengnian	任彭年
Richard Poh (Bu Wancang)	卜万苍
Sang Hu	桑弧
Shui Hua	水华
Stanley Kwan (Guan Jinpeng)	关锦鹏
Sun Yu	孙瑜
Tian Zhuangzhuang	田壮壮
Tsai Ming-liang (Cai Mingliang)	蔡明亮
Wang Haowei	王好为
Wang Jiayi	王家乙
Wang Xiaoshuai	王小帅
Wu Lan	乌兰
Wu Wenguang	吴文光
Xie Fei	谢飞
Xie Jin	谢晋
Xie Tieli	谢铁骊
Xu Xingzhi	许幸之
Yan Xueshu	颜学恕
Ye Daying	叶大鹰
Yuan Muzhi	袁牧之
Zhang Nuanxin	张暖忻
Zhang Yimou	张艺谋
Zhang Yuan	张元
Zhang Yuqiang	张郁强
Zhao Ming	赵明
Zhou Xiaowen	周晓文

Cihui biao (Chinese terms)	词汇表
baochan daohu	包产到户
fei nongmin	非农民
fengjing	风景

funü	妇女
gemenr	哥们儿
geming yangban xi	革命样板戏
geti hu	个体户
guanxi	关系
gui	鬼
guohua	国画
hei	黑
hong xiao bing	红小兵
houxue	后学
huangse	黄色
hukou nongmin	户口农民
hutong	胡同
jingyi	敬意
ketou	磕头
ku ger	苦歌儿
li	礼
liumang	流氓
mangliu	盲流
mianqiang	勉强
mofan gongren	模范工人
naili naiqi	奶哩奶气
nüxing	女性
qigong	气功
qingbai	清白
ren	仁
shanghen	伤痕
shanshui	山水
shi	史
tansuo	探索
tongxue	同学
wo xin ni	我信你
xin	信
yiwu suoyou	一无所有
ziran	自然

Index

197

About the Author

Stephanie Hemelryk Donald is Senior Lecturer in Media Studies at Murdoch University. She has also worked as an actor for several years in London and around the U.K. She has published three other books: *Belief in China*; *Art and Politics, Deities and Mortality, The State of China Atlas* (with Robert Benewick), and *Picturing Power in the People's Republic of China: Posters of the Cultural Revolution* (with Harriet Evans). She lives in Fremantle, Western Australia, with James, Morag, and Ellen.